"Michael Sandel is . . . one of the world's most interesting political philosophers. Politicians and commentators tend to ask two questions of policy: will it make voters better off, and will it affect their liberty? Sandel rightly points out the shallowness of that debate and adds a third criterion: how will it affect the common good?"   —*The Guardian*

"Sandel practices the best kind of academic populism, managing to simplify John Stuart Mill and John Rawls without being simplistic . . . Sandel sets out to confront the most difficult moral issues in politics. He ends up clarifying a basic political divide—not between left and right, but between those who recognize nothing greater than individual rights and choices, and those who affirm a 'politics of the common good,' rooted in moral beliefs that can't be ignored."
—**MICHAEL GERSON**, *The Washington Post*

"Reading *Justice* by Michael Sandel is an intoxicating invitation to take apart and examine how we arrive at our notions of right and wrong . . . A sly current of wit animates his new book and helps pry open our habitual ways of ordering the universe."
—**KAREN R. LONG**, *The Plain Dealer* (Cleveland)

"[A] road map for negotiating modern moral dilemmas . . . For those seeking a short course through moral philosophy from a witty writer, fast on his feet, and nimble with his pen, this thin volume is difficult to beat."   —**KEVIN J. HAMILTON**, *The Seattle Times*

"Sandel explains theories of justice . . . with clarity and immediacy honed by years of classroom presentation; the ideas of Aristotle, Jer-

emy Bentham, Immanuel Kant, John Stuart Mill, Robert Nozick and John Rawls have rarely, if ever, been set out as accessibly."
—**JONATHAN RAUCH**, *The New York Times Book Review*

"Sandel belongs to the tradition, dating back to ancient Greece, which sees moral philosophy as an outgrowth and refinement of civic debate. Like Aristotle, he seeks to systematise educated common sense, not to replace it with expert knowledge or abstract principles. This accounts for one of the most striking and attractive features of *Justice*—its use of examples drawn from real legal and political controversies . . . Sandel's insistence on the inescapably ethical character of political debate is enormously refreshing." —**EDWARD SKIDELSKY**, *New Statesman*

"Sandel dazzles in this sweeping survey of hot topics—the recent government bailouts, the draft, surrogate pregnancies, same-sex marriage, immigration reform and reparations for slavery—that situates various sides in the debates in the context of timeless philosophical questions . . . [He] has a rare gift for making complex issues comprehensible, even entertaining, without compromising their gravity . . . Erudite, conversational and deeply humane, this is truly transformative reading."
—*Publishers Weekly* (starred review)

"Using a compelling, entertaining mix of hypotheticals, news stories, episodes from history, pop-culture tidbits, literary examples, legal cases and teachings from the great philosophers—principally, Aristotle, Kant, Bentham, Mill and Rawls—Sandel takes on a variety of controversial issues—abortion, same-sex marriage, affirmative action—and forces us to confront our own assumptions, biases and lazy thought . . . His relentless, though never oppressive, reason shines throughout the narrative. Sparkling commentary from the professor we all wish we had."
—*Kirkus Reviews* (starred review)

ALSO BY MICHAEL J. SANDEL

Liberalism and the Limits of Justice (1982; 2nd ed., 1998)

Liberalism and Its Critics, editor (1984)

Democracy's Discontent: America in Search of a Public Philosophy (1996)

Public Philosophy: Essays on Morality in Politics (2005)

The Case Against Perfection: Ethics in the Age of Genetic Engineering (2007)

Justice: A Reader, editor (2007)

MICHAEL J. SANDEL
JUSTICE

Michael J. Sandel is the Anne T. and Robert M. Bass Professor of Government at Harvard University, where he has taught political philosophy since 1980. He lives in Brookline, Massachusetts.

Go online to debate, discuss, and share your thoughts with other readers of *Justice*. Visit www.justiceharvard.org.

JUSTICE

WHAT'S

THE

RIGHT THING

TO DO?

MICHAEL J. SANDEL

FARRAR, STRAUS AND GIROUX

NEW YORK

Farrar, Straus and Giroux
18 West 18th Street, New York 10011

Printed in the United States of America
Published in 2009 by Farrar, Straus and Giroux
First paperback edition, 2010

The Library of Congress has cataloged the hardcover edition as follows:
Sandel, Michael J.
    Justice : what's the right thing to do? / Michael J. Sandel.— 1st ed.
        p.   cm.
    Includes bibliographical references and index.
    ISBN: 978-0-374-18065-2 (hardcover : alk. paper)
    1. Justice.   2. Values.   3. Ethics.   I. Title.

JC578.S25 2009
172'.2—dc22

                                                            2009025438

Paperback ISBN: 978-0-374-53250-5

Designed by Abby Kagan

www.fsgbooks.com

19 20 18

For Kiku, with love

CONTENTS

JUSTICE

1. DOING THE RIGHT THING

In the summer of 2004, Hurricane Charley roared out of the Gulf of Mexico and swept across Florida to the Atlantic Ocean. The storm claimed twenty-two lives and caused $11 billion in damage.[1] It also left in its wake a debate about price gouging.

At a gas station in Orlando, they were selling two-dollar bags of ice for ten dollars. Lacking power for refrigerators or air-conditioning in the middle of August, many people had little choice but to pay up. Downed trees heightened demand for chain saws and roof repairs. Contractors offered to clear two trees off a homeowner's roof—for $23,000. Stores that normally sold small household generators for $250 were now asking $2,000. A seventy-seven-year-old woman fleeing the hurricane with her elderly husband and handicapped daughter was charged $160 per night for a motel room that normally goes for $40.[2]

Many Floridians were angered by the inflated prices. "After Storm Come the Vultures," read a headline in *USA Today*. One resident, told it would cost $10,500 to remove a fallen tree from his roof, said it was wrong for people to "try to capitalize on other people's hardship and misery." Charlie Crist, the state's attorney general, agreed: "It is astounding to me, the level of greed that someone must have in their soul to be willing to take advantage of someone suffering in the wake of a hurricane."[3]

Florida has a law against price gouging, and in the aftermath of the hurricane, the attorney general's office received more than two thousand complaints. Some led to successful lawsuits. A Days Inn in West Palm Beach had to pay $70,000 in penalties and restitution for overcharging customers.[4]

But even as Crist set about enforcing the price-gouging law, some economists argued that the law—and the public outrage—were misconceived. In medieval times, philosophers and theologians believed that the exchange of goods should be governed by a "just price," determined by tradition or the intrinsic value of things. But in market societies, the economists observed, prices are set by supply and demand. There is no such thing as a "just price."

Thomas Sowell, a free-market economist, called price gouging an "emotionally powerful but economically meaningless expression that most economists pay no attention to, because it seems too confused to bother with." Writing in the *Tampa Tribune*, Sowell sought to explain "how 'price gouging' helps Floridians." Charges of price gouging arise "when prices are significantly higher than what people have been used to," Sowell wrote. But "the price levels that you happen to be used to" are not morally sacrosanct. They are no more "special or 'fair'" than other prices" that market conditions—including those prompted by a hurricane—may bring about.[5]

Higher prices for ice, bottled water, roof repairs, generators, and motel rooms have the advantage, Sowell argued, of limiting the use of such things by consumers and increasing incentives for suppliers in far-off places to provide the goods and services most needed in the hurricane's aftermath. If ice fetches ten dollars a bag when Floridians are facing power outages in the August heat, ice manufacturers will find it worth their while to produce and ship more of it. There is nothing unjust about these prices, Sowell explained; they simply reflect the value that buyers and sellers choose to place on the things they exchange.[6]

Jeff Jacoby, a pro-market commentator writing in the *Boston Globe*, argued against price-gouging laws on similar grounds: "It isn't gouging to charge what the market will bear. It isn't greedy or brazen. It's how goods and services get allocated in a free society." Jacoby acknowledged that the "price spikes are infuriating, especially to someone whose life has just been thrown into turmoil by a deadly storm." But public anger is no justification for interfering with the free market. By providing incentives for suppliers to produce more of the needed goods, the seemingly exorbitant prices "do far more good than harm." His conclusion: "Demonizing vendors won't speed Florida's recovery. Letting them go about their business will."[7]

Attorney General Crist (a Republican who would later be elected governor of Florida) published an op-ed piece in the Tampa paper defending the law against price gouging: "In times of emergency, government cannot remain on the sidelines while people are charged unconscionable prices as they flee for their lives or seek the basic commodities for their families after a hurricane."[8] Crist rejected the notion that these "unconscionable" prices reflected a truly free exchange:

> This is not the normal free market situation where willing buyers freely elect to enter into the marketplace and meet willing sellers, where a price is agreed upon based on supply and demand. In an emergency, buyers under duress have no freedom. Their purchases of necessities like safe lodging are forced.[9]

The debate about price gouging that arose in the aftermath of Hurricane Charley raises hard questions of morality and law: Is it wrong for sellers of goods and services to take advantage of a natural disaster by charging whatever the market will bear? If so, what, if anything, should the law do about it? Should the state prohibit price gouging, even if doing so interferes with the freedom of buyers and sellers to make whatever deals they choose?

Welfare, Freedom, and Virtue

These questions are not only about how individuals should treat one another. They are also about what the law should be, and about how society should be organized. They are questions about justice. To answer them, we have to explore the meaning of justice. In fact, we've already begun to do so. If you look closely at the price-gouging debate, you'll notice that the arguments for and against price-gouging laws revolve around three ideas: maximizing welfare, respecting freedom, and promoting virtue. Each of these ideas points to a different way of thinking about justice.

The standard case for unfettered markets rests on two claims—one about welfare, the other about freedom. First, markets promote the welfare of society as a whole by providing incentives for people to work hard supplying the goods that other people want. (In common parlance, we often equate welfare with economic prosperity, though welfare is a broader concept that can include noneconomic aspects of social well-being.) Second, markets respect individual freedom; rather than impose a certain value on goods and services, markets let people choose for themselves what value to place on the things they exchange.

Not surprisingly, the opponents of price-gouging laws invoke these two familiar arguments for free markets. How do defenders of price gouging laws respond? First, they argue that the welfare of society as whole is not really served by the exorbitant prices charged in hard times. Even if high prices call forth a greater supply of goods, this benefit has to be weighed against the burden such prices impose on those least able to afford them. For the affluent, paying inflated prices for a gallon of gas or a motel room in a storm may be an annoyance; but for those of modest means, such prices pose a genuine hardship, one that might lead them to stay in harm's way rather than flee to safety. Proponents of price-gouging laws argue that any estimate of the general welfare must include the pain and suffering of those who may be priced out of basic necessities during an emergency.

Second, defenders of price-gouging laws maintain that, under certain conditions, the free market is not truly free. As Crist points out, "buyers under duress have no freedom. Their purchases of necessities like safe lodging are forced." If you're fleeing a hurricane with your family, the exorbitant price you pay for gas or shelter is not really a voluntary exchange. It's something closer to extortion. So to decide whether price-gouging laws are justified, we need to assess these competing accounts of welfare and of freedom.

But we also need to consider one further argument. Much public support for price-gouging laws comes from something more visceral than welfare or freedom. People are outraged at "vultures" who prey on the desperation of others and want them punished—not rewarded with windfall profits. Such sentiments are often dismissed as atavistic emotions that should not interfere with public policy or law. As Jacoby writes, "demonizing vendors won't speed Florida's recovery."[10]

But the outrage at price-gougers is more than mindless anger. It gestures at a moral argument worth taking seriously. Outrage is the special kind of anger you feel when you believe that people are getting things they don't deserve. Outrage of this kind is anger at injustice.

Crist touched on the moral source of the outrage when he described the "greed that someone must have in their soul to be willing to take advantage of someone suffering in the wake of a hurricane." He did not explicitly connect this observation to price-gouging laws. But implicit in his comment is something like the following argument, which might be called the virtue argument:

Greed is a vice, a bad way of being, especially when it makes people oblivious to the suffering of others. More than a personal vice, it is at odds with civic virtue. In times of trouble, a good society pulls together. Rather than press for maximum advantage, people look out for one another. A society in which people exploit their neighbors for financial gain in times of crisis is not a good society. Excessive greed is therefore a vice that a good society should discourage if it can. Price-gouging laws cannot banish greed, but they can at least restrain its most brazen expression, and signal society's disapproval of it. By punishing greedy behavior rather than rewarding it, society affirms the civic virtue of shared sacrifice for the common good.

To acknowledge the moral force of the virtue argument is not to insist that it must always prevail over competing considerations. You might conclude, in some instances, that a hurricane-stricken community should make a devil's bargain—allow price gouging in hopes of attracting an army of roofers and contractors from far and wide, even at the moral cost of sanctioning greed. Repair the roofs now and the social fabric later. What's important to notice, however, is that the debate about price-gouging laws is not simply about welfare and freedom. It is also about virtue—about cultivating the attitudes and dispositions, the qualities of character, on which a good society depends.

Some people, including many who support price-gouging laws, find the virtue argument discomfiting. The reason: It seems more judgmental than arguments that appeal to welfare and freedom. To ask whether a policy will speed economic recovery or spur economic growth does not involve judging people's preferences. It assumes that everyone prefers more income rather than less, and it doesn't pass judgment on how they spend their money. Similarly, to ask whether, under conditions of duress, people are actually free to choose doesn't require evaluating their choices. The question is whether, or to what extent, people are free rather than coerced.

The virtue argument, by contrast, rests on a judgment that greed is a vice that the state should discourage. But who is to judge what is virtue and what is vice? Don't citizens of pluralist societies disagree about such things? And isn't it dangerous to impose judgments about virtue through law? In the face of these worries, many people hold that government should be neutral on matters of virtue and vice; it should not try to cultivate good attitudes or discourage bad ones.

So when we probe our reactions to price gouging, we find ourselves pulled in two directions: We are outraged when people get things they don't deserve; greed that preys on human misery, we think, should be punished, not rewarded. And yet we worry when judgments about virtue find their way into law.

This dilemma points to one of the great questions of political philosophy: Does a just society seek to promote the virtue of its citizens? Or should law be neutral toward competing conceptions of virtue, so that citizens can be free to choose for themselves the best way to live?

According to the textbook account, this question divides ancient and modern political thought. In one important respect, the textbook is right. Aristotle teaches that justice means giving people what they deserve. And in order to determine who deserves what, we have to determine what virtues are worthy of honor and reward. Aristotle maintains that we can't figure out what a just constitution is without first reflecting on the most desirable way of life. For him, law can't be neutral on questions of the good life.

By contrast, modern political philosophers—from Immanuel Kant in the eighteenth century to John Rawls in the twentieth century— argue that the principles of justice that define our rights should not rest on any particular conception of virtue, or of the best way to live. Instead, a just society respects each person's freedom to choose his or her own conception of the good life.

So you might say that ancient theories of justice start with virtue, while modern theories start with freedom. And in the chapters to come, we explore the strengths and weaknesses of each. But it's worth noticing at the outset that this contrast can mislead.

For if we turn our gaze to the arguments about justice that animate contemporary politics—not among philosophers but among ordinary men and women—we find a more complicated picture. It's true that most of our arguments are about promoting prosperity and respecting individual freedom, at least on the surface. But underlying these arguments, and sometimes contending with them, we can often glimpse another set of convictions—about what virtues are worthy of honor and reward, and what way of life a good society should promote. Devoted though we are to prosperity and freedom, we can't quite shake off the judgmental strand of justice. The conviction that justice involves virtue as well as choice runs deep. Thinking about justice seems inescapably to engage us in thinking about the best way to live.

What Wounds Deserve the Purple Heart?

On some issues, questions of virtue and honor are too obvious to deny. Consider the recent debate over who should qualify for the Purple Heart. Since 1932, the U.S. military has awarded the medal to soldiers wounded or killed in battle by enemy action. In addition to the honor, the medal entitles recipients to special privileges in veterans' hospitals.

Since the beginning of the current wars in Iraq and Afghanistan, growing numbers of veterans have been diagnosed with post-traumatic stress disorder and treated for the condition. Symptoms include recurring nightmares, severe depression, and suicide. At least three hundred thousand veterans reportedly suffer from traumatic stress or major depression. Advocates for these veterans have proposed that they, too, should qualify for the Purple Heart. Since psychological injuries can be at least as debilitating as physical ones, they argue, soldiers who suffer these wounds should receive the medal.[11]

After a Pentagon advisory group studied the question, the Pentagon announced, in 2009, that the Purple Heart would be reserved for soldiers with physical injuries. Veterans suffering from mental disorders and psychological trauma would not be eligible, even though they qualify for government-supported medical treatment and disability payments. The Pentagon offered two reasons for its decision: traumatic stress disorders are not intentionally caused by enemy action, and they are difficult to diagnose objectively.[12]

Did the Pentagon make the right decision? Taken by themselves, its reasons are unconvincing. In the Iraq War, one of the most common injuries recognized with the Purple Heart has been a punctured eardrum, caused by explosions at close range.[13] But unlike bullets and bombs, such explosions are not a deliberate enemy tactic intended to injure or kill; they are (like traumatic stress) a damaging side effect of battlefield action. And while traumatic disorders may be more difficult to diagnose than a broken limb, the injury they inflict can be more severe and long-lasting.

As the wider debate about the Purple Heart revealed, the real issue is about the meaning of the medal and the virtues it honors. What, then, are the relevant virtues? Unlike other military medals, the Purple Heart honors sacrifice, not bravery. It requires no heroic act, only an injury inflicted by the enemy. The question is what kind of injury should count.

A veteran's group called the Military Order of the Purple Heart opposed awarding the medal for psychological injuries, claiming that doing so would "debase" the honor. A spokesman for the group stated that "shedding blood" should be an essential qualification.[14] He didn't explain why bloodless injuries shouldn't count. But Tyler E. Boudreau, a former Marine captain who favors including psychological injuries, offers a compelling analysis of the dispute. He attributes the opposition to a deep-seated attitude in the military that views post-traumatic stress as a kind of weakness. "The same culture that demands tough-mindedness also encourages skepticism toward the suggestion that the violence of war can hurt the healthiest of minds . . . Sadly, as long as our military culture bears at least a quiet contempt for the psychological wounds of war, it is unlikely those veterans will ever see a Purple Heart."[15]

So the debate over the Purple Heart is more than a medical or clinical dispute about how to determine the veracity of injury. At the heart of the disagreement are rival conceptions of moral character and military valor. Those who insist that only bleeding wounds should count believe that post-traumatic stress reflects a weakness of character unworthy of honor. Those who believe that psychological wounds should qualify argue that veterans suffering long-term trauma and severe depression have sacrificed for their country as surely, and as honorably, as those who've lost a limb.

The dispute over the Purple Heart illustrates the moral logic of Aristotle's theory of justice. We can't determine who deserves a military medal without asking what virtues the medal properly honors. And to answer that question, we have to assess competing conceptions of character and sacrifice.

It might be argued that military medals are a special case, a throwback to an ancient ethic of honor and virtue. These days, most of our arguments about justice are about how to distribute the fruits of prosperity, or the burdens of hard times, and how to define the basic rights of citizens. In these domains, considerations of welfare and freedom predominate. But arguments about the rights and wrongs of economic arrangements often lead us back to Aristotle's question of what people morally deserve, and why.

Bailout Outrage

The public furor over the financial crisis of 2008–09 is a case in point. For years, stock prices and real estate values had climbed. The reckoning came when the housing bubble burst. Wall Street banks and financial institutions had made billions of dollars on complex investments backed by mortgages whose value now plunged. Once proud Wall Street firms teetered on the edge of collapse. The stock market tanked, devastating not only big investors but also ordinary Americans, whose retirement accounts lost much of their value. The total wealth of American families fell by $11 trillion in 2008, an amount equal to the combined annual output of Germany, Japan, and the UK.[16]

In October 2008, President George W. Bush asked Congress for $700 billion to bail out the nation's big banks and financial firms. It didn't seem fair that Wall Street had enjoyed huge profits during the good times and was now asking taxpayers to foot the bill when things had gone bad. But there seemed no alternative. The banks and financial firms had grown so vast and so entwined with every aspect of the economy that their collapse might bring down the entire financial system. They were "too big to fail."

No one claimed that the banks and investment houses deserved the money. Their reckless bets (enabled by inadequate government regulation) had created the crisis. But here was a case where the welfare of the economy as a whole seemed to outweigh considerations of fairness. Congress reluctantly appropriated the bailout funds.

Then came the bonuses. Shortly after the bailout money began to flow, news accounts revealed that some of the companies now on the public dole were awarding millions of dollars in bonuses to their executives. The most egregious case involved the American International Group (A.I.G.), an insurance giant brought to ruin by the risky investments of its financial products unit. Despite having been rescued with massive infusions of government funds (totaling $173 billion), the company paid $165 million in bonuses to executives in the very division that had precipitated the crisis. Seventy-three employees received bonuses of $1 million or more.[17]

News of the bonuses set off a firestorm of public protest. This time, the outrage was not about ten-dollar bags of ice or overpriced motel rooms. It was about lavish rewards subsidized with taxpayer funds to members of the division that had helped bring the global financial system to near meltdown. Something was wrong with this picture. Although the U.S. government now owned 80 percent of the company, the treasury secretary pleaded in vain with A.I.G.'s government-appointed CEO to rescind the bonuses. "We cannot attract and retain the best and the brightest talent," the CEO replied, "if employees believe their compensation is subject to continued and arbitrary adjustment by the U.S. Treasury." He claimed the employees' talents were needed to unload the toxic assets for the benefit of the taxpayers, who, after all, owned most of the company.[18]

The public reacted with fury. A full-page headline in the tabloid *New York Post* captured the sentiments of many: "Not So Fast You Greedy

Bastards."[19] The U.S. House of Representatives sought to claw back the payments by approving a bill that would impose a 90 percent tax on bonuses paid to employees of companies that received substantial bailout funds.[20] Under pressure from New York attorney general Andrew Cuomo, fifteen of the top twenty A.I.G. bonus recipients agreed to return the payments, and some $50 million was recouped in all.[21] This gesture assuaged public anger to some degree, and support for the punitive tax measure faded in the Senate.[22] But the episode left the public reluctant to spend more to clean up the mess the financial industry had created.

At the heart of the bailout outrage was a sense of injustice. Even before the bonus issue erupted, public support for the bailout was hesitant and conflicted. Americans were torn between the need to prevent an economic meltdown that would hurt everyone and their belief that funneling massive sums to failed banks and investment companies was deeply unfair. To avoid economic disaster, Congress and the public acceded. But morally speaking, it had felt all along like a kind of extortion.

Underlying the bailout outrage was a belief about moral desert: The executives receiving the bonuses (and the companies receiving the bailouts) didn't deserve them. But why didn't they? The reason may be less obvious than it seems. Consider two possible answers—one is about greed, the other about failure.

One source of outrage was that the bonuses seemed to reward greed, as the tabloid headline indelicately suggested. The public found this morally unpalatable. Not only the bonuses but the bailout as a whole seemed, perversely, to reward greedy behavior rather than punish it. The derivatives traders had landed their company, and the country, in dire financial peril—by making reckless investments in pursuit of ever-greater profits. Having pocketed the profits when times were good, they saw nothing wrong with million-dollar bonuses even after their investments had come to ruin.[23]

The greed critique was voiced not only by the tabloids, but also (in more decorous versions) by public officials. Senator Sherrod Brown

(D-Ohio) said that A.I.G.'s behavior "smacks of greed, arrogance, and worse."[24] President Obama stated that A.I.G. "finds itself in financial distress due to recklessness and greed."[25]

The problem with the greed critique is that it doesn't distinguish the rewards bestowed by the bailout after the crash from the rewards bestowed by markets when times were flush. Greed is a vice, a bad attitude, an excessive, single-minded desire for gain. So it's understandable that people aren't keen to reward it. But is there any reason to assume that the recipients of bailout bonuses are any greedier now than they were a few years ago, when they were riding high and reaping even greater rewards?

Wall Street traders, bankers, and hedge fund managers are a hard-charging lot. The pursuit of financial gain is what they do for a living. Whether or not their vocation taints their character, their virtue is unlikely to rise or fall with the stock market. So if it's wrong to reward greed with big bailout bonuses, isn't it also wrong to reward it with market largess? The public was outraged when, in 2008, Wall Street firms (some on taxpayer-subsidized life support) handed out $16 billion in bonuses. But this figure was less than half the amounts paid out in 2006 ($34 billion) and 2007 ($33 billion).[26] If greed is the reason they don't deserve the money now, on what basis can it be said they deserved the money then?

One obvious difference is that bailout bonuses come from the taxpayer while the bonuses paid in good times come from company earnings. If the outrage is based on the conviction that the bonuses are undeserved, however, the source of the payment is not morally decisive. But it does provide a clue: the reason the bonuses are coming from the taxpayer is that the companies have failed. This takes us to the heart of the complaint. The American public's real objection to the bonuses—and the bailout—is not that they reward greed but that they reward failure.

Americans are harder on failure than on greed. In market-driven societies, ambitious people are expected to pursue their interests vigorously, and the line between self-interest and greed often blurs. But the line between success and failure is etched more sharply. And the idea that people deserve the rewards that success bestows is central to the American dream.

Notwithstanding his passing reference to greed, President Obama understood that rewarding failure was the deeper source of dissonance and outrage. In announcing limits on executive pay at companies receiving bailout funds, Obama identified the real source of bailout outrage:

> This is America. We don't disparage wealth. We don't begrudge anybody for achieving success. And we certainly believe that success should be rewarded. But what gets people upset—and rightfully so—are executives being rewarded for failure, especially when those rewards are subsidized by U.S. taxpayers.[27]

One of the most bizarre statements about bailout ethics came from Senator Charles Grassley (R-Iowa), a fiscal conservative from the heartland. At the height of the bonus furor, Grassley said in an Iowa radio interview that what bothered him most was the refusal of the corporate executives to take any blame for their failures. He would "feel a bit better towards them if they would follow the Japanese example and come before the American people and take that deep bow and say, 'I'm sorry,' and then either do one of two things—resign or go commit suicide."[28]

Grassley later explained that he was not calling on the executives to commit suicide. But he did want them to accept responsibility for their failure, to show contrition, and to offer a public apology. "I haven't heard this from CEOs, and it just makes it very difficult for the taxpayers of my district to just keep shoveling money out the door."[29]

Grassley's comments support my hunch that the bailout anger was not mainly about greed; what most offended Americans' sense of justice was that their tax dollars were being used to reward failure.

If that's right, it remains to ask whether this view of the bailouts was justified. Were the CEOs and top executives of the big banks and investment firms really to blame for the financial crisis? Many of the executives didn't think so. Testifying before congressional committees investigating the financial crisis, they insisted they had done all they could with the information available to them. The former chief executive of Bear Stearns, a Wall Street investment firm that collapsed in 2008, said he'd pondered long and hard whether he could have done anything differently. He concluded he'd done all he could. "I just simply have not been able to come up with anything . . . that would have made a difference to the situation we faced."[30]

Other CEOs of failed companies agreed, insisting that they were victims "of a financial tsunami" beyond their control.[31] A similar attitude extended to young traders, who had a hard time understanding the public's fury about their bonuses. "There's no sympathy for us anywhere," a Wall Street trader told a reporter for *Vanity Fair*. "But it's not as if we weren't working hard."[32]

The tsunami metaphor became part of bailout vernacular, especially in financial circles. If the executives are right that the failure of their companies was due to larger economic forces, not their own decisions, this would explain why they didn't express the remorse that Senator Grassley wanted to hear. But it also raises a far-reaching question about failure, success, and justice.

If big, systemic economic forces account for the disastrous loses of 2008 and 2009, couldn't it be argued that they also account for the dazzling gains of earlier years? If the weather is to blame for the bad years, how can it be that the talent, wisdom, and hard work of bankers, traders, and Wall Street executives are responsible for the stupendous returns that occurred when the sun was shining?

Confronted with public outrage over paying bonuses for failure, the CEOs argued that financial returns are not wholly their own doing, but the product of forces beyond their control. They may have a point.

But if this is true, there's good reason to question their claim to out-sized compensation when times are good. Surely the end of the cold war, the globalization of trade and capital markets, the rise of personal computers and the Internet, and a host of other factors help explain the success of the financial industry during its run in the 1990s and in the early years of the twenty-first century.

In 2007, CEOs at major U.S. corporations were paid 344 times the pay of the average worker.[33] On what grounds, if any, do executives deserve to make that much more than their employees? Most of them work hard and bring talent to their work. But consider this: In 1980, CEOs earned only 42 times what their workers did.[34] Were executives less talented and hardworking in 1980 than they are today? Or do pay differentials reflect contingencies unrelated to talents and skills?

Or compare the level of executive compensation in the United States with that in other countries. CEOs at top U.S. companies earn an average of $13.3 million per year (using 2004–2006 data), compared to $6.6 million for European chief executives and $1.5 million for CEOs in Japan.[35] Are American executives twice as deserving as their European counterparts, and nine times as deserving as Japanese CEOs? Or do these differences also reflect factors unrelated to the effort and talent that executives bring to their jobs?

The bailout outrage that gripped the United States in early 2009 expressed the widely held view that people who wreck the companies they run with risky investments don't deserve to be rewarded with millions of dollars in bonuses. But the argument over the bonuses raises questions about who deserves what when times are good. Do the successful deserve the bounty that markets bestow upon them, or does that bounty depend on factors beyond their control? And what are the implications for the mutual obligations of citizens—in good times and hard times? Whether the financial crisis will prompt public debate on these broader questions remains to be seen.

Three Approaches to Justice

To ask whether a society is just is to ask how it distributes the things we prize—income and wealth, duties and rights, powers and opportunities, offices and honors. A just society distributes these goods in the right way; it gives each person his or her due. The hard questions begin when we ask what people are due, and why.

We've already begun to wrestle with these questions. As we've pondered the rights and wrongs of price gouging, competing claims to the Purple Heart, and financial bailouts, we've identified three ways of approaching the distribution of goods: welfare, freedom, and virtue. Each of these ideals suggests a different way of thinking about justice.

Some of our debates reflect disagreement about what it means to maximize welfare or respect freedom or cultivate virtue. Others involve disagreement about what to do when these ideals conflict. Political philosophy cannot resolve these disagreements once and for all. But it can give shape to the arguments we have, and bring moral clarity to the alternatives we confront as democratic citizens.

This book explores the strengths and weaknesses of these three ways of thinking about justice. We begin with the idea of maximizing welfare. For market societies such as ours, it offers a natural starting point. Much contemporary political debate is about how to promote prosperity, or improve our standard of living, or spur economic growth. Why do we care about these things? The most obvious answer is that we think prosperity makes us better off than we would otherwise be— as individuals and as a society. Prosperity matters, in other words, because it contributes to our welfare. To explore this idea, we turn to utilitarianism, the most influential account of how and why we should maximize welfare, or (as the utilitarians put it) seek the greatest happiness for the greatest number.

Next, we take up a range of theories that connect justice to freedom. Most of these theories emphasize respect for individual rights, though they disagree among themselves about which rights are most important. The idea that justice means respecting freedom and individual rights is at least as familiar in contemporary politics as the utilitarian idea of maximizing welfare. For example, the U.S. Bill of Rights sets out certain liberties—including rights to freedom of speech and religious liberty—that even majorities may not violate. And around the world, the idea that justice means respecting certain universal human rights is increasingly embraced (in theory, if not always in practice).

The approach to justice that begins with freedom is a capacious school. In fact, some of the most hard-fought political arguments of our time take place between two rival camps within it—the laissez-faire camp and the fairness camp. Leading the laissez-faire camp are free-market libertarians who believe that justice consists in respecting and upholding the voluntary choices made by consenting adults. The fairness camp contains theorists of a more egalitarian bent. They argue that unfettered markets are neither just nor free. In their view, justice requires policies that remedy social and economic disadvantages and give everyone a fair chance at success.

Finally, we turn to theories that see justice as bound up with virtue and the good life. In contemporary politics, virtue theories are often identified with cultural conservatives and the religious right. The idea of legislating morality is anathema to many citizens of liberal societies, as it risks lapsing into intolerance and coercion. But the notion that a just society affirms certain virtues and conceptions of the good life has inspired political movements and arguments across the ideological spectrum. Not only the Taliban, but also abolitionists and Martin Luther King, Jr., have drawn their visions of justice from moral and religious ideals.

Before attempting to assess these theories of justice, it's worth asking how philosophical arguments can proceed—especially in so contested a domain as moral and political philosophy. They often begin with concrete situations. As we've seen in our discussion of price gouging, Purple Hearts, and bailouts, moral and political reflection finds its occasion in disagreement. Often the disagreements are among partisans or rival advocates in the public realm. Sometimes the disagree-ments are within us as individuals, as when we find ourselves torn or conflicted about a hard moral question.

But how exactly can we reason our way from the judgments we make about concrete situations to the principles of justice we believe should apply in all situations? What, in short, does moral reasoning consist in?

To see how moral reasoning can proceed, let's turn to two situa-tions—one a fanciful hypothetical story much discussed by philoso-phers, the other an actual story about an excruciating moral dilemma.

Consider first this philosopher's hypothetical.[36] Like all such tales, it involves a scenario stripped of many realistic complexities, so that we can focus on a limited number of philosophical issues.

The Runaway Trolley

Suppose you are the driver of a trolley car hurtling down the track at sixty miles an hour. Up ahead you see five workers standing on the track, tools in hand. You try to stop, but you can't. The brakes don't work. You feel desperate, because you know that if you crash into these five workers, they will all die. (Let's assume you know that for sure.)

Suddenly, you notice a side track, off to the right. There is a worker on that track, too, but only one. You realize that you can turn the trolley car onto the side track, killing the one worker, but sparing the five.

What should you do? Most people would say, "Turn! Tragic though it is to kill one innocent person, it's even worse to kill five." Sacrificing one life in order to save five does seem the right thing to do.

Now consider another version of the trolley story. This time, you are not the driver but an onlooker, standing on a bridge overlooking the track. (This time, there is no side track.) Down the track comes a trolley, and at the end of the track are five workers. Once again, the brakes don't work. The trolley is about to crash into the five workers. You feel helpless to avert this disaster—until you notice, standing next to you on the bridge, a very heavy man. You could push him off the bridge, onto the track, into the path of the oncoming trolley. He would die, but the five workers would be saved. (You consider jumping onto the track yourself, but realize you are too small to stop the trolley.)

Would pushing the heavy man onto the track be the right thing to do? Most people would say, "Of course not. It would be terribly wrong to push the man onto the track."

Pushing someone off a bridge to a certain death does seem an awful thing to do, even if it saves five innocent lives. But this raises a moral puzzle: Why does the principle that seems right in the first case—sacrifice one life to save five—seem wrong in the second?

If, as our reaction to the first case suggests, numbers count—if it is better to save five lives than one—then why shouldn't we apply this principle in the second case, and push? It does seem cruel to push a man to his death, even for a good cause. But is it any less cruel to kill a man by crashing into him with a trolley car?

Perhaps the reason it is wrong to push is that doing so uses the man on the bridge against his will. He didn't choose to be involved, after all. He was just standing there.

But the same could be said of the person working on the side track. He didn't choose to be involved, either. He was just doing his job, not volunteering to sacrifice his life in the event of a runaway trolley. It might be argued that railway workers willingly incur a risk that by-standers do not. But let's assume that being willing to die in an emergency to save other people's lives is not part of the job description, and that the worker has no more consented to give his life than the by-stander on the bridge has consented to give his.

Maybe the moral difference lies not in the effect on the victims—both wind up dead—but in the intention of the person making the decision. As the driver of the trolley, you might defend your choice to divert the trolley by pointing out that you didn't *intend* the death of the worker on the side track, foreseeable though it was; your purpose would still have been achieved if, by a great stroke of luck, the five workers were spared and the sixth also managed to survive.

But the same is true in the pushing case. The death of the man you push off the bridge is not essential to your purpose. All he needs to do is block the trolley; if he can do so and somehow survive, you would be delighted.

Or perhaps, on reflection, the two cases should be governed by the same principle. Both involve a deliberate choice to take the life of one innocent person in order to prevent an even greater loss of life. Perhaps your reluctance to push the man off the bridge is mere squeamishness, a hesitation you should overcome. Pushing a man to his death with your bare hands does seem more cruel than turning the steering wheel of a trolley. But doing the right thing is not always easy.

We can test this idea by altering the story slightly. Suppose you, as the onlooker, could cause the large man standing next to you to fall onto the track without pushing him; imagine he is standing on a trap door that you could open by turning a steering wheel. No pushing, same result. Would that make it the right thing to do? Or is it still morally worse than for you, as the trolley driver, to turn onto the side track?

It is not easy to explain the moral difference between these cases— why turning the trolley seems right, but pushing the man off the bridge seems wrong. But notice the pressure we feel to reason our way to a convincing distinction between them—and if we cannot, to reconsider our judgment about the right thing to do in each case. We sometimes think of moral reasoning as a way of persuading other people. But it is also a way of sorting out our own moral convictions, of figuring out what we believe and why.

Some moral dilemmas arise from conflicting moral principles. For example, one principle that comes into play in the trolley story says we should save as many lives as possible, but another says it is wrong to kill an innocent person, even for a good cause. Confronted with a situation in which saving a number of lives depends on killing an innocent person, we face a moral quandary. We must try to figure out which principle has greater weight, or is more appropriate under the circumstances.

Other moral dilemmas arise because we are uncertain how events will unfold. Hypothetical examples such as the trolley story remove the uncertainty that hangs over the choices we confront in real life. They assume we know for sure how many will die if we don't turn— or don't push. This makes such stories imperfect guides to action. But it also makes them useful devices for moral analysis. By setting aside contingencies—"What if the workers noticed the trolley and jumped aside in time?"—hypothetical examples help us to isolate the moral principles at stake and examine their force.

The Afghan Goatherds

Consider now an actual moral dilemma, similar in some ways to the fanciful tale of the runaway trolley, but complicated by uncertainty about how things will turn out:

In June 2005, a special forces team made up of Petty Officer Marcus Luttrell and three other U.S. Navy SEALs set out on a secret reconnaissance mission in Afghanistan, near the Pakistan border, in search of a Taliban leader, a close associate of Osama bin Laden.[37] According to intelligence reports, their target commanded 140 to 150 heavily armed fighters and was staying in a village in the forbidding mountainous region.

Shortly after the special forces team took up a position on a mountain ridge overlooking the village, two Afghan farmers with about a hundred bleating goats happened upon them. With them was a boy about fourteen years old. The Afghans were unarmed. The American soldiers trained their rifles on them, motioned for them to sit on the ground, and then debated what to do about them. On the one hand, the goatherds appeared to be unarmed civilians. On the other hand, letting them go would run the risk that they would inform the Taliban of the presence of the U.S. soldiers.

As the four soldiers contemplated their options, they realized that they didn't have any rope, so tying up the Afghans to allow time to find a new hideout was not feasible. The only choice was to kill them or let them go free.

One of Luttrell's comrades argued for killing the goatherds: "We're on active duty behind enemy lines, sent here by our senior commanders. We have a right to do everything we can to save our own lives. The military decision is obvious. To turn them loose would be wrong."[38] Luttrell was torn. "In my soul, I knew he was right," he wrote in retrospect. "We could not possibly turn them loose. But my trouble is, I have another soul. My Christian soul. And it was crowding in on me. Something kept whispering in the back of my mind, it would be wrong to execute these unarmed men in cold blood."[39] Luttrell didn't say what he meant by his Christian soul, but in the end, his conscience didn't allow him to kill the goatherds. He cast the deciding vote to release them. (One of his three comrades had abstained.) It was a vote he came to regret.

About an hour and a half after they released the goatherds, the four soldiers found themselves surrounded by eighty to a hundred Taliban fighters armed with AK-47s and rocket-propelled grenades. In the fierce firefight that followed, all three of Luttrell's comrades were killed. The Taliban fighters also shot down a U.S. helicopter that sought to rescue the SEAL unit, killing all sixteen soldiers on board.

Luttrell, severely injured, managed to survive by falling down the mountainside and crawling seven miles to a Pashtun village, whose residents protected him from the Taliban until he was rescued.

In retrospect, Luttrell condemned his own vote not to kill the goatherds. "It was the stupidest, most southern-fried, lamebrained decision I ever made in my life," he wrote in a book about the experience. "I must have been out of my mind. I had actually cast a vote which I knew could sign our death warrant. . . . At least, that's how I look back on those moments now. . . . The deciding vote was mine, and it will haunt me till they rest me in an East Texas grave."[40]

Part of what made the soldiers' dilemma so difficult was uncertainty about what would happen if they released the Afghans. Would they simply go on their way, or would they alert the Taliban? But suppose Luttrell knew that freeing the goatherds would lead to a devastating battle resulting in the loss of his comrades, nineteen American deaths, injury to himself, and the failure of his mission? Would he have decided differently?

For Luttrell, looking back, the answer is clear: he should have killed the goatherds. Given the disaster that followed, it is hard to disagree. From the standpoint of numbers, Luttrell's choice is similar to the trolley case. Killing the three Afghans would have saved the lives of his three comrades and the sixteen U.S. troops who tried to rescue them. But which version of the trolley story does it resemble? Would killing the goatherds be more like turning the trolley or pushing the man off the bridge? The fact that Luttrell anticipated the danger and still could not bring himself to kill unarmed civilians in cold blood suggests it may be closer to the pushing case.

And yet the case for killing the goatherds seems somehow stronger than the case for pushing the man off the bridge. This may be because we suspect that—given the outcome—they were not innocent bystanders, but Taliban sympathizers. Consider an analogy: If we had reason to believe that the man on the bridge was responsible for disabling the brakes of the trolley in hopes of killing the workers on the track (let's say they were his enemies), the moral argument for pushing him onto the track would begin to look stronger. We would still need to know who his enemies were, and why he wanted to kill them. If we learned that the workers on the track were members of the French resistance and the heavy man on the bridge a Nazi who had sought to kill them by disabling the trolley, the case for pushing him to save them would become morally compelling.

It is possible, of course, that the Afghan goatherds were not Taliban sympathizers, but neutrals in the conflict, or even Taliban opponents, who were forced by the Taliban to reveal the presence of the American troops. Suppose Luttrell and his comrades knew for certain that the goatherds meant them no harm, but would be tortured by the Taliban to reveal their location. The Americans might have killed the goatherds to protect their mission and themselves. But the decision to do so would have been more wrenching (and morally more questionable) than if they knew the goatherds to be pro-Taliban spies.

Moral Dilemmas

Few of us face choices as fateful as those that confronted the soldiers on the mountain or the witness to the runaway trolley. But wrestling with their dilemmas sheds light on the way moral argument can proceed, in our personal lives and in the public square.

Life in democratic societies is rife with disagreement about right and wrong, justice and injustice. Some people favor abortion rights, and others consider abortion to be murder. Some believe fairness requires taxing the rich to help the poor, while others believe it is unfair to tax away money people have earned through their own efforts. Some defend affirmative action in college admissions as a way of righting past wrongs, whereas others consider it an unfair form of reverse discrimination against people who deserve admission on their merits. Some people reject the torture of terror suspects as a moral abomination unworthy of a free society, while others defend it as a last resort to prevent a terrorist attack.

Elections are won and lost on these disagreements. The so-called culture wars are fought over them. Given the passion and intensity with which we debate moral questions in public life, we might be tempted to think that our moral convictions are fixed once and for all, by upbringing or faith, beyond the reach of reason.

But if this were true, moral persuasion would be inconceivable, and what we take to be public debate about justice and rights would be nothing more than a volley of dogmatic assertions, an ideological food fight.

At its worst, our politics comes close to this condition. But it need not be this way. Sometimes, an argument can change our minds.

How, then, can we reason our way through the contested terrain of justice and injustice, equality and inequality, individual rights and the common good? This book tries to answer that question.

One way to begin is to notice how moral reflection emerges naturally from an encounter with a hard moral question. We start with an opinion, or a conviction, about the right thing to do: "Turn the trolley onto the side track." Then we reflect on the reason for our conviction, and seek out the principle on which it is based: "Better to sacrifice one life to avoid the death of many." Then, confronted with a situation that confounds the principle, we are pitched into confusion: "I thought it was always right to save as many lives as possible, and yet it seems wrong to push the man off the bridge (or to kill the unarmed goatherds)." Feeling the force of that confusion, and the pressure to sort it out, is the impulse to philosophy.

Confronted with this tension, we may revise our judgment about the right thing to do, or rethink the principle we initially espoused. As we encounter new situations, we move back and forth between our judgments and our principles, revising each in light of the other. This turning of mind, from the world of action to the realm of reasons and back again, is what moral reflection consists in.

This way of conceiving moral argument, as a dialectic between our judgments about particular situations and the principles we affirm on reflection, has a long tradition. It goes back to the dialogues of Socrates and the moral philosophy of Aristotle. But notwithstanding its ancient lineage, it is open to the following challenge:

If moral reflection consists in seeking a fit between the judgments we make and the principles we affirm, how can such reflection lead us to justice, or moral truth? Even if we succeed, over a lifetime, in bringing our moral intuitions and principled commitments into alignment, what confidence can we have that the result is anything more than a self-consistent skein of prejudice?

The answer is that moral reflection is not a solitary pursuit but a public endeavor. It requires an interlocutor—a friend, a neighbor, a comrade, a fellow citizen. Sometimes the interlocutor can be imagined rather than real, as when we argue with ourselves. But we cannot discover the meaning of justice or the best way to live through introspection alone.

In Plato's *Republic*, Socrates compares ordinary citizens to a group of prisoners confined in a cave. All they ever see is the play of shadows on the wall, a reflection of objects they can never apprehend. Only the philosopher, in this account, is able to ascend from the cave to the bright light of day, where he sees things as they really are. Socrates suggests that, having glimpsed the sun, only the philosopher is fit to rule the cave dwellers, if he can somehow be coaxed back into the darkness where they live.

Plato's point is that to grasp the meaning of justice and the nature of the good life, we must rise above the prejudices and routines of everyday life. He is right, I think, but only in part. The claims of the cave must be given their due. If moral reflection is dialectical—if it moves back and forth between the judgments we make in concrete situations and the principles that inform those judgments—it needs opinions and convictions, however partial and untutored, as ground and grist. A philosophy untouched by the shadows on the wall can only yield a sterile utopia.

When moral reflection turns political, when it asks what laws should govern our collective life, it needs some engagement with the tumult of the city, with the arguments and incidents that roil the public mind. Debates over bailouts and price gouging, income inequality and affirmative action, military service and same-sex marriage, are the stuff of political philosophy. They prompt us to articulate and justify our moral and political convictions, not only among family and friends but also in the demanding company of our fellow citizens.

More demanding still is the company of political philosophers, ancient and modern, who thought through, in sometimes radical and surprising ways, the ideas that animate civic life—justice and rights, obligation and consent, honor and virtue, morality and law. Aristotle,

Immanuel Kant, John Stuart Mill, and John Rawls all figure in these pages. But their order of appearance is not chronological. This book is not a history of ideas, but a journey in moral and political reflection. Its goal is not to show who influenced whom in the history of political thought, but to invite readers to subject their own views about justice to critical examination—to figure out what they think, and why.

2. THE GREATEST HAPPINESS PRINCIPLE / UTILITARIANISM

In the summer of 1884, four English sailors were stranded at sea in a small lifeboat in the South Atlantic, over a thousand miles from land. Their ship, the *Mignonette*, had gone down in a storm, and they had escaped to the lifeboat, with only two cans of preserved turnips and no fresh water. Thomas Dudley was the captain, Edwin Stephens was the first mate, and Edmund Brooks was a sailor—"all men of excellent character," according to newspaper accounts.[1]

The fourth member of the crew was the cabin boy, Richard Parker, age seventeen. He was an orphan, on his first long voyage at sea. He had signed up against the advice of his friends, "in the hopefulness of youthful ambition," thinking the journey would make a man of him. Sadly, it was not to be.

From the lifeboat, the four stranded sailors watched the horizon, hoping a ship might pass and rescue them. For the first three days, they ate small rations of turnips. On the fourth day, they caught a turtle. They subsisted on the turtle and the remaining turnips for the next few days. And then for eight days, they ate nothing.

By now Parker, the cabin boy, was lying in the corner of the lifeboat. He had drunk seawater, against the advice of the others, and become ill. He appeared to be dying. On the nineteenth day of their ordeal, Dudley, the captain, suggested drawing lots to determine who would die so that the others might live. But Brooks refused, and no lots were drawn.

The next day came, and still no ship was in sight. Dudley told Brooks to avert his gaze and motioned to Stephens that Parker had to be killed. Dudley offered a prayer, told the boy his time had come, and then killed him with a penknife, stabbing him in the jugular vein. Brooks emerged from his conscientious objection to share in the gruesome bounty. For four days, the three men fed on the body and blood of the cabin boy.

And then help came. Dudley describes their rescue in his diary, with staggering euphemism: "On the 24th day, as we were having our breakfast," a ship appeared at last. The three survivors were picked up. Upon their return to England, they were arrested and tried. Brooks turned state's witness. Dudley and Stephens went to trial. They freely confessed that they had killed and eaten Parker. They claimed they had done so out of necessity.

Suppose you were the judge. How would you rule? To simplify things, put aside the question of law and assume that you were asked to decide whether killing the cabin boy was morally permissible.

The strongest argument for the defense is that, given the dire circumstances, it was necessary to kill one person in order to save three. Had no one been killed and eaten, all four would likely have died. Parker, weakened and ill, was the logical candidate, since he would soon have died anyway. And unlike Dudley and Stephens, he had no dependents. His death deprived no one of support and left no grieving wife or children.

This argument is open to at least two objections: First, it can be asked whether the benefits of killing the cabin boy, taken as a whole, really did outweigh the costs. Even counting the number of lives saved and the happiness of the survivors and their families, allowing such a killing might have bad consequences for society as a whole—weakening the norm against murder, for example, or increasing people's tendency to take the law into their own hands, or making it more difficult for captains to recruit cabin boys.

Second, even if, all things considered, the benefits do outweigh the costs, don't we have a nagging sense that killing and eating a defenseless cabin boy is wrong for reasons that go beyond the calculation of social costs and benefits? Isn't it wrong to use a human being in this way—exploiting his vulnerability, taking his life without his consent— even if doing so benefits others?

To anyone appalled by the actions of Dudley and Stephens, the first objection will seem a tepid complaint. It accepts the utilitarian assumption that morality consists in weighing costs and benefits, and simply wants a fuller reckoning of the social consequences.

If the killing of the cabin boy is worthy of moral outrage, the second objection is more to the point. It rejects the idea that the right thing to do is simply a matter of calculating consequences—costs and benefits. It suggests that morality means something more—something to do with the proper way for human beings to treat one another.

These two ways of thinking about the lifeboat case illustrate two rival approaches to justice. The first approach says the morality of an action depends solely on the consequences it brings about; the right thing to do is whatever will produce the best state of affairs, all things considered. The second approach says that consequences are not all we should care about, morally speaking; certain duties and rights should command our respect, for reasons independent of the social consequences.

In order to resolve the lifeboat case, as well as many less extreme dilemmas we commonly encounter, we need to explore some big questions of moral and political philosophy: Is morality a matter of counting lives and weighing costs and benefits, or are certain moral duties and human rights so fundamental that they rise above such calculations? And if certain rights are fundamental in this way—be they natural, or sacred, or inalienable, or categorical—how can we identify them? And what makes them fundamental?

Jeremy Bentham's Utilitarianism

Jeremy Bentham (1748–1832) left no doubt where he stood on this question. He heaped scorn on the idea of natural rights, calling them "nonsense upon stilts." The philosophy he launched has had an influential career. In fact, it exerts a powerful hold on the thinking of policy-makers, economists, business executives, and ordinary citizens to this day.

Bentham, an English moral philosopher and legal reformer, founded the doctrine of utilitarianism. Its main idea is simply stated and intuitively appealing: The highest principle of morality is to maximize happiness, the overall balance of pleasure over pain. According to Bentham, the right thing to do is whatever will maximize utility. By "utility," he means whatever produces pleasure or happiness, and whatever prevents pain or suffering.

Bentham arrives at his principle by the following line of reasoning: We are all governed by the feelings of pain and pleasure. They are our "sovereign masters." They govern us in everything we do and also determine what we ought to do. The standard of right and wrong is "fastened to their throne."[2]

We all like pleasure and dislike pain. The utilitarian philosophy recognizes this fact, and makes it the basis of moral and political life. Maximizing utility is a principle not only for individuals but also for legislators. In deciding what laws or policies to enact, a government should do whatever will maximize the happiness of the community as a whole. What, after all, is a community? According to Bentham, it is "a fictitious body," composed of the sum of the individuals who comprise it. Citizens and legislators should therefore ask themselves this question: If we add up all of the benefits of this policy, and subtract all the costs, will it produce more happiness than the alternative?

Bentham's argument for the principle that we should maximize utility takes the form of a bold assertion: There are no possible grounds for rejecting it. Every moral argument, he claims, must implicitly draw on the idea of maximizing happiness. People may say they believe in certain absolute, categorical duties or rights. But they would have no basis for defending these duties or rights unless they believed that respecting them would maximize human happiness, at least in the long run.

"When a man attempts to combat the principle of utility," Bentham writes, "it is with reasons drawn, without his being aware of it, from that very principle itself." All moral quarrels, properly understood, are disagreements about how to apply the utilitarian principle of maximizing pleasure and minimizing pain, not about the principle itself. "Is it possible for a man to move the earth?" Bentham asks. "Yes; but he must first find out another earth to stand upon." And the only earth, the only premise, the only starting point for moral argument, according to Bentham, is the principle of utility.[3]

Bentham thought his utility principle offered a science of morality that could serve as the basis of political reform. He proposed a number of projects designed to make penal policy more efficient and humane. One was the Panopticon, a prison with a central inspection tower that would enable the supervisor to observe the inmates without their seeing him. He suggested that the Panopticon be run by a private contractor (ideally himself), who would manage the prison in exchange for the profits to be made from the labor of the convicts, who would work sixteen hours per day. Although Bentham's plan was ultimately rejected, it was arguably ahead of its time. Recent years have seen a revival, in the United States and Britain, of the idea of outsourcing prisons to private companies.

Rounding up beggars

Another of Bentham's schemes was a plan to improve "pauper management" by establishing a self-financing workhouse for the poor. The plan, which sought to reduce the presence of beggars on the streets, offers a vivid illustration of the utilitarian logic. Bentham observed, first of all, that encountering beggars on the streets reduces the happiness of passersby, in two ways. For tenderhearted souls, the sight of a beggar produces the pain of sympathy; for hardhearted folk, it generates the pain of disgust. Either way, encountering beggars reduces the utility of the general public. So Bentham proposed removing beggars from the streets and confining them in a workhouse.[4]

Some may think this unfair to the beggars. But Bentham does not neglect their utility. He acknowledges that some beggars would be happier begging than working in a poorhouse. But he notes that for every happy and prosperous beggar, there are many miserable ones. He concludes that the sum of the pains suffered by the public is greater than whatever unhappiness is felt by beggars hauled off to the workhouse.[5]

Some might worry that building and running the workhouse would impose an expense on taxpayers, reducing their happiness and thus their utility. But Bentham proposed a way to make his pauper management plan entirely self-financing. Any citizen who encountered a beggar would be empowered to apprehend him and take him to the nearest workhouse. Once confined there, each beggar would have to work to pay off the cost of his or her maintenance, which would be tallied in a "self-liberation account." The account would include food, clothing, bedding, medical care, and a life insurance policy, in case the beggar died before the account was paid up. To give citizens an incentive to take the trouble to apprehend beggars and deliver them to the workhouse, Bentham proposed a reward of twenty shillings per apprehension—to be added, of course, to the beggar's tab.[6]

Bentham also applied utilitarian logic to rooming assignments within the facility, to minimize the discomfort inmates suffered from their neighbors: "Next to every class, from which any inconvenience is to be apprehended, station a class unsusceptible of that inconvenience." So, for example, "next to raving lunatics, or persons of profligate conversation, place the deaf and dumb . . . Next to prostitutes and loose women, place the aged women." As for "the shockingly deformed," Bentham proposed housing them alongside inmates who were blind.[7]

Harsh though his proposal may seem, Bentham's aim was not punitive. It was meant simply to promote the general welfare by solving a problem that diminished social utility. His scheme for pauper management was never adopted. But the utilitarian spirit that informed it is alive and well today. Before considering some present-day instances of utilitarian thinking, it is worth asking whether Bentham's philosophy is objectionable, and if so, on what grounds.

Objection 1: Individual Rights

The most glaring weakness of utilitarianism, many argue, is that it fails to respect individual rights. By caring only about the sum of satisfactions, it can run roughshod over individual people. For the utilitarian, individuals matter, but only in the sense that each person's preferences should be counted along with everyone else's. But this means that the utilitarian logic, if consistently applied, could sanction ways of treating persons that violate what we think of as fundamental norms of decency and respect, as the following cases illustrate:

Throwing Christians to lions

In ancient Rome, they threw Christians to the lions in the Coliseum for the amusement of the crowd. Imagine how the utilitarian calculus would go: Yes, the Christian suffers excruciating pain as the lion mauls and devours him. But think of the collective ecstasy of the cheering spectators packing the Coliseum. If enough Romans derive enough pleasure from the violent spectacle, are there any grounds on which a utilitarian can condemn it?

The utilitarian may worry that such games will coarsen habits and breed more violence in the streets of Rome; or lead to fear and trembling among prospective victims that they, too, might one day be tossed to the lions. If these effects are bad enough, they could conceivably outweigh the pleasure the games provide, and give the utilitarian a

reason to ban them. But if these calculations are the only reasons to
desist from subjecting Christians to violent death for the sake of entertainment, isn't something of moral importance missing?

Is torture ever justified?

A similar question arises in contemporary debates about whether torture is ever justified in the interrogation of suspected terrorists. Consider the ticking time bomb scenario: Imagine that you are the head of
the local CIA branch. You capture a terrorist suspect who you believe
has information about a nuclear device set to go off in Manhattan later
the same day. In fact, you have reason to suspect that he planted the
bomb himself. As the clock ticks down, he refuses to admit to being a
terrorist or to divulge the bomb's location. Would it be right to torture
him until he tells you where the bomb is and how to disarm it?

The argument for doing so begins with a utilitarian calculation.
Torture inflicts pain on the suspect, greatly reducing his happiness or
utility. But thousands of innocent lives will be lost if the bomb ex-
plodes. So you might argue, on utilitarian grounds, that it's morally
justified to inflict intense pain on one person if doing so will prevent
death and suffering on a massive scale. Former Vice President Richard
Cheney's argument that the use of harsh interrogation techniques
against suspected Al-Qaeda terrorists helped avert another terrorist
attack on the United States rests on this utilitarian logic.

This is not to say that utilitarians necessarily favor torture. Some
utilitarians oppose torture on practical grounds. They argue that it seldom works, since information extracted under duress is often unreliable. So pain is inflicted, but the community is not made any safer:
there is no increase in the collective utility. Or they worry that if our
country engages in torture, our soldiers will face harsher treatment if
taken prisoner. This result could actually reduce the overall utility associated with our use of torture, all things considered.

These practical considerations may or may not be true. As reasons to oppose torture, however, they are entirely compatible with utilitarian thinking. They do not assert that torturing a human being is intrinsically wrong, only that practicing torture will have bad effects that, taken as a whole, will do more harm than good.

Some people reject torture on principle. They believe that it violates human rights and fails to respect the intrinsic dignity of human beings. Their case against torture does not depend on utilitarian considerations. They argue that human rights and human dignity have a moral basis that lies beyond utility. If they are right, then Bentham's philosophy is wrong.

On the face of it, the ticking time bomb scenario seems to support Bentham's side of the argument. Numbers do seem to make a moral difference. It is one thing to accept the possible death of three men in a lifeboat to avoid killing one innocent cabin boy in cold blood. But what if thousands of innocent lives are at stake, as in the ticking time bomb scenario? What if hundreds of thousands of lives were at risk? The utilitarian would argue that, at a certain point, even the most ardent advocate of human rights would have a hard time insisting it is morally preferable to let vast numbers of innocent people die than to torture a single terrorist suspect who may know where the bomb is hidden.

As a test of utilitarian moral reasoning, however, the ticking time bomb case is misleading. It purports to prove that numbers count, so that if enough lives are at stake, we should be willing to override our scruples about dignity and rights. And if that is true, then morality is about calculating costs and benefits after all.

But the torture scenario does not show that the prospect of saving many lives justifies inflicting severe pain on one innocent person. Recall that the person being tortured to save all those lives is a suspected terrorist, in fact the person we believe may have planted the bomb. The moral force of the case for torturing him depends heavily on the assumption that he is in some way responsible for creating the danger we

now seek to avert. Or if he is not responsible for this bomb, we assume
he has committed other terrible acts that make him deserving of harsh
treatment. The moral intuitions at work in the ticking time bomb case
are not only about costs and benefits, but also about the non-utilitarian
idea that terrorists are bad people who deserve to be punished.

We can see this more clearly if we alter the scenario to remove any
element of presumed guilt. Suppose the only way to induce the terrorist
suspect to talk is to torture his young daughter (who has no knowledge
of her father's nefarious activities). Would it be morally permissible to
do so? I suspect that even a hardened utilitarian would flinch at the notion. But this version of the torture scenario offers a truer test of the utilitarian principle. It sets aside the intuition that the terrorist deserves to
be punished anyhow (regardless of the valuable information we hope
to extract), and forces us to assess the utilitarian calculus on its own.

The city of happiness

The second version of the torture case (the one involving the innocent
daughter) brings to mind a short story by Ursula K. Le Guin. The story
("The Ones Who Walked Away from Omelas") tells of a city called
Omelas—a city of happiness and civic celebration, a place without
kings or slaves, without advertisements or a stock exchange, a place
without the atomic bomb. Lest we find this place too unrealistic to
imagine, the author tells us one more thing about it: "In a basement
under one of the beautiful public buildings of Omelas, or perhaps in
the cellar of one of its spacious private homes, there is a room. It has
one locked door, and no window." And in this room sits a child. The
child is feeble-minded, malnourished, and neglected. It lives out its
days in wretched misery.

> They all know it is there, all the people of Omelas . . . They all know
> that it has to be there . . . [T]hey all understand that their happiness,
> the beauty of their city, the tenderness of their friendships, the health

of their children, . . . even the abundance of their harvest and the kindly weathers of their skies, depend wholly on this child's abominable misery. . . . If the child were brought up into the sunlight out of the vile place, if it were cleaned and fed and comforted, that would be a good thing, indeed; but if it were done, in that day and hour all the prosperity and beauty and delight of Omelas would wither and be destroyed. Those are the terms.[8]

Are those terms morally acceptable? The first objection to Bentham's utilitarianism, the one that appeals to fundamental human rights, says they are not—even if they lead to a city of happiness. It would be wrong to violate the rights of the innocent child, even for the sake of the happiness of the multitude.

Objection 2: A Common Currency of Value

Utilitarianism claims to offer a science of morality, based on measuring, aggregating, and calculating happiness. It weighs preferences without judging them. Everyone's preferences count equally. This nonjudgmental spirit is the source of much of its appeal. And its promise to make moral choice a science informs much contemporary economic reasoning. But in order to aggregate preferences, it is necessary to measure them on a single scale. Bentham's idea of utility offers one such common currency.

But is it possible to translate all moral goods into a single currency of value without losing something in the translation? The second objection to utilitarianism doubts that it is. According to this objection, all values can't be captured by a common currency of value.

To explore this objection, consider the way utilitarian logic is applied in cost-benefit analysis, a form of decision-making that is widely used by governments and corporations. Cost-benefit analysis tries to bring rationality and rigor to complex social choices by translating all costs and benefits into monetary terms—and then comparing them.

The benefits of lung cancer

Philip Morris, the tobacco company, does big business in the Czech Republic, where cigarette smoking remains popular and socially acceptable. Worried about the rising health care costs of smoking, the Czech government recently considered raising taxes on cigarettes. In hopes of fending off the tax increase, Philip Morris commissioned a cost-benefit analysis of the effects of smoking on the Czech national budget. The study found that the government actually gains more money than it loses from smoking. The reason: although smokers impose higher medical costs on the budget while they are alive, they die early, and so save the government considerable sums in health care, pensions, and housing for the elderly. According to the study, once the "positive effects" of smoking are taken into account—including cigarette tax revenues and savings due to the premature deaths of smokers—the net gain to the treasury is $147 million per year.[9]

The cost-benefit analysis proved to be a public relations disaster for Philip Morris. "Tobacco companies used to deny that cigarettes killed people," one commentator wrote. "Now they brag about it."[10] An anti-smoking group ran newspaper ads showing the foot of a cadaver in a morgue with a $1,227 price tag attached to the toe, representing the savings to the Czech government of each smoking-related death. Faced with public outrage and ridicule, the chief executive of Philip Morris apologized, saying the study showed "a complete and unacceptable disregard of basic human values."[11]

Some would say the Philip Morris smoking study illustrates the moral folly of cost-benefit analysis and the utilitarian way of thinking that underlies it. Viewing lung cancer deaths as a boon for the bottom line does display a callous disregard for human life. Any morally defensible policy toward smoking would have to consider not only the fiscal effects but also the consequences for public health and human well-being.

But a utilitarian would not dispute the relevance of these broader consequences—the pain and suffering, the grieving families, the loss of life. Bentham invented the concept of utility precisely to capture, on a single scale, the disparate range of things we care about, including the value of human life. For a Benthamite, the smoking study does not embarrass utilitarian principles but simply misapplies them. A fuller cost-benefit analysis would add to the moral calculus an amount representing the cost of dying early for the smoker and his family, and would weigh these against the savings the smoker's early death would provide the government.

This takes us back to the question of whether all values can be translated into monetary terms. Some versions of cost-benefit analysis try to do so, even to the point of placing a dollar value on human life. Consider two uses of cost-benefit analysis that generated moral outrage, not because they didn't calculate the value of human life, but because they did.

Exploding gas tanks

During the 1970s, the Ford Pinto was one of the best-selling subcompact cars in the United States. Unfortunately, its fuel tank was prone to explode when another car collided with it from the rear. More than five hundred people died when their Pintos burst into flames, and many more suffered severe burn injuries. When one of the burn victims sued Ford Motor Company for the faulty design, it emerged that Ford engineers had been aware of the danger posed by the gas tank. But company executives had conducted a cost-benefit analysis and determined that the benefits of fixing it (in lives saved and injuries prevented) were not worth the eleven dollars per car it would have cost to equip each car with a device that would have made the gas tank safer.

To calculate the benefits to be gained by a safer gas tank, Ford estimated that 180 deaths and 180 burn injuries would result if no changes were made. It then placed a monetary value on each life lost and injury suffered—$200,000 per life, and $67,000 per injury. It added to these amounts the number and value of the Pintos likely to go up in flames, and calculated that the overall benefit of the safety improvement would be $49.5 million. But the cost of adding an $11 device to 12.5 million vehicles would be $137.5 million. So the company concluded that the cost of fixing the fuel tank was not worth the benefits of a safer car.[12]

Upon learning of the study, the jury was outraged. It awarded the plaintiff $2.5 million in compensatory damages and $125 million in punitive damages (an amount later reduced to $3.5 million).[13] Perhaps the jurors considered it wrong for a corporation to assign a monetary value to human life, or perhaps they thought that $200,000 was egregiously low. Ford had not come up with that figure on its own, but had taken it from a U.S. government agency. In the early 1970s, the National Highway Traffic Safety Administration had calculated the cost of a traffic fatality. Counting future productivity losses, medical costs, funeral costs, and the victim's pain and suffering, the agency arrived at $200,000 per fatality.

If the jury's objection was to the price tag, not the principle, a utilitarian could agree. Few people would choose to die in a car crash for $200,000. Most people like living. To measure the full effect on utility of a traffic fatality, one would have to include the victim's loss of future happiness, not only lost earnings and funeral costs. What, then, would be a truer estimate of the dollar value of a human life?

A discount for seniors

When the U.S. Environmental Protection Agency tried to answer this question, it, too, prompted moral outrage, but of a different kind. In 2003, the EPA presented a cost-benefit analysis of new air pollution standards. The agency assigned a more generous value to human life than did Ford, but with an age-adjusted twist: $3.7 million per life saved due to cleaner air, except for those older than seventy, whose lives were valued at $2.3 million. Lying behind the different valuations was a utilitarian notion: saving an older person's life produces less utility than saving a younger person's life. (The young person has longer to live, and therefore more happiness still to enjoy.) Advocates for the elderly did not see it that way. They protested the "senior citizen discount," and argued that government should not assign greater value to the lives of the young than of the old. Stung by the protest, the EPA quickly renounced the discount and withdrew the report.[14]

Critics of utilitarianism point to such episodes as evidence that cost-benefit analysis is misguided, and that placing a monetary value on human life is morally obtuse. Defenders of cost-benefit analysis disagree. They argue that many social choices implicitly trade off some number of lives for other goods and conveniences. Human life has its price, they insist, whether we admit it or not.

For example, the use of the automobile exacts a predictable toll in human lives—more than forty thousands deaths annually in the United States. But that does not lead us as a society to give up cars. In fact, it does not even lead us to lower the speed limit. During an oil crisis in 1974, the U.S. Congress mandated a national speed limit of fifty-five miles per hour. Although the goal was to save energy, an effect of the lower speed limit was fewer traffic fatalities.

In the 1980s, Congress removed the restriction, and most states raised the speed limit to sixty-five miles per hour. Drivers saved time, but traffic deaths increased. At the time, no one did a cost-benefit analysis to determine whether the benefits of faster driving were worth the cost in lives. But some years later, two economists did the math. They defined one benefit of a higher speed limit as a quicker commute to and from work, calculated the economic benefit of the time saved (valued at an average wage of $20 an hour) and divided the savings by the number of additional deaths. They discovered that, for the convenience of driving faster, Americans were effectively valuing human life at the rate of $1.54 million per life. That was the economic gain, per fatality, of driving ten miles an hour faster.[15]

Advocates of cost-benefit analysis point out that by driving sixty-five miles an hour rather than fifty-five, we implicitly value human life at $1.54 million—much less than the $6 million per life figure typically used by U.S. government agencies in setting pollution standards and health-and-safety regulations. So why not be explicit about it? If trading off certain levels of safety for certain benefits and conveniences is unavoidable, they argue, we should do so with our eyes open, and should compare the costs and benefits as systematically as possible— even if that means putting a price tag on human life.

Utilitarians see our tendency to recoil at placing a monetary value on human life as an impulse we should overcome, a taboo that obstructs clear thinking and rational social choice. For critics of utilitarianism, however, our hesitation points to something of moral importance— the idea that it is not possible to measure and compare all values and goods on a single scale.

Pain for pay

It is not obvious how this dispute can be resolved. But some empirically minded social scientists have tried. In the 1930s, Edward Thorndike, a social psychologist, tried to prove what utilitarianism assumes: namely, that it is possible to translate our seemingly disparate desires and aversions into a common currency of pleasure and pain. He conducted a survey of young recipients of government relief, asking them how much they would have to be paid to suffer various experiences. For example: "How much would you have to be paid to have one upper front tooth pulled out?" Or "to have the little toe of one foot cut off?" Or "to eat a live earthworm six inches long?" Or "to choke a stray cat to death with your bare hands?" Or "to live all the rest of your life on a farm in Kansas, ten miles from any town?"[16]

Which of these items do you think commanded the highest price, and which the least? Here is the price list his survey produced (in 1937 dollars):

Tooth	$4,500
Toe	$57,000
Worm	$100,000
Cat	$10,000
Kansas	$300,000

Thorndike thought his findings lent support to the idea that all goods can be measured and compared on a single scale. "Any want or satisfaction which exists at all, exists in some amount and is therefore measurable," he wrote. "The life of a dog or a cat or a chicken . . . consists largely of and is determined by appetites, cravings, desires and their gratification. . . . So also does the life of man, though the appetites and desires are more numerous, subtle, and complicated."[17]

But the preposterous character of Thorndike's price list suggests the absurdity of such comparisons. Can we really conclude that the respondents considered the prospect of life on a farm in Kansas to be three times as disagreeable as eating an earthworm, or do these experiences differ in ways that don't admit meaningful comparison? Thorndike conceded that up to one-third of the respondents stated that no sum would induce them to suffer some of these experiences, suggesting that they considered them "immeasurably repugnant."[18]

St. Anne's girls

There may be no knock-down argument for or against the claim that all moral goods can be translated without loss into a single measure of value. But here is a further case that calls the claim into question:

In the 1970s, when I was a graduate student at Oxford, there were separate colleges for men and women. The women's colleges had parietal rules against male guests staying overnight in women's rooms. These rules were rarely enforced and easily violated, or so I was told. Most college officials no longer saw it as their role to enforce traditional notions of sexual morality. Pressure grew to relax these rules, which became a subject of debate at St. Anne's College, one of the all-women colleges.

Some older women on the faculty were traditionalists. They opposed allowing male guests, on conventional moral grounds; it was immoral, they thought, for unmarried young women to spend the night with men. But times had changed, and the traditionalists were embarrassed to give the real grounds for their objection. So they translated their arguments into utilitarian terms. "If men stay overnight," they argued, "the costs to the college will increase." How, you might wonder? "Well, they'll want to take baths, and that will use more hot water." Furthermore, they argued, "we will have to replace the mattresses more often."

The reformers met the traditionalists' arguments by adopting the following compromise: Each woman could have a maximum of three overnight guests each week, provided each guest paid fifty pence per night to defray the costs to the college. The next day, the headline in the *Guardian* read, "St. Anne's Girls, Fifty Pence a Night." The language of virtue had not translated very well into the language of utility. Soon thereafter, the parietal rules were waived altogether, and so was the fee.

John Stuart Mill

We have considered two objections to Bentham's "greatest happiness" principle—that it does not give adequate weight to human dignity and individual rights, and that it wrongly reduces everything of moral importance to a single scale of pleasure and pain. How compelling are these objections?

John Stuart Mill (1806–1873) believed they could be answered. A generation after Bentham, he tried to save utilitarianism by recasting it as a more humane, less calculating doctrine. Mill was the son of James Mill, a friend and disciple of Bentham. James Mill home-schooled his son, and the young Mill became a child prodigy. He studied Greek at the age of three and Latin at eight. At age eleven, he wrote a history of Roman law. When he was twenty, he suffered a nervous breakdown, which left him depressed for several years. Shortly thereafter he met Harriet Taylor. She was a married woman at the time, with two children, but she and Mill became close friends. When her husband died twenty years later, she and Mill married. Mill credited Taylor as his greatest intellectual companion and collaborator as he set about revising Bentham's doctrine.

The case for liberty

Mill's writings can be read as a strenuous attempt to reconcile individual rights with the utilitarian philosophy he inherited from his father and adopted from Bentham. His book *On Liberty* (1859) is the classic defense of individual freedom in the English-speaking world. Its central principle is that people should be free to do whatever they want, provided they do no harm to others. Government may not interfere with individual liberty in order to protect a person from himself, or to impose the majority's beliefs about how best to live. The only actions for which a person is accountable to society, Mill argues, are those that affect others. As long as I am not harming anyone else, my "independence is, of right, absolute. Over himself, over his own body and mind, the individual is sovereign."[19]

This unyielding account of individual rights would seem to require something stronger than utility as its justification. For consider: Suppose a large majority despises a small religion and wants it banned. Isn't it possible, even likely, that banning the religion will produce the greatest happiness for the greatest number? True, the banned minority would suffer unhappiness and frustration. But if the majority is big enough and passionate enough in its hatred of the heretics, its collective happiness could well outweigh their suffering. If that scenario is possible, then it appears that utility is a shaky, unreliable foundation for religious liberty. Mill's principle of liberty would seem to need a sturdier moral basis than Bentham's principle of utility.

Mill disagrees. He insists that the case for individual liberty rests entirely on utilitarian considerations: "It is proper to state that I forego any advantage which could be derived to my argument from the idea of abstract right, as a thing independent of utility. I regard utility as the ultimate appeal on all ethical questions; but it must be utility in the largest sense, grounded on the permanent interests of man as a progressive being."[20]

Mill thinks we should maximize utility, not case by case, but in the long run. And over time, he argues, respecting individual liberty will lead to the greatest human happiness. Allowing the majority to silence dissenters or censor free-thinkers might maximize utility today, but it will make society worse off—less happy—in the long run.

Why should we assume that upholding individual liberty and the right to dissent will promote the welfare of society in the long run? Mill offers several reasons: The dissenting view may turn out to be true, or partially true, and so offer a corrective to prevailing opinion. And even if it is not, subjecting prevailing opinion to a vigorous contest of ideas will prevent it from hardening into dogma and prejudice. Finally, a society that forces its members to embrace custom and convention is likely to fall into a stultifying conformity, depriving itself of the energy and vitality that prompt social improvement.

Mill's speculations about the salutary social effects of liberty are plausible enough. But they do not provide a convincing moral basis for individual rights, for at least two reasons: First, respecting individual rights for the sake of promoting social progress leaves rights hostage to contingency. Suppose we encounter a society that achieves a kind of long-term happiness by despotic means. Wouldn't the utilitarian have to conclude that, in such a society, individual rights are not morally required? Second, basing rights on utilitarian considerations misses the sense in which violating someone's rights inflicts a wrong on the individual, whatever its effect on the general welfare. If the majority persecutes adherents of an unpopular faith, doesn't it do an injustice *to them*, as individuals, regardless of any bad effects such intolerance may produce for society as a whole over time?

Mill has an answer to these challenges, but it carries him beyond the confines of utilitarian morality. Forcing a person to live according to custom or convention or prevailing opinion is wrong, Mill explains, because it prevents him from achieving the highest end of human life— the full and free development of his human faculties. Conformity, in Mill's account, is the enemy of the best way to live.

> The human faculties of perception, judgment, discriminative feeling, mental activity, and even moral preference, are exercised only in making a choice. He who does anything because it is the custom, makes no choice. He gains no practice either in discerning or in desiring what is best. The mental and moral, like the muscular powers, are improved only by being used . . . He who lets the world, or his own portion of it, choose his plan of life for him, has no need of any other faculty than the ape-like one of imitation. He who chooses his plan for himself, employs all his faculties.[21]

Mill concedes that following convention may lead a person to a satisfying life path and keep him out of harm's way. "But what will be his comparative worth as a human being?" he asks. "It really is of importance, not only what men do, but also what manner of men they are that do it."[22]

So actions and consequences are not all that matter after all. Character also counts. For Mill, individuality matters less for the pleasure it brings than for the character it reflects. "One whose desires and impulses are not his own, has no character, no more than a steam engine has character."[23]

Mill's robust celebration of individuality is the most distinctive contribution of *On Liberty*. But it is also a kind of heresy. Since it appeals to moral ideals beyond utility—ideals of character and human flourishing—it is not really an elaboration of Bentham's principle but a renunciation of it, despite Mill's claim to the contrary.

Higher pleasures

Mill's response to the second objection to utilitarianism—that it reduces all values to a single scale—also turns out to lean on moral ideals independent of utility. In *Utilitarianism* (1861), a long essay Mill wrote shortly after *On Liberty*, he tries to show that utilitarians can distinguish higher pleasures from lower ones.

For Bentham, pleasure is pleasure and pain is pain. The only basis for judging one experience better or worse than another is the intensity and duration of the pleasure or pain it produces. The so-called higher pleasures or nobler virtues are simply those that produce stronger, longer pleasure. Bentham recognizes no qualitative distinction among pleasures. "The quantity of pleasure being equal," he writes, "push-pin is as good as poetry."[24] (Push-pin was a children's game.)

Part of the appeal of Bentham's utilitarianism is this nonjudgmental spirit. It takes people's preferences as they are, without passing judgment on their moral worth. All preferences count equally. Bentham thinks it is presumptuous to judge some pleasures as inherently better than others. Some people like Mozart, others Madonna. Some like ballet, others like bowling. Some read Plato, others *Penthouse*. Who is to say, Bentham might ask, which pleasures are higher, or worthier, or nobler than others?

The refusal to distinguish higher from lower pleasures is connected to Bentham's belief that all values can be measured and compared on a single scale. If experiences differ only in the quantity of pleasure or pain they produce, not qualitatively, then it makes sense to weigh them on a single scale. But some object to utilitarianism on precisely this point: they believe that some pleasures really are "higher" than others. If some pleasures are worthy and others base, they say, why should society weigh all preferences equally, much less regard the sum of such preferences as the greatest good?

Think again about the Romans throwing Christians to the lions in the Coliseum. One objection to the bloody spectacle is that it violates the rights of the victims. But a further objection is that it caters to perverse pleasures rather than noble ones. Wouldn't it be better to change those preferences than to satisfy them?

It is said that the Puritans banned bearbaiting, not because of the pain it caused the bears but because of the pleasure it gave the onlookers. Bearbaiting is no longer a popular pastime, but dogfighting and cock-fighting hold a persistent allure, and some jurisdictions ban them. One justification for such bans is to prevent cruelty to animals. But such laws may also reflect a moral judgment that deriving pleasure from dogfights is abhorrent, something a civilized society should discourage. You don't need to be a Puritan to have some sympathy with this judgment.

Bentham would count all preferences, regardless of their worth, in determining what the law should be. But if more people would rather watch dogfights than view Rembrandt paintings, should society subsidize dogfight arenas rather than art museums? If certain pleasures are base and degrading, why should they have any weight at all in deciding what laws should be adopted?

Mill tries to save utilitarianism from this objection. Unlike Bentham, Mill believes it is possible to distinguish between higher and lower pleasures—to assess the quality, not just the quantity or intensity, of our desires. And he thinks he can make this distinction without relying on any moral ideas other than utility itself.

Mill begins by pledging allegiance to the utilitarian creed: "Actions are right in proportion as they tend to promote happiness; wrong as they tend to produce the reverse of happiness. By happiness is intended pleasure and the absence of pain; by unhappiness, pain and the privation of pleasure." He also affirms the "theory of life on which this theory of morality is grounded—namely, that pleasure and freedom from pain are the only things desirable as ends; and that all desirable things . . . are desirable either for pleasure inherent in themselves or as means to the promotion of pleasure and the prevention of pain."[25]

Despite insisting that pleasure and pain are all that matter, Mill acknowledges that "some kinds of pleasure are more desirable and more valuable than others." How can we know which pleasures are qualitatively higher? Mill proposes a simple test: "Of two pleasures, if there be one to which all or almost all who have experience of both give a decided preference, irrespective of any feeling of moral obligation to prefer it, that is the more desirable pleasure."[26]

This test has one clear advantage: It does not depart from the utilitarian idea that morality rests wholly and simply on our actual desires. "[T]he sole evidence it is possible to produce that anything is desirable is that people actually desire it," Mill writes.[27] But as a way of arriving at qualitative distinctions among pleasures, his test seems open to an obvious objection: Isn't it often the case that we prefer lower pleasures to higher ones? Don't we sometimes prefer lying on the sofa watching sitcoms to reading Plato or going to the opera? And isn't it possible to prefer these undemanding experiences without considering them to be particularly worthwhile?

Shakespeare versus The Simpsons

When I discuss Mill's account of higher pleasures with my students, I try out a version of his test. I show the students three examples of popular entertainment: a World Wrestling Entertainment fight (a raucous spectacle in which the so-called wrestlers attack one another with folding chairs); a Hamlet soliloquy performed by a Shakespearean actor; and an excerpt from The Simpsons. I then ask two questions: Which of these performances did you enjoy most—find most pleasurable—and which do you think is the highest, or worthiest?

Invariably The Simpsons gets the most votes as most enjoyable, followed by Shakespeare. (A few brave souls confess their fondness for the WWE.) But when asked which experience they consider qualitatively highest, the students vote overwhelmingly for Shakespeare.

The results of this experiment pose a challenge to Mill's test. Many students prefer watching Homer Simpson, but still think a *Hamlet* soliloquy offers a higher pleasure. Admittedly, some may say Shakespeare is better because they are sitting in a classroom and don't want to seem philistine. And some students argue that *The Simpsons*, with its subtle mix of irony, humor, and social commentary, does rival Shakespeare's art. But if most people who have experienced both prefer watching *The Simpsons*, then Mill would be hard pressed to conclude that Shakespeare is qualitatively higher.

And yet Mill does not want to give up the idea that some ways of life are nobler than others, even if the people who live them are less easily satisfied. "A being of higher faculties requires more to make him happy, is capable probably of more acute suffering . . . than one of an inferior type; but in spite of these liabilities, he can never really wish to sink into what he feels to be a lower grade of existence." Why are we unwilling to trade a life that engages our higher faculties for a life of base contentment? Mill thinks the reason has something to do with "the love of liberty and personal independence," and concludes that "its most appropriate appellation is a sense of dignity, which all human beings possess in one form or other."[28]

Mill concedes that "occasionally, under the influence of temptation," even the best of us postpone higher pleasures to lower ones. Everyone gives in to the impulse to be a couch potato once in a while. But this does not mean we don't know the difference between Rembrandt and reruns. Mill makes this point in a memorable passage: "It is better to be a human being dissatisfied than a pig satisfied; better to be Socrates dissatisfied than a fool satisfied. And if the fool, or the pig, are of a different opinion, it is because they only know their own side of the question."[29]

This expression of faith in the appeal of the higher human faculties is compelling. But in relying on it, Mill strays from the utilitarian premise. No longer are de facto desires the sole basis for judging what is noble and what is base. Now the standard derives from an ideal of human dignity independent of our wants and desires. The higher pleasures are not higher *because* we prefer them; we prefer them because we recognize them as higher. We judge *Hamlet* as great art not because we like it more than lesser entertainments, but because it engages our highest faculties and makes us more fully human.

As with individual rights, so with higher pleasures: Mill saves utilitarianism from the charge that it reduces everything to a crude calculus of pleasure and pain, but only by invoking a moral ideal of human dignity and personality independent of utility itself.

Of the two great proponents of utilitarianism, Mill was the more humane philosopher, Bentham the more consistent one. Bentham died in 1832, at the age of eighty-four. But if you go to London, you can visit him today. He provided in his will that his body be preserved, embalmed, and displayed. And so he can be found at University College London, where he sits pensively in a glass case, dressed in his actual clothing.

Shortly before he died, Bentham asked himself a question consistent with his philosophy: Of what use could a dead man be to the living? One use, he concluded, would be to make one's corpse available for the study of anatomy. In the case of great philosophers, however, better yet to preserve one's physical presence in order to inspire future generations of thinkers.[30] Bentham put himself in this second category.

In fact, modesty was not one of Bentham's obvious character traits. Not only did he provide strict instructions for his body's preservation and display, he also suggested that his friends and disciples meet every year "for the purpose of commemorating the founder of the greatest happiness system of morals and legislation," and that when they did, they should bring Bentham out for the occasion.[31]

His admirers have obliged. Bentham's "auto icon," as he dubbed it, was on hand for the founding of the International Bentham Society in the 1980s. And the stuffed Bentham is reportedly wheeled in for meetings of the governing council of the college, whose minutes record him as "present but not voting."[32]

Despite Bentham's careful planning, the embalming of his head went badly, so he now keeps his vigil with a wax head in place of the real one. His actual head, now kept in a cellar, was displayed for a time on a plate between his feet. But students stole the head and ransomed it back to the college for a charitable donation.[33]

Even in death, Jeremy Bentham promotes the greatest good for the greatest number.

3. DO WE OWN OURSELVES? / LIBERTARIANISM

Each fall, *Forbes* magazine publishes a list of the four hundred richest Americans. For over a decade, Microsoft founder Bill Gates III has topped the list, as he did in 2008, when *Forbes* estimated his net worth at $57 billion. Other members of the club include investor Warren Buffett (ranked 2nd, with $50 billion), the owners of Wal-Mart, the founders of Google and Amazon, assorted oilmen, hedge fund managers, media moguls, and real-estate tycoons, television talk show host Oprah Winfrey (in 155th place, with $2.7 billion), and New York Yankees owner George Steinbrenner (tied for last place, with $1.3 billion).[1]

So vast is the wealth at the top of the American economy, even in a weakened state, that being a mere billionaire is barely enough to gain admission to the Forbes 400. In fact, the richest 1 percent of Americans possess over a third of the country's wealth, more than the combined wealth of the bottom *90 percent* of American families. The top 10 percent of American households take in 42 percent of all income and hold 71 percent of all wealth.[2]

Economic inequality is steeper in the United States than in other democracies. Some people think that such inequality is unjust, and favor taxing the rich to help the poor. Others disagree. They say there is nothing unfair about economic inequality, provided it arises without force or fraud, through the choices people make in a market economy.

Who is right? If you think justice means maximizing happiness, you might favor wealth redistribution, on the following grounds: Suppose we take $1 million from Bill Gates and disperse it among a hundred needy recipients, giving each of them $10,000. Overall happiness would likely increase. Gates would scarcely miss the money, while each of the recipients would derive great happiness from the $10,000 windfall. Their collective utility would go up more than his would go down.

This utilitarian logic could be extended to support quite a radical redistribution of wealth; it would tell us to transfer money from the rich to the poor until the last dollar we take from Gates hurts him as much as it helps the recipient.

This Robin Hood scenario is open to at least two objections—one from within utilitarian thinking, the other from outside it. The first objection worries that high tax rates, especially on income, reduce the incentive to work and invest, leading to a decline in productivity. If the economic pie shrinks, leaving less to redistribute, the overall level of utility might go down. So before taxing Bill Gates and Oprah Winfrey too heavily, the utilitarian would have to ask whether doing so would lead them to work less and so to earn less, eventually reducing the amount of money available for redistribution to the needy.

The second objection regards these calculations as beside the point. It argues that taxing the rich to help the poor is unjust because it violates a fundamental right. According to this objection, taking money from Gates and Winfrey without their consent, even for a good cause, is coercive. It violates their liberty to do with their money whatever they please. Those who object to redistribution on these grounds are often called "libertarians."

Libertarians favor unfettered markets and oppose government regulation, not in the name of economic efficiency but in the name of human freedom. Their central claim is that each of us has a fundamen-

tal right to liberty—the right to do whatever we want with the things
we own, provided we respect other people's rights to do the same.

The Minimal State

If the libertarian theory of rights is correct, then many activities of the
modern state are illegitimate, and violations of liberty. Only a minimal
state—one that enforces contracts, protects private property from
theft, and keeps the peace—is compatible with the libertarian theory
of rights. Any state that does more than this is morally unjustified.

The libertarian rejects three types of policies and laws that modern
states commonly enact:

1. No Paternalism. Libertarians oppose laws to protect people
from harming themselves. Seatbelt laws are a good example; so are
motorcycle helmet laws. Even if riding a motorcycle without a helmet
is reckless, and even if helmet laws save lives and prevent devastating
injuries, libertarians argue that such laws violate the right of the individual to decide what risks to assume. As long as no third parties are
harmed, and as long as motorcycle riders are responsible for their own
medical bills, the state has no right to dictate what risks they may take
with their bodies and lives.

2. No Morals Legislation. Libertarians oppose using the coercive
force of law to promote notions of virtue or to express the moral convictions of the majority. Prostitution may be morally objectionable to
many people, but that does not justify laws that prevent consenting
adults from engaging in it. Majorities in some communities may disap-
prove of homosexuality, but that does not justify laws that deprive
gay men and lesbians of the right to choose their sexual partners for
themselves.

3. No Redistribution of Income or Wealth. The libertarian theory
of rights rules out any law that requires some people to help others,
including taxation for redistribution of wealth. Desirable though it
may be for the affluent to support the less fortunate—by subsidizing

their health care or housing or education—such help should be left up to the individual to undertake, not mandated by the government. According to the libertarian, redistributive taxes are a form of coercion, even theft. The state has no more right to force affluent taxpayers to support social programs for the poor than a benevolent thief has the right to steal money from a rich person and give it to the homeless.

The libertarian philosophy does not map neatly onto the political spectrum. Conservatives who favor laissez-faire economic policies often part company with libertarians on cultural issues such as school prayer, abortion, and restrictions on pornography. And many proponents of the welfare state hold libertarian views on issues such as gay rights, reproductive rights, freedom of speech, and the separation of church and state.

During the 1980s, libertarian ideas found prominent expression in the pro-market, antigovernment rhetoric of Ronald Reagan and Margaret Thatcher. As an intellectual doctrine, libertarianism emerged earlier, in opposition to the welfare state. In *The Constitution of Liberty* (1960), the Austrian-born economist-philosopher Friedrich A. Hayek (1899–1992) argued that any attempt to bring about greater economic equality was bound to be coercive and destructive of a free society.[3] In *Capitalism and Freedom* (1962), the American economist Milton Friedman (1912–2006) argued that many widely accepted state activities are illegitimate infringements on individual freedom. Social Security, or any mandatory, government-run retirement program, is one of his prime examples: "If a man knowingly prefers to live for today, to use his resources for current enjoyment, deliberately choosing a penurious old age, by what right do we prevent him from doing so?" Friedman asks. We might urge such a person to save for his retirement, "but are we entitled to use coercion to prevent him from doing what he chooses to do?"[4]

Friedman objects to minimum wage laws on similar grounds. Government has no right to prevent employers from paying any wage, however low, that workers are prepared to accept. The government

also violates individual freedom when it makes laws against employment discrimination. If employers want to discriminate on the basis of
race, religion, or any other factor, the state has no right to prevent
them from doing so. In Friedman's view, "such legislation clearly involves interference with the freedom of individuals to enter into voluntary contracts with one another."[5]

Occupational licensing requirements also wrongly interfere with
freedom of choice. If an untrained barber wants to offer his less-than-
expert services to the public, and if some customers are willing to take
their chances on a cheap haircut, the state has no business forbidding
the transaction. Friedman extends this logic even to physicians. If I
want a bargain appendectomy, I should be free to hire anyone I choose,
certified or not, to do the job. While it is true that most people want
assurance of their doctor's competence, the market can provide such
information. Instead of relying on state licensing of doctors, Friedman
suggests, patients can use private rating services such as *Consumer Reports* or the *Good Housekeeping* seal of approval.[6]

Free-Market Philosophy

In *Anarchy, State and Utopia* (1974), Robert Nozick offers a philosophical defense of libertarian principles and a challenge to familiar ideas of
distributive justice. He begins with the claim that individuals have
rights "so strong and far-reaching" that "they raise the question of what,
if anything, the state may do." He concludes that "only a minimal state,
limited to enforcing contracts and protecting people against force,
theft, and fraud, is justified. Any more extensive state violates persons'
rights not to be forced to do certain things, and is unjustified."[7]

Prominent among the things that no one should be forced to do is
help other people. Taxing the rich to help the poor coerces the rich. It
violates their right to do what they want with the things they own.

According to Nozick, there is nothing wrong with economic inequality as such. Simply knowing that the Forbes 400 have billions

while others are penniless doesn't enable you to conclude anything about the justice or injustice of the arrangement. Nozick rejects the idea that a just distribution consists of a certain pattern—such as equal income, or equal utility, or equal provision of basic needs. What matters is how the distribution came about.

Nozick rejects patterned theories of justice in favor of those that honor the choices people make in free markets. He argues that distributive justice depends on two requirements—justice in initial holdings and justice in transfer.[8]

The first asks if the resources you used to make your money were legitimately yours in the first place. (If you made a fortune selling stolen goods, you would not be entitled to the proceeds.) The second asks if you made your money either through free exchanges in the marketplace or from gifts voluntarily bestowed upon you by others. If the answer to both questions is yes, you are entitled to what you have, and the state may not take it without your consent. Provided no one starts out with ill-gotten gains, any distribution that results from a free market is just, however equal or unequal it turns out to be.

Nozick concedes that it is not easy to determine whether the initial holdings that gave rise to today's economic positions were themselves just or ill-gotten. How can we know to what extent today's distribution of income and wealth reflects illegitimate seizures of land or other assets through force, theft, or fraud generations ago? If it can be shown that those who have landed on top are the beneficiaries of past injustices—such as the enslavement of African Americans or the expropriation of Native Americans—then, according to Nozick, a case can be made for remedying the injustice through taxation, reparations, or other means. But it is important to notice that these measures are for the sake of redressing past wrongs, not for the sake of bringing about greater equality for its own sake.

Nozick illustrates the folly (as he sees it) of redistribution with a hypothetical example about the basketball great Wilt Chamberlain, whose salary in the early 1970s reached the then lofty sum of $200,000 per season. Since Michael Jordan is the iconic basketball star of recent times, we can update Nozick's example with Jordan, who in his last year with the Chicago Bulls was paid $31 million—more per game than Chamberlain made in a season.

Michael Jordan's Money

To set aside any question about initial holdings, let's imagine, Nozick suggests, that you set the initial distribution of income and wealth according to whatever pattern you consider just—a perfectly equal distribution, if you like. Now the basketball season begins. Those who want to see Michael Jordan play deposit five dollars in a box each time they buy a ticket. The proceeds in the box go to Jordan. (In real life, of course, Jordan's salary is paid by the owners, from team revenues. Nozick's simplifying assumption—that the fans pay Jordan directly—is a way of focusing on the philosophical point about voluntary exchange.)

Since many people are eager to see Jordan play, attendance is high and the box becomes full. By the end of the season, Jordan has $31 million, far more than anyone else. As a result, the initial distribution—the one you consider just—no longer obtains. Jordan has more and others less. But the new distribution arose through wholly voluntary choices. Who has grounds for complaint? Not those who paid to see Jordan play; they freely chose to buy tickets. Not those who dislike basketball and stayed at home; they didn't spend a penny on Jordan, and are no worse off than before. Surely not Jordan; he chose to play basketball in exchange for a handsome income.[9]

Nozick believes this scenario illustrates two problems with patterned theories of distributive justice. First, liberty upsets patterns. Anyone who believes that economic inequality is unjust will have to intervene in the free market, repeatedly and continuously, to undo the effects of the choices people make. Second, intervening in this way— taxing Jordan to support programs that help the disadvantaged—not only overturns the results of voluntary transactions; it also violates Jordan's rights by taking his earnings. It forces him, in effect, to make a charitable contribution against his will.

What exactly is wrong with taxing Jordan's earnings? According to Nozick, the moral stakes go beyond money. At issue, he believes, is nothing less than human freedom. He reasons as follows: "Taxation of earnings from labor is on a par with forced labor."[10] If the state has the right to claim some portion of my earnings, it also has the right to claim some portion of my time. Instead of taking, say, 30 percent of my income, it might just as well direct me to spend 30 percent of my time working for the state. But if the state can force me to labor on its behalf, it essentially asserts a property right in me.

> Seizing the results of someone's labor is equivalent to seizing hours from him and directing him to carry on various activities. If people force you to do certain work, or unrewarded work, for a certain period of time, they decide what you are to do and what purposes your work is to serve apart from your decisions. This . . . makes them a part-owner of you; it gives them a property right in you.[11]

This line of reasoning takes us to the moral crux of the libertarian claim—the idea of self-ownership. If I own myself, I must own my labor. (If someone else could order me to work, that person would be my master, and I would be a slave.) But if I own my labor, I must be entitled to the fruits of my labor. (If someone else were entitled to my earnings, that person would own my labor and would therefore own me.) That is why, according to Nozick, taxing some of Michael Jordan's $31 million to help the poor violates his rights. It asserts, in effect, that the state, or the community, is a part owner of him.

The libertarian sees a moral continuity from taxation (taking my earnings) to forced labor (taking my labor) to slavery (denying that I own myself):

Self-Ownership	Taking
person	slavery
labor	forced labor
fruits of labor	taxation

Of course, even the most steeply progressive income tax does not claim 100 percent of anyone's income. So the government does not claim to own its taxpaying citizens entirely. But Nozick maintains that it does claim to own part of us—whatever part corresponds to the portion of income we must pay to support causes beyond the minimal state.

Do We Own Ourselves?

When, in 1993, Michael Jordan announced his retirement from basketball, Chicago Bulls fans were bereft. He would later come out of retirement and lead the Bulls to three more championships. But suppose that, in 1993, the Chicago City Council, or, for that matter, Congress, sought to ease the distress of Chicago Bulls fans by voting to require Jordan to play basketball for one-third of the next season. Most people would consider such a law unjust, a violation of Jordan's liberty. But if Congress may not force Jordan to return to the basketball court (for even a third of the season), by what right does it force him to give up one-third of the money he makes playing basketball?

Those who favor the redistribution of income through taxation offer various objections to the libertarian logic. Most of these objections can be answered.

Objection 1: Taxation is not as bad as forced labor.

If you are taxed, you can always choose to work less and pay lower taxes; but if you are forced to labor, you have no such choice.

Libertarian reply: Well, yes. But why should the state force you to make that choice? Some people like watching sunsets, while others prefer activities that cost money—going to the movies, eating out, sailing on yachts, and so on. Why should people who prefer leisure be taxed less than those who prefer activities that cost money?

Consider an analogy: A thief breaks into your home, and has time to take either your $1,000 flat-screen television or the $1,000 in cash you have hidden in your mattress. You might hope he steals the television, because you could then choose whether or not to spend $1,000 to replace it. If the thief stole the cash, he would leave you no such choice (assuming it's too late to return the television for a full refund). But this preference for losing the television (or working less) is beside the point; the thief (and the state) do wrong in both cases, whatever adjustments the victims might make to mitigate their losses.

Objection 2: The poor need the money more.

Libertarian reply: Maybe so. But this is a reason to persuade the affluent to support the needy through their own free choice. It does not justify forcing Jordan and Gates to give to charity. Stealing from the rich and giving to the poor is still stealing, whether it's done by Robin Hood or the state.

Consider this analogy: Just because a patient on dialysis *needs* one of my kidneys more than I do (assuming I have two healthy ones) doesn't mean he has a right to it. Nor may the state lay claim to one of my kidneys to help the dialysis patient, however urgent and pressing his needs may be. Why not? Because it's mine. Needs don't trump my fundamental right to do what I want with the things I own.

Objection 3: Michael Jordan doesn't play alone. He therefore owes a debt to those who contribute to his success.

Libertarian reply: It's true that Jordan's success depends on other people. Basketball is a team sport. People would not have paid $31 million to watch him shoot free-throws by himself on an empty court. He could never have made all that money without teammates, coaches, trainers, referees, broadcasters, stadium maintenance workers, and so on.

But these people have already been paid the market value of their services. Although they make less than Jordan, they voluntarily accepted compensation for the jobs they perform. So there is no reason to suppose that Jordan owes them a portion of his earnings. And even if Jordan owes something to his teammates and coaches, it is hard to see how this debt justifies taxing his earnings to provide food stamps for the hungry or public housing for the homeless.

Objection 4: Jordan is not really being taxed without his consent. As a citizen of a democracy, he has a voice in making the tax laws to which he is subject.

Libertarian reply: Democratic consent is not enough. Suppose Jordan voted against the tax law, but it passed anyway. Wouldn't the IRS still insist that he pay? It certainly would. You might argue that by living in this society, Jordan gives his consent (at least implicitly) to abide by the majority's will and obey the laws. But does this mean that simply by living here as citizens, we write the majority a blank check, and consent in advance to all laws, however unjust?

If so, the majority may tax the minority, even confiscate its wealth and property, against its will. What then becomes of individual rights? If democratic consent justifies the taking of property, does it also justify the taking of liberty? May the majority deprive me of freedom of speech and of religion, claiming that, as a democratic citizen, I have already given my consent to whatever it decides?

The libertarian has a ready response to each of the first four objections. But a further objection is less easy to dismiss:

Objection 5: Jordan is lucky.

He is fortunate to possess the talent to excel at basketball, and lucky to live in a society that prizes the ability to soar through the air and put a ball through a hoop. No matter how hard he has worked to develop his skills, Jordan cannot claim credit for his natural gifts, or for living at a time when basketball is popular and richly rewarded. These things are not his doing. So it cannot be said that he is morally entitled to keep all the money his talents reap. The community does him no injustice by taxing his earnings for the public good.

Libertarian reply: This objection questions whether Jordan's talents are really his. But this line of argument is potentially dangerous. If Jordan is not entitled to the benefits that result from the exercise of his talents, then he doesn't really own them. And if he doesn't own his talents and skills, then he doesn't really own himself. But if Jordan doesn't own himself, who does? Are you sure you want to attribute to the political community a property right in its citizens?

The notion of self-ownership is appealing, especially for those who seek a strong foundation for individual rights. The idea that I belong to myself, not to the state or political community, is one way of explaining why it is wrong to sacrifice my rights for the welfare of others. Recall our reluctance to push the heavy man off the bridge to block a runaway trolley. Don't we hesitate to push him because we recognize that his life belongs to him? Had the heavy man jumped to his death to save the workers on the track, few would object. It is, after all, his life. But his life is not for us to take and use, even for a good cause. The same can be said of the unfortunate cabin boy. Had Parker chosen to sacrifice his life to save his starving shipmates, most people would say he had a right to do so. But his mates had no right to help themselves to a life that did not belong to them.

Many who reject laissez-faire economics invoke the idea of self-ownership in other domains. This may explain the persisting appeal of libertarian ideas, even for people who are sympathetic to the welfare state. Consider the way self-ownership figures in arguments about reproductive freedom, sexual morality, and privacy rights. Government should not ban contraceptives or abortion, it is often said, because women should be free to decide what to do with their own bodies. The law should not punish adultery, prostitution, or homosexuality, many argue, because consenting adults should be free to choose their sexual partners for themselves. Some favor markets in kidneys for transplantation on the grounds that I own my own body, and should therefore be free to sell my body parts. Some extend this principle to defend a right to assisted suicide. Since I own my own life, I should be free to end it if I wish, and to enlist a willing physician (or anyone else) to assist. The state has no right to prevent me from using my body or disposing of my life as I please.

The idea that we own ourselves figures in many arguments for freedom of choice. If I own my body, my life, and my person, I should be free to do whatever I want with them (provided I don't harm others). Despite the appeal of this idea, its full implications are not easy to embrace.

If you are tempted by libertarian principles and want to see how far you would take them, consider these cases:

Selling kidneys

Most countries ban the buying and selling of organs for transplantation. In the United States, people may donate one of their kidneys but not sell it on the open market. But some people argue that such laws should be changed. They point out that thousands of people die each year waiting for kidney transplants—and that the supply would be increased if there existed a free market for kidneys. They also argue that people in need of money should be free to sell their kidneys if they wish.

One argument for permitting the buying and selling of kidneys rests on the libertarian notion of self-ownership: If I own my own body, I should be free to sell my body parts as I please. As Nozick writes, "The central core of the notion of a property right in X . . . is the right to determine what shall be done with X."[12] But few advocates of organ sales actually embrace the full libertarian logic.

Here's why: Most proponents of markets in kidneys emphasize the moral importance of saving lives, and the fact that most people who donate one of their kidneys can manage with the other one. But if you believe that your body and life are your property, neither of these considerations really matters. If you own yourself, your right to use your body as you please is reason enough to let you sell your body parts. The lives you save or the good you do is beside the point.

To see how this is so, imagine two atypical cases:

First, suppose the prospective buyer of your spare kidney is perfectly healthy. He is offering you (or more likely a peasant in the developing world) $8,000 for a kidney, not because he desperately needs an organ transplant but because he is an eccentric art dealer who sells human organs to affluent clients as coffee table conversation pieces. Should people be allowed to buy and sell kidneys for this purpose? If you believe that we own ourselves, you would be hard pressed to say no. What matters is not the purpose but the right to dispose of our property as we please. Of course, you might abhor the frivolous use of body parts and favor organ sales for life-saving purposes only. But if you held this view, your defense of the market would not rest on libertarian premises. You would concede that we do not have an unlimited property right in our bodies.

Consider a second case. Suppose a subsistence farmer in an Indian village wants more than anything else in the world to send his child to college. To raise the money, he sells his spare kidney to an affluent

American in need of a transplant. A few years later, as the farmer's second child approaches college age, another buyer comes to his village and offers a handsome price for his second kidney. Should he be free to sell that one, too, even if going without a kidney would kill him? If the moral case for organ sales rests on the notion of self-ownership, the answer must be yes. It would be odd to think that the farmer owns one of his kidneys but not the other. Some might object that no one should be induced to give up his life for money. But if we own our bodies and lives, then the farmer has every right to sell his second kidney, even if this amounts to selling his life. (The scenario is not wholly hypothetical. In the 1990s, a California prison inmate wanted to donate a second kidney to his daughter. The ethics board of the hospital refused.)

It is possible, of course, to permit only those organ sales that save lives and that do not imperil the life of the seller. But such a policy would not rest on the principle of self-ownership. If we truly own our bodies and lives, it should be up to us to decide whether to sell our body parts, for what purposes, and at what risk to ourselves.

Assisted suicide

In 2007, Dr. Jack Kevorkian, age seventy-nine, emerged from a Michigan prison having served eight years for administering lethal drugs to terminally ill patients who wanted to die. As a condition of his parole, he agreed not to assist any more patients in committing suicide. During the 1990s, Dr. Kevorkian (who became known as "Dr. Death") campaigned for laws allowing assisted suicide and practiced what he preached, helping 130 people end their lives. He was charged, tried, and convicted of second-degree murder only after he gave the CBS television program *60 Minutes* a video that showed him in action, giving a lethal injection to a man suffering from Lou Gehrig's disease.[13]

Assisted suicide is illegal in Michigan, Dr. Kevorkian's home state, and in every other state except Oregon and Washington. Many countries prohibit assisted suicide, and only a few (most famously the Netherlands) expressly permit it.

At first glance, the argument for assisted suicide seems a textbook application of libertarian philosophy. For the libertarian, laws banning assisted suicide are unjust, for the following reason: If my life belongs to me, I should be free to give it up. And if I enter into a voluntary agreement with someone to help me die, the state has no right to interfere.

But the case for permitting assisted suicide does not necessarily depend on the idea that we own ourselves, or that our lives belong to us. Many who favor assisted suicide do not invoke property rights, but argue in the name of dignity and compassion. They say that terminally ill patients who are suffering greatly should be able to hasten their deaths, rather than linger in excruciating pain. Even those who believe we have a general duty to preserve human life may conclude that, at a certain point, the claims of compassion outweigh our duty to carry on.

With terminally ill patients, the libertarian rationale for assisted suicide is hard to disentangle from the compassion rationale. To assess the moral force of the self-ownership idea, consider a case of assisted suicide that does not involve a terminally ill patient. It is, admittedly, a weird case. But its weirdness allows us to assess the libertarian logic on its own, unclouded by considerations of dignity and compassion.

Consensual cannibalism

In 2001, a strange encounter took place in the German village of Rotenburg. Bernd-Jurgen Brandes, a forty-three-year-old software engineer, responded to an Internet ad seeking someone willing to be killed and eaten. The ad had been posted by Armin Meiwes, forty-two, a computer technician. Meiwes was offering no monetary compensation, only the experience itself. Some two hundred people replied to the ad. Four traveled to Meiwes's farmhouse for an interview, but decided they were not interested. But when Brandes met with Meiwes and considered his proposal over coffee, he gave his consent. Meiwes proceeded to kill his guest, carve up the corpse, and store it in plastic bags in his freezer. By the time he was arrested, the "Cannibal of Rotenburg" had consumed over forty pounds of his willing victim, cooking some of him in olive oil and garlic.[14]

When Meiwes was brought to trial, the lurid case fascinated the public and confounded the court. Germany has no law against cannibalism. The perpetrator could not be convicted of murder, the defense maintained, because the victim was a willing participant in his own death. Meiwes's lawyer argued that his client could be guilty only of "killing on request," a form of assisted suicide that carries a maximum five-year sentence. The court attempted to resolve the conundrum by convicting Meiwes of manslaughter and sentencing him to eight and a half years in prison.[15] But two years later, an appeals court overturned the conviction as too lenient, and sentenced Meiwes to life in prison.[16] In a bizarre denouement to the sordid tale, the cannibal killer has reportedly become a vegetarian in prison, on the grounds that factory farming is inhumane.[17]

Cannibalism between consenting adults poses the ultimate test for the libertarian principle of self-ownership and the idea of justice that follows from it. It is an extreme form of assisted suicide. Since it has nothing to do with relieving the pain of a terminally ill patient, it can be justified only on the grounds that we own our bodies and lives, and may do with them what we please. If the libertarian claim is right, banning consensual cannibalism is unjust, a violation of the right to liberty. The state may no more punish Armin Meiwes than it may tax Bill Gates and Michael Jordan to help the poor.

4. HIRED HELP / MARKETS AND MORALS

Many of our most heated debates about justice involve the role of markets: Is the free market fair? Are there some goods that money can't buy— or shouldn't? If so, what are these goods, and what's wrong with buying and selling them?

The case for free markets typically rests on two claims—one about freedom, the other about welfare. The first is the libertarian case for markets. It says that letting people engage in voluntary exchanges respects their freedom; laws that interfere with the free market violate individual liberty. The second is the utilitarian argument for markets. It says that free markets promote the general welfare; when two people make a deal, both gain. As long as their deal makes them better off without hurting anyone else, it must increase overall utility.

Market skeptics question these claims. They argue that market choices are not always as free as they may seem. And they argue that certain goods and social practices are corrupted or degraded if bought and sold for money.

In this chapter, we'll consider the morality of paying people to perform two very different kinds of work—fighting wars and bearing children. Thinking through the rights and wrongs of markets in these contested cases will help us clarify the differences among leading theories of justice.

What's Just—Drafting Soldiers or Hiring Them?

In the early months of the U.S. Civil War, festive rallies and patriotic sentiment prompted tens of thousands of men in the Northern states to volunteer for the Union army. But with the Union defeat at Bull Run, followed by the failure the following spring of General George B. McClellan's drive to capture Richmond, Northerners began to doubt that the conflict would end quickly. More troops had to be raised, and in July 1862, Abraham Lincoln signed the Union's first draft law. A Confederate draft was already in place.

Conscription ran against the grain of the American individualist tradition, and the Union draft made a striking concession to that tradition: Anyone who was drafted and didn't want to serve could hire someone else to take his place.[1]

Draftees seeking substitutes ran ads in newspapers, offering payments as high as $1,500, a considerable sum at the time. The Confederacy's draft law also allowed for paid substitutes, giving rise to the slogan "rich man's war and poor man's fight," a complaint that echoed in the North. In March 1863, Congress passed a new draft law that sought to address the complaint. Although it did not eliminate the right to hire a substitute, it provided that any draftee could pay the government a fee of $300 instead of serving. Although the commutation fee represented close to a year's wages for an unskilled laborer, the provision sought to bring the price of exemption within reach of ordinary workers. Some cities and counties subsidized the fee for their draftees. And insurance societies enabled subscribers to pay a monthly premium for a policy that would cover the fee in the event of conscription.[2]

Though intended to offer exemption from service at a bargain rate, the commutation fee was politically more unpopular than substitution—perhaps because it seemed to put a price on human life (or the risk of death) and to give that price government sanction. Newspaper headlines proclaimed, "Three Hundred Dollars or Your Life." Anger over the draft and the $300 commutation fee prompted violence against enrollment officers, most notably in the New York City draft riots of July 1863, which lasted several days and claimed more than a hundred lives. The following year, Congress enacted a new draft law that eliminated the commutation fee. The right to hire a substitute, however, was retained in the North (though not in the South) throughout the war.[3]

In the end, relatively few draftees wound up fighting in the Union army. (Even after conscription was established, the bulk of the army consisted of volunteers, prompted to enlist by bounty payments and the threat of being drafted.) Many whose numbers were drawn in draft lotteries either fled or were exempted for disability. Of the roughly 207,000 men who were actually drafted, 87,000 paid the commutation fee, 74,000 hired substitutes, and only 46,000 served.[4] Those who hired substitutes to fight in their place included Andrew Carnegie and J. P. Morgan, the fathers of Theodore and Franklin Roosevelt, and future presidents Chester A. Arthur and Grover Cleveland.[5]

Was the Civil War system a just way of allocating military service? When I put this question to my students, almost all of them say no. They say it's unfair to allow the affluent to hire substitutes to fight in their place. Like many Americans who protested in the 1860s, they consider this system a form of class discrimination.

I then ask the students whether they favor a draft or the all-volunteer army we have today. Almost all favor the volunteer army (as do most Americans). But this raises a hard question: If the Civil War system was unfair because it let the affluent hire other people to fight their wars, doesn't the same objection apply to the volunteer army?

The method of hiring differs, of course. Andrew Carnegie had to find his own substitute and pay him directly; today the military recruits the soldiers to fight in Iraq or Afghanistan, and we, the taxpayers, collectively pay them. But it remains the case that those of us who'd rather not enlist hire other people to fight our wars and risk their lives. So what's the difference, morally speaking? If the Civil War system of hiring substitutes was unjust, isn't the volunteer army unjust as well?

To examine this question, let's set aside the Civil War system and consider the two standard ways of recruiting soldiers—conscription and the market.

In its simplest form, conscription fills the ranks of the military by requiring all eligible citizens to serve, or, if not all are needed, by holding a lottery to determine who will be called. This was the system used by the United States during the First and Second World Wars. A draft was also used during the Vietnam War, though the system was complex and riddled with deferments for students and people in certain occupations, allowing many to avoid having to fight.

The existence of the draft fueled opposition to the Vietnam War, especially on college campuses. Partly in response, President Richard Nixon proposed doing away with conscription, and in 1973, as the United States wound down its presence in Vietnam, the all-volunteer military force replaced the draft. Since military service was no longer compulsory, the military increased pay and other benefits to attract the soldiers it needed.

A volunteer army, as we use the term today, fills its ranks through the use of the labor market—as do restaurants, banks, retail stores, and other businesses. The term volunteer is something of a misnomer. The volunteer army is not like a volunteer fire department, in which people serve without pay, or the local soup kitchen, where volunteer workers donate their time. It is a professional army in which soldiers work for pay. The soldiers are "volunteers" only in the sense that paid employees in any profession are volunteers. No one is conscripted, and the job is performed by those who agree to do so in exchange for money and other benefits.

The debate over how a democratic society should fill the ranks of the military is at its most intense during times of war, as the Civil War draft riots and Vietnam-era protests attest. After the United States adopted an all-volunteer force, the question of justice in the allocation of military service faded from public attention. But the U.S.-led wars in Iraq and Afghanistan have revived public discussion about whether it is right for a democratic society to recruit its soldiers by means of the market.

Most Americans favor the volunteer army, and few want to go back to conscription. (In September 2007, in the midst of the Iraq War, a Gallup poll found that Americans opposed reinstating the draft by 80 to 18 percent.[6]) But the renewed debate over the volunteer army and the draft brings us face-to-face with some big questions of political philosophy—questions about individual liberty and civic obligation.

To explore these questions, let's compare the three ways of allocating military service we have considered—conscription, conscription with a provision for hiring substitutes (the Civil War system), and the market system. Which is most just?

1. conscription
2. conscription allowing paid substitutes (Civil War system)
3. market system (volunteer army)

The Case for the Volunteer Army

If you are a libertarian, the answer is obvious. Conscription (policy 1) is unjust because it is coercive, a form of slavery. It implies that the state owns its citizens and can do with them what it pleases, including forcing them to fight and risk their lives in war. Ron Paul, a Republican member of Congress and a leading libertarian, recently made this claim in opposing calls to reinstate the draft to fight the Iraq War: "Conscription is slavery, plain and simple. And it was made illegal under the 13th amendment, which prohibits involuntary servitude. One may well be killed as a military draftee, which makes conscription a very dangerous kind of enslavement."[7]

But even if you don't consider conscription equivalent to slavery, you might oppose it on the grounds that it limits people's choices, and therefore reduces overall happiness. This is a utilitarian argument against conscription. It holds that, compared to a system that permits the hiring of substitutes, conscription reduces people's welfare by preventing mutually advantageous trades. If Andrew Carnegie and his substitute both want to make a deal, why prevent them from doing so? The freedom to enter into the exchange seems to increase each party's utility without reducing anyone else's. Therefore, for utilitarian reasons, the Civil War system (policy 2) is better than pure conscription (policy 1).

It's easy to see how utilitarian assumptions can support market reasoning. If you assume that a voluntary exchange makes both parties better off, without harming anyone else, you have a good utilitarian case for letting markets rule.

We can see this if we now compare the Civil War system (policy 2) with the volunteer army (policy 3). The same logic that argues for letting draftees hire substitutes also argues for a full-market solution: If you're going to let people hire substitutes, why draft anyone in the first place? Why not simply recruit troops through the labor market? Set whatever wage and benefits are necessary to attract the number and quality of soldiers required, and let people choose for themselves whether to take the job. No one is forced to serve against his or her will, and those willing to serve can decide if military service is preferable, all things considered, to their other alternatives.

So, from a utilitarian point of view, the volunteer army seems the best of the three options. Letting people freely choose to enlist based on the compensation being offered enables them to serve only if doing so maximizes their own utility; and those who don't want to serve don't suffer the utility loss of being forced into the military against their will.

A utilitarian could conceivably object that the volunteer army is more expensive than a conscript army. To attract the requisite number and quality of soldiers, pay and benefits must be higher than when soldiers are forced to serve. So a utilitarian might worry that the increased happiness of better-paid soldiers would be offset by the unhappiness of taxpayers who now pay more for military service.

But this objection is not very convincing, especially if the alternative is conscription (with or without substitution). It would be odd to insist, on utilitarian grounds, that the cost to taxpayers of other government services, such as police and fire protection, should be reduced by forcing randomly chosen people to perform these tasks at below-market pay; or that the cost of highway maintenance should be reduced by requiring a subset of taxpayers chosen by lottery either to perform the work themselves or hire others to do so. The unhappiness that would result from such coercive measures would probably outweigh the benefit to the taxpayers of cheaper government services.

So, from the standpoint of both libertarian and utilitarian reasoning, the volunteer army seems best, the Civil War hybrid system second best, and conscription the least desirable way of allocating military service. But at least two objections can be made to this line of argument. One objection is about fairness and freedom; the other is about civic virtue and the common good.

Objection 1: Fairness and freedom

The first objection holds that, for those with limited alternatives, the free market is not all that free. Consider an extreme case: A homeless person sleeping under a bridge may have chosen, in some sense, to do so; but we would not necessarily consider his choice to be a free one. Nor would we be justified in assuming that he must prefer sleeping under a bridge to sleeping in an apartment. In order to know whether his choice reflects a preference for sleeping out of doors or an inability to afford an apartment, we need to know something about his circumstances. Is he doing this freely or out of necessity?

The same question can be asked of market choices generally—including the choices people make when they take on various jobs. How does this apply to military service? We can't determine the justice or injustice of the volunteer army without knowing more about the background conditions that prevail in the society: Is there a reasonable degree of equal opportunity, or do some people have very few options in life? Does everyone have a chance to get a college education, or is it the case that, for some people, the only way to afford college is to enlist in the military?

From the standpoint of market reasoning, the volunteer army is attractive because it avoids the coercion of conscription. It makes military service a matter of consent. But some people who wind up serving in the all-volunteer army may be as averse to military service as those who stay away. If poverty and economic disadvantage are widespread, the choice to enlist may simply reflect the lack of alternatives.

According to this objection, the volunteer army may not be as voluntary as it seems. In fact, it may involve an element of coercion. If some in the society have no other good options, those who choose to enlist may be conscripted, in effect, by economic necessity. In that case, the difference between conscription and the volunteer army is not that one is compulsory while the other is free; it's rather that each employs a different form of compulsion—the force of law in the first case and the pressure of economic necessity in the second. Only if people have a reasonable range of decent job options can it be said that the choice to serve for pay reflects their preferences rather than their limited alternatives.

The class composition of today's volunteer army bears out this objection, at least to some extent. Young people from low- to middle-income neighborhoods (median household income of $30,850 to $57,836) are disproportionately represented in the ranks of active-duty army recruits.[8] Least represented are the poorest 10 percent of the population (many of whom may lack the requisite education and skills) and the most affluent 20 percent (those from neighborhoods with median household incomes of $66,329 and above).[9] In recent years, over 25 percent of army recruits have lacked a regular high school diploma.[10] And while 46 percent of the civilian population has had some college education, only 6.5 percent of the 18-to-24-year-olds in the military's enlisted ranks have ever been to college.[11]

In recent years, the most privileged young people in American society have not opted for military service. The title of a recent book about the class composition of the armed forces captures this well: *AWOL: The Unexcused Absence of America's Upper Classes from Military Service.*[12] Of the 750 members of Princeton's class of 1956, the majority— 450 students —joined the military after graduation. Of the 1,108 members of Princeton's class of 2006, only 9 students enlisted.[13] A similar pattern is found at other elite universities—and in the nation's capital. Only 2 percent of members of Congress have a son or daughter serving in the military.[14]

Congressman Charles Rangel, a Democrat from Harlem who is a decorated Korean War veteran, considers this unfair, and has called for reinstatement of the draft. "As long as Americans are being shipped off to war," he wrote, "then everyone should be vulnerable, not just those who, because of economic circumstances, are attracted by lucrative enlistment bonuses and educational incentives." He points out that, in New York City, "the disproportionate burden of service is dramatic. In 2004, 70% of the volunteers in the city were black or Hispanic, recruited from lower income communities."[15]

Rangel opposed the Iraq War, and believes it never would have been launched if the children of policy-makers had had to share the burden of fighting it. He also argues that, given the unequal opportunities in American society, allocating military service by the market is unfair to those with the fewest alternatives:

The great majority of people bearing arms for this country in Iraq are from the poorer communities in our inner cities and rural areas, places where enlistment bonuses of up to $40,000 and thousands in educational benefits are very attractive. For people who have college as an option, those incentives—at the risk to one's life—don't mean a thing.[16]

So the first objection to the market rationale for a volunteer army is concerned with unfairness and coercion—the unfairness of class discrimination and the coercion that can occur if economic disadvantage compels young people to risk their lives in exchange for a college education and other benefits.

Notice that the coercion objection is not an objection to the volunteer army as such. It only applies to a volunteer army that operates in a society with substantial inequalities. Alleviate those inequalities, and you remove the objection. Imagine, for example, a perfectly equal society, in which everyone had access to the same educational opportunities. In such a society, no one could complain that the choice to enlist in the military was less than free, because unfairly pressured by economic necessity.

Of course, no society is perfectly equal. So the risk of coercion always hovers over the choices people make in the labor market. How much equality is needed to ensure that market choices are free rather than coerced? At what point do inequalities in the background conditions of society undermine the fairness of social institutions (such as the volunteer army) based on individual choice? Under what conditions is the free market really free? To answer these questions, we'll need to examine moral and political philosophies that see freedom—not utility—at the heart of justice. So let's postpone these questions until we turn to Immanuel Kant and John Rawls in later chapters.

Objection 2: Civic virtue and the common good

In the meantime, let's consider a second objection to the use of markets in allocating military service—the objection in the name of civic virtue and the common good.

This objection says that military service is not just another job; it's a civic obligation. According to this argument, all citizens have a duty to serve their country. Some proponents of this view believe this obligation can be discharged only through military service, while others say it can be fulfilled through other forms of national service, such as the Peace Corps, AmeriCorps, or Teach for America. But if military service (or national service) is a civic duty, it's wrong to put it up for sale on the market.

Consider another civic responsibility—jury duty. No one dies performing jury duty, but being called to serve on a jury can be onerous, especially if it conflicts with work or other pressing commitments. And yet we don't let people hire substitutes to take their place on juries. Nor do we use the labor market to create a paid, professional, "all-volunteer" jury system. Why not? From the standpoint of market reasoning, a case could be made for doing so. The same utilitarian arguments raised against drafting soldiers can be made against drafting jurors: Allowing a busy person to get out of jury duty by hiring a substitute would make both parties better off. Doing away with mandatory jury duty would be better still; letting the labor market recruit the requisite number of qualified jurors would enable those who want the work to have it and those who dislike the work to avoid it.

So why do we forego the increased social utility of a market for jurors? Perhaps because we worry that paid jurors would come disproportionately from disadvantaged backgrounds, and that the quality of justice would suffer. But there's no reason to assume that the affluent make better jurors than those from modest backgrounds. In any case, the wages and benefits could always be adjusted (as the army has done) to attract those with the necessary education and skills.

The reason we draft jurors rather than hire them is that we regard the activity of dispensing justice in the courts as a responsibility all citizens should share. Jurors don't simply vote; they deliberate with one another about the evidence and the law. And the deliberations draw on the disparate life experiences that jurors from various walks of life bring with them. Jury duty is not only a way of resolving cases. It is also a form of civic education, and an expression of democratic citizenship. Although jury duty is not always edifying, the idea that all citizens are obligated to perform it preserves a connection between the courts and the people.

Something similar could be said of military service. The civic argument for conscription claims that military service, like jury duty, is a civic responsibility; it expresses, and deepens, democratic citizenship. From this point of view, turning military service into a commodity—a task we hire other people to perform—corrupts the civic ideals that should govern it. According to this objection, hiring soldiers to fight our wars is wrong, not because it's unfair to the poor but because it allows us to abdicate a civic duty.

The historian David M. Kennedy has offered a version of this argument. He argues that "the U.S. armed forces today have many of the attributes of a mercenary army," by which he means a paid, professional army that is separated to a significant degree from the society on whose behalf it fights.[17] He doesn't mean to disparage the motives of those who enlist. His worry is that hiring a relatively small number of our fellow citizens to fight our wars lets the rest of us off the hook. It severs the link between the majority of democratic citizens and the soldiers who fight in their name.

Kennedy observes that, "proportionate to the population, today's active-duty military establishment is about 4 percent of the size of the force that won World War II." This makes it relatively easy for policymakers to commit the country to war without having to secure the broad and deep consent of the society as a whole. "History's most powerful military force can now be sent into battle in the name of a society that scarcely breaks a sweat when it does so."[18] The volunteer army absolves most Americans of the responsibility to fight and die for their country. While some see this as an advantage, this exemption from shared sacrifice comes at the price of eroding political accountability:

A hugely preponderant majority of Americans with no risk whatsoever of exposure to military service have, in effect, hired some of the least advantaged of their fellow countrymen to do some of their most dangerous business while the majority goes on with their own affairs unbloodied and undistracted.[19]

One of the most famous statements of the civic case for conscription was offered by Jean-Jacques Rousseau (1712–1778), the Geneva-born Enlightenment political theorist. In *The Social Contract* (1762), he argues that turning a civic duty into a marketable good does not increase freedom, but rather undermines it:

> As soon as public service ceases to be the chief business of the citizens, and they would rather serve with their money than with their persons, the state is not far from its fall. When it is necessary to march out to war, they pay troops and stay at home. . . . In a country that is truly free, the citizens do everything with their own arms and nothing by means of money; so far from paying to be exempted from their duties, they would even pay for the privilege of fulfilling them themselves. I am far from taking the common view: I hold enforced labor to be less opposed to liberty than taxes.[20]

Rousseau's robust notion of citizenship, and his wary view of markets, may seem distant from the assumptions of our day. We are inclined to view the state, with its binding laws and regulations, as the realm of force; and to see the market, with its voluntary exchanges, as the realm of freedom. Rousseau would say this has things backward— at least where civic goods are concerned.

Market advocates might defend the volunteer army by rejecting Rousseau's strenuous notion of citizenship, or by denying its relevance to military service. But the civic ideals he invoked retain a certain resonance, even in a market-driven society such as the United States. Most supporters of the volunteer army vehemently deny that it amounts to a mercenary army. They rightly point out that many of those who serve are motivated by patriotism, not only by the pay and benefits. But why do we consider this important? Provided the soldiers do their jobs well, why should we care about their motivation? Even as we relegate recruitment to the market, we find it hard to detach military service from older notions of patriotism and civic virtue.

For, consider: What, really, is the difference between the contemporary volunteer army and an army of mercenaries? Both pay soldiers to fight. Both entice people to enlist by the promise of salary and other benefits. If the market is an appropriate way of raising an army, what exactly is wrong with mercenaries?

One might reply that mercenaries are foreign nationals who fight only for pay, whereas the American volunteer army hires only Americans. But if the labor market is an appropriate way of raising troops, it's not clear why the U.S. military should discriminate in hiring on the basis of nationality. Why shouldn't it actively recruit soldiers from among citizens of other countries who want the work and possess the relevant qualifications? Why not create a foreign legion of soldiers from the developing world, where wages are low and good jobs are scarce?

It is sometimes argued that foreign soldiers would be less loyal than Americans. But national origin is no guarantee of loyalty on the battlefield, and military recruiters could screen foreign applicants to determine their reliability. Once you accept the notion that the army should use the labor market to fill its ranks, there is no reason in principle to restrict eligibility to American citizens—no reason, that is, unless you believe military service is a civic responsibility after all, an expression of citizenship. But if you believe that, then you have reason to question the market solution.

Two generations after ending the draft, Americans hesitate to apply the full logic of market reasoning to military service. The French Foreign Legion has a long tradition of recruiting foreign soldiers to fight for France. Although French law prohibits the Legion from active recruiting outside of France, the Internet has made that restriction meaningless. Online recruiting in thirteen languages now attracts recruits from throughout the world. About a quarter of the force now comes from Latin America, and a growing proportion comes from China and other Asian countries.[21]

The United States has not established a foreign legion, but it has taken a step in that direction. Faced with difficulties meeting recruiting goals as the wars in Iraq and Afghanistan have stretched on, the military has begun recruiting foreign immigrants currently living in the United States on temporary visas. The inducements include good pay and a fast track to American citizenship. About thirty thousand noncitizens now serve in the U.S. armed forces. The new program will extend eligibility from permanent residents with green cards to temporary immigrants, foreign students, and refugees.[22]

The recruitment of foreign troops is not the only way the logic of the market plays out. Once you view military service as a job like any other, there is no reason to assume the hiring must be done by the government. In fact, the United States now outsources military functions to private enterprise on a large scale. Private military contractors play an increasing role in conflicts around the world, and form a substantial part of the U.S. military presence in Iraq.

In July 2007, the *Los Angeles Times* reported that the number of U.S.-paid private contractors in Iraq (180,000) exceeded the number of U.S. military personnel stationed there (160,000).[23] Many of the contractors perform non-combat logistical support—building bases, repairing vehicles, delivering supplies, and providing food services. But about 50,000 are armed security operatives whose work guarding bases, convoys, and diplomats often draws them into combat.[24] More than 1,200 private contractors have been killed in Iraq, though they do not return in flag-draped coffins, and their numbers are not included in the U.S. military's casualty count.[25]

One of the leading private military companies is Blackwater Worldwide. Erik Prince, the company's CEO, is a former Navy SEAL with an ardent faith in the free market. He rejects the suggestion that his soldiers are "mercenaries," a term he considers "slanderous."[26] Prince explains: "We're trying to do for the national security apparatus what Federal Express did for the postal service."[27] Blackwater received over $1 billion in government contracts for its services in Iraq, but has often been at the center of controversy.[28] Its role first came to public attention in 2004, when four of its employees were ambushed and killed in

Fallujah and two of the bodies were strung from a bridge. The incident led President George W. Bush to order the Marines into Fallujah in a massive and costly battle with insurgents.

In 2007, six Blackwater guards opened fire on a crowd in a Baghdad square, killing seventeen civilians. The guards, who claimed they had been fired upon first, were immune from prosecution under Iraqi law because of rules laid down by the American governing authority after the invasion. The contractors were eventually indicted for manslaughter by the U.S. Justice Department, and the incident led the Iraqi government to demand the withdrawal of Blackwater from the country.[29]

Many in Congress and in the public at large object to the outsourcing of war to for-profit companies such as Blackwater. Much of the criticism focuses on the unaccountability of these companies, and their involvement in abuses. Several years before the Blackwater shooting incident, private contractors from other companies were among those who abused detainees at Abu Ghraib prison. Although the army soldiers involved were court-martialed, the private contractors were not punished.[30]

But suppose Congress tightened regulations on private military companies to make them more accountable, and to hold their employees to the same standards of behavior that apply to U.S. troops. Would the use of private companies to fight our wars cease to be objectionable? Or is there a moral difference between paying Federal Express to deliver the mail and hiring Blackwater to deliver lethal force on the battlefield?

To answer this question, we have to resolve a prior one: Is military service (and perhaps national service generally) a civic obligation that all citizens have a duty to perform, or is it a hard and risky job like others (coal mining, for example, or commercial fishing) that is properly governed by the labor market? And to answer this question, we have to ask a broader one: What obligations do citizens of a democratic society owe to one another, and how do such obligations arise? Different theories of justice offer different answers to this question. We'll be in a better position to decide whether we should draft soldiers or hire them once we explore, later in the book, the basis and scope of civic obligation. In the meantime, consider another controversial use of the labor market.

Pregnancy for Pay

William and Elizabeth Stern were a professional couple living in Tenafly, New Jersey—he a biochemist, she a pediatrician. They wanted a baby, but couldn't have one on their own, at least not without medical risk to Elizabeth, who had multiple sclerosis. So they contacted an infertility center that arranged "surrogate" pregnancies. The center ran ads seeking "surrogate mothers"—women willing to carry a baby to term for someone else, in exchange for a monetary payment.[31]

One of the women who had answered the ads was Mary Beth Whitehead, a twenty-nine-year-old mother of two children, and the wife of a sanitation worker. In February 1985, William Stern and Mary Beth Whitehead signed a contract. Mary Beth agreed to be artificially inseminated with William's sperm, to bear the child, and to hand it over to William upon birth. She also agreed to give up her maternal rights, so that Elizabeth Stern could adopt the child. For his part, William agreed to pay Mary Beth a fee of $10,000 (payable on delivery), plus medical expenses. (He also paid a fee of $7,500 to the infertility center for arranging the deal.)

After several artificial inseminations, Mary Beth became pregnant, and in March 1986 she gave birth to a baby girl. The Sterns, anticipating their soon-to-be adopted daughter, named her Melissa. But Mary Beth Whitehead decided she could not part with the child, and wanted to keep it. She fled to Florida with the baby, but the Sterns got a court order requiring her to turn over the child. Florida police found Mary Beth, the baby was given to the Sterns, and the custody fight went to court in New Jersey.

The trial judge had to decide whether to enforce the contract. What do you think would be the right thing to do? To simplify matters, let's focus on the moral issue, rather than the law. (As it happens, New Jersey had no law either permitting or prohibiting surrogacy contracts at the time.) William Stern and Mary Beth Whitehead had made a contract. Morally speaking, should it have been enforced?

The strongest argument in favor of upholding the contract is that a deal is a deal. Two consenting adults had entered into a voluntary agreement that offered benefits to both parties: William Stern would get a genetically related child, and Mary Beth Whitehead would earn $10,000 for nine months of work.

Admittedly, this was no ordinary commercial deal. So you might hesitate to enforce it on one of two grounds: First, you might doubt that a woman's agreement to have a baby and give it up for money is fully informed. Can she really anticipate how she'll feel once the time comes to give up the child? If not, it might be argued that her initial consent was beclouded by the need for money, and by the lack of adequate knowledge about what it would be like to part with her child. Second, you might find it objectionable to buy and sell babies, or to rent the reproductive capacity of women, even if both parties freely agree to do so. It could be argued that this practice turns children into commodities and exploits women by treating pregnancy and child-bearing as a money-making business.

Judge Harvey R. Sorkow, the trial judge in the "Baby M" case, as it came to be known, was not persuaded by either of these objections.[32] He upheld the agreement, invoking the sanctity of contracts. A deal was a deal, and the birth mother had no right to break the contract simply because she'd changed her mind.[33]

The judge addressed both objections. First, he rejected the notion that Mary Beth's agreement was less than voluntary, her consent somehow tainted:

Neither party has a superior bargaining position. Each had what the other wanted. A price for the service each was to perform was struck and a bargain reached. One did not force the other. Neither had ex-

pertise that left the other at a disadvantage. Neither had disproportionate bargaining power.[34]

Second, he rejected the notion that surrogacy amounts to baby-
selling. The judge held that William Stern, the biological father, had not
bought a baby from Mary Beth Whitehead; he'd paid her for the service
of carrying his child to term. "At birth, the father does not purchase
the child. It is his own biological genetically related child. He cannot
purchase what is already his."[35] Since the baby was conceived with
William's sperm, it was his baby to begin with, the judge reasoned.
Therefore, no baby-selling was involved. The $10,000 payment was for
a service (the pregnancy), not a product (the child).

As for the claim that providing such a service exploits women,
Judge Sorkow disagreed. He compared paid pregnancy to paid sperm
donation. Since men are allowed to sell their sperm, women should be
allowed to sell their reproductive capacities: "If a man may offer the
means for procreation then a woman must equally be allowed to do
so."[36] To hold otherwise, he stated, would be to deny women the
equal protection of the law.

Mary Beth Whitehead appealed the case to the New Jersey Supreme
Court. In a unanimous opinion, the court overturned Judge Sorkow
and ruled that the surrogacy contract was invalid.[37] The court awarded
custody of Baby M to William Stern, on the grounds that this was in
the best interest of the child. Contract aside, the court believed the
Sterns would do a better job of raising Melissa. But it restored Mary
Beth Whitehead's status as the child's mother, and asked the lower
court to determine visitation rights.

Writing for the court, Chief Justice Robert Wilentz rejected the
surrogacy contract. He argued that it was not truly voluntary, and that
it constituted baby-selling.

First, the consent was flawed. Mary Beth's agreement to bear a
child and surrender it at birth was not truly voluntary, because it was
not fully informed:

Under the contract, the natural mother is irrevocably committed before she knows the strength of her bond with her child. She never makes a totally voluntary, informed decision, for quite clearly any decision prior to the baby's birth is, in the most important sense, uninformed.[38]

Once the baby is born, the mother is in a better position to make an informed choice. But by then, her decision is not free, but is compelled by "the threat of a lawsuit, and the inducement of a $10,000 payment," making it "less than totally voluntary."[39] Moreover, the need for money makes it likely that poor women will "choose" to become surrogate mothers for the affluent, rather than the other way around. Justice Wilentz suggested that this, too, called into question the voluntary character of such agreements: "We doubt that infertile couples in the low-income bracket will find upper income surrogates."[40]

So one reason for voiding the contract was tainted consent. But Wilentz also offered a second, more fundamental reason:

Putting aside the issue of how compelling her need for money may have been, and how significant her understanding of the consequences, we suggest that her consent is irrelevant. There are, in a civilized society, some things that money cannot buy.[41]

Commercial surrogacy amounts to baby-selling, Wilentz argued, and baby-selling is wrong, however voluntary it may be. He rejected the argument that the payment is for the surrogate's service rather than for the child. According to the contract, the $10,000 was payable only upon surrender of custody and the termination by Mary Beth of her parental rights.

This is the sale of a child, or, at the very least, the sale of a mother's right to her child, the only mitigating factor being that one of the purchasers is the father. . . . [A] middle man, propelled by profit, promotes the sale. Whatever idealism may have motivated any of the participants, the profit motive predominates, permeates, and ultimately governs the transaction.[42]

Surrogacy Contracts and Justice

So who was right in the Baby M case—the trial court that enforced the contract, or the higher court that invalidated it? To answer this question, we need to assess the moral force of contracts, and the two objections that were raised against the surrogacy contract.

The argument for upholding the surrogacy contract draws on the two theories of justice we've considered so far—libertarianism and utilitarianism. The libertarian case for contracts is that they reflect freedom of choice; to uphold a contract between two consenting adults is to respect their liberty. The utilitarian case for contracts is that they promote the general welfare; if both parties agree to a deal, both must derive some benefit or happiness from the agreement—otherwise, they wouldn't have made it. So, unless it can be shown that the deal reduces someone else's utility (and by more than it benefits the parties), mutually advantageous exchanges—including surrogacy contracts— should be upheld.

What about the objections? How convincing are they?

Objection 1: Tainted consent

The first objection, about whether Mary Beth Whitehead's agreement was truly voluntary, raises a question about the conditions under which people make choices. It argues that we can exercise free choice only if we're not unduly pressured (by the need for money, say), and if we're reasonably well informed about the alternatives. Exactly what counts as undue pressure or the lack of informed consent is open to argument. But the point of such arguments is to determine when a supposedly voluntary agreement is really voluntary—and when it's not. This question loomed large in the Baby M case, as it does in debates about the volunteer army.

Stepping back from the cases, it's worth noticing that this debate, about the background conditions necessary for meaningful consent, is actually a family quarrel within one of the three approaches to justice we consider in this book—the one that says justice means respecting freedom. As we've already seen, libertarianism is one member of this family. It holds that justice requires respect for whatever choices people make, provided the choices don't violate anyone's rights. Other theories that view justice as respecting freedom impose some restrictions on the conditions of choice. They say—as did Justice Wilentz in the Baby M case—that choices made under pressure, or in the absence of informed consent, are not truly voluntary. We'll be better equipped to assess this debate when we turn to the political philosophy of John Rawls—a member of the freedom camp who rejects the libertarian account of justice.

Objection 2: Degradation and higher goods

What about the second objection to surrogacy contracts—the one that says there are some things money shouldn't buy, including babies and women's reproductive capacities? What exactly is wrong with buying and selling these things? The most compelling answer is that treating babies and pregnancy as commodities degrades them, or fails to value them appropriately.

Underlying this answer is a far-reaching idea: The right way of valuing goods and social practices is not simply up to us. Certain modes of valuation are appropriate to certain goods and practices. In the case of commodities, such as cars and toasters, the proper way of valuing them is to use them, or to make them and sell them for profit. But it's a mistake to treat all things as if they were commodities. It would be wrong, for example, to treat human beings as commodities, mere things to be bought and sold. That's because human beings are persons worthy of respect, not objects to be used. Respect and use are two different modes of valuation.

Elizabeth Anderson, a contemporary moral philosopher, has applied a version of this argument to the surrogacy debate. She argues that surrogacy contracts degrade children and women's labor by treating them as if they were commodities.[43] By degradation, she means treating something "in accordance with a lower mode of valuation than is proper to it. We value things not just 'more' or 'less,' but in qualitatively higher and lower ways. To love or respect someone is to value her in a higher way than one would if one merely used her. . . . Commercial surrogacy degrades children insofar as it treats them as commodities."[44] It uses them as instruments of profit rather than cherishes them as persons worthy of love and care.

Commercial surrogacy also degrades women, Anderson argues, by treating their bodies as factories and by paying them not to bond with the children they bear. It replaces "the parental norms which usually govern the practice of gestating children with the economic norms which govern ordinary production." By requiring the surrogate mother "to repress whatever parental love she feels for the child," Anderson writes, surrogacy contracts "convert women's labor into a form of alienated labor."[45]

> In the surrogate contract, [the mother] agrees not to form or to attempt to form a parent-child relationship with her offspring. Her labor is alienated, because she must divert it from the end which the social practices of pregnancy rightly promote—an emotional bond with her child.[46]

Central to Anderson's argument is the idea that goods differ in kind; it's therefore a mistake to value all goods in the same way, as instruments of profit or objects of use. If this idea is right, it explains why there are some things money shouldn't buy.

It also poses a challenge to utilitarianism. If justice is simply a matter of maximizing the balance of pleasure over pain, we need a single, uniform way of weighing and valuing all goods and the pleasure or pain they give us. Bentham invented the concept of utility for precisely this purpose. But Anderson argues that valuing everything according to utility (or money) degrades those goods and social practices—including children, pregnancy, and parenting—that are properly valued according to higher norms.

But what are those higher norms, and how can we know what modes of valuation are appropriate to what goods and social practices? One approach to this question begins with the idea of freedom. Since human beings are capable of freedom, we shouldn't be used as if we were mere objects, but should be treated instead with dignity and respect. This approach emphasizes the distinction between persons (worthy of respect) and mere objects or things (open to use) as the fundamental distinction in morality. The greatest defender of this approach is Immanuel Kant, to whom we turn in the next chapter.

Another approach to higher norms begins with the idea that the right way of valuing goods and social practices depends on the purposes and ends those practices serve. Recall that, in opposing surrogacy, Anderson argues that "the social practices of pregnancy rightly promote" a certain end, namely an emotional bond of a mother with her child. A contract that requires the mother not to form such a bond is degrading because it diverts her from this end. It replaces a "norm of parenthood" with a "norm of commercial production." The notion that we identify the norms appropriate to social practices by trying to grasp the characteristic end, or purpose, of those practices is at the heart of Aristotle's theory of justice. We will examine his approach in a later chapter.

Until we examine these theories of morality and justice, we can't really determine what goods and social practices should be governed by markets. But the debate over surrogacy, like the argument over the volunteer army, gives us a glimpse of what's at stake.

Outsourcing Pregnancy

Melissa Stern, once known as Baby M, recently graduated from George Washington University, where she majored in religion.[47] Over two decades have passed since her celebrated custody battle in New Jersey, but the debate over surrogate motherhood continues. Many European countries ban commercial surrogacy. In the United States, more than a dozen states have legalized the practice, about a dozen states prohibit it, while in other states its legal status is unclear.[48]

New reproductive technologies have changed the economics of surrogacy in ways that sharpen the ethical quandary it presents. When Mary Beth Whitehead agreed to undertake a pregnancy for pay, she provided both egg and womb. She was therefore the biological mother of the child she bore. But the advent of in vitro fertilization (IVF) makes it possible for one woman to provide the egg and another to gestate it. Deborah Spar, a professor of business administration at the Harvard Business School, has analyzed the commercial advantages of the new surrogacy.[49] Traditionally, those who contracted for surrogacy "essentially needed to purchase a single package of egg-bundled-with-womb." Now they can acquire "the egg from one source (including, in many cases, the intended mother) and the womb from another."[50]

This "unbundling" of the supply chain, Spar explains, has prompted growth in the surrogacy market.[51] "By removing the traditional link between egg, womb, and mother, gestational surrogacy [has] reduced the legal and emotional risks that had surrounded traditional surrogacy and allowed a new market to thrive." "Freed from the constraints of the egg-and-womb package," surrogacy brokers are now "more discriminating" in the surrogates they choose, "looking for eggs with particular genetic traits and wombs attached to a certain personality."[52] Prospective parents no longer need to worry about the genetic characteristics of the woman they hire to carry their child, "because they're acquiring those elsewhere."[53]

They don't care what she looks like, and they are less worried that she will claim the child at birth or that courts would be inclined to find in her favor. All they really need is a healthy woman, willing to undergo pregnancy and to adhere to certain standards of behavior—no drinking, no smoking, no drugs—during its course.[54]

Although gestational surrogacy has increased the supply of prospective surrogates, demand has increased as well. Surrogates now receive about $20,000 to $25,000 per pregnancy. The total cost of the arrangement (including medical bills and legal fees) is typically $75,000 to $80,000.

With prices this steep, it's not surprising to find that prospective parents have begun to seek less expensive alternatives. As with other products and services in a global economy, paid pregnancy is now outsourced to low-cost providers. In 2002, India legalized commercial surrogacy in hopes of attracting foreign customers.[55]

The western Indian city of Anand may soon be to paid pregnancy what Bangalore is to call centers. In 2008, more than fifty women in the city were carrying pregnancies for couples in the United States, Taiwan, Britain, and elsewhere.[56] One clinic there provides group housing, complete with maids, cooks, and doctors, for fifteen pregnant women serving as surrogates for clients around the world.[57] The money the women earn, from $4,500 to $7,500, is often more than they would otherwise make in fifteen years, and enables them to buy a house or to finance their own children's education.[58] For the prospective parents who go to Anand, the arrangement is a bargain. At around $25,000 (including medical costs, the surrogate's payment, round-trip airfare, and hotel expenses for two trips), the total cost is about a third of what it would be for gestational surrogacy in the United States.[59]

Some suggest that commercial surrogacy as practiced today is less morally troubling than the arrangement that led to the Baby M case. Since the surrogate does not provide the egg, only the womb and the labor of pregnancy, it is argued, the child is not genetically hers. According to this view, no baby is being sold, and the claim to the child is less likely to be contested.

But gestational surrogacy does not resolve the moral quandary. It may be true that gestational surrogates will be less attached to the children they bear than surrogates who also provide the egg. But dividing the role of mother three ways (adopting parent, egg donor, and gestational surrogate) rather than two does not settle the question of who has the superior claim to the child.

If anything, the outsourcing of pregnancy that has occurred due in part to IVF has cast the moral issues in sharper relief. The substantial cost savings for prospective parents, and the enormous economic benefits, relative to local wages, that Indian surrogates derive from the practice, make it undeniable that commercial surrogacy can increase the general welfare. So, from a utilitarian point of view, it's hard to argue with the rise of paid pregnancy as a global industry.

But the global outsourcing of pregnancy also dramatizes the moral qualms. Suman Dodia, a twenty-six-year-old Indian who was a gestational surrogate for a British couple, had previously earned $25 per month working as a maid. For her, the prospect of earning $4,500 for nine months' work must have been almost too compelling to resist.[60] The fact that she had delivered her own three children at home and never visited a doctor adds poignancy to her role as a surrogate. Referring to her paid pregnancy, she said, "I'm being more careful now than I was with my own pregnancies."[61] Although the economic benefits of her choice to become a surrogate are clear, it's not obvious that we would call it free. Moreover, the creation of a paid pregnancy industry on global scale—as a deliberate policy in poor countries, no less— heightens the sense that surrogacy degrades women by instrumentalizing their bodies and reproductive capacities.

It is hard to imagine two human activities more dissimilar than bearing children and fighting wars. But the pregnant surrogates in India and the soldier Andrew Carnegie hired to take his place in the Civil War have something in common. Thinking through the rights and wrongs of their situations brings us face to face with two of the questions that divide competing conceptions of justice: How free are the choices we make in the free market? And are there certain virtues and higher goods that markets do not honor and money cannot buy?

5. WHAT MATTERS IS THE MOTIVE / IMMANUEL KANT

If you believe in universal human rights, you are probably not a utilitarian. If all human beings are worthy of respect, regardless of who they are or where they live, then it's wrong to treat them as mere instruments of the collective happiness. (Recall the story of the malnourished child languishing in the cellar for the sake of the "city of happiness.")

You might defend human rights on the grounds that respecting them will maximize utility in the long run. In that case, however, your reason for respecting rights is not to respect the person who holds them but to make things better for everyone. It is one thing to condemn the scenario of the suffering child because it reduces overall utility, and something else to condemn it as an intrinsic moral wrong, an injustice to the child.

If rights don't rest on utility, what is their moral basis? Libertarians offer a possible answer: Persons should not be used merely as means to the welfare of others, because doing so violates the fundamental right of self-ownership. My life, labor, and person belong to me and me alone. They are not at the disposal of the society as a whole.

As we have seen, however, the idea of self-ownership, consistently applied, has implications that only an ardent libertarian can love—an unfettered market without a safety net for those who fall behind; a minimal state that rules out most measures to ease inequality and promote the common good; and a celebration of consent so complete that it permits self-inflicted affronts to human dignity such as consensual cannibalism or selling oneself into slavery.

Even John Locke (1632–1704), the great theorist of property rights and limited government, does not assert an unlimited right of self-possession. He rejects the notion that we may dispose of our life and liberty however we please. But Locke's theory of unalienable rights invokes God, posing a problem for those who seek a moral basis for rights that does not rest on religious assumptions.

Kant's Case for Rights

Immanuel Kant (1724–1804) offers an alternative account of duties and rights, one of the most powerful and influential accounts any philosopher has produced. It does not depend on the idea that we own ourselves, or on the claim that our lives and liberties are a gift from God. Instead, it depends on the idea that we are rational beings, worthy of dignity and respect.

Kant was born in the East Prussian city of Konigsberg in 1724, and died there, almost eighty years later. He came from a family of modest means. His father was a harness-maker and his parents were Pietists, members of a Protestant faith that emphasized the inner religious life and the doing of good works.[1]

He excelled at the University of Konigsberg, which he entered at age sixteen. For a time, he worked as a private tutor, and then, at thirty-one, he received his first academic job, as an unsalaried lecturer, for which he was paid based on the number of students who showed up at his lectures. He was a popular and industrious lecturer, giving about twenty lectures a week on subjects including metaphysics, logic, ethics, law, geography, and anthropology.

In 1781, at age fifty-seven, he published his first major book, *The Critique of Pure Reason*, which challenged the empiricist theory of knowledge associated with David Hume and John Locke. Four years later, he published the *Groundwork for the Metaphysics of Morals*, the first of his several works on moral philosophy. Five years after Jeremy Bentham's *Principles of Morals and Legislation* (1780), Kant's *Groundwork* launched a devastating critique of utilitarianism. It argues that morality is not about maximizing happiness or any other end. Instead, it is about respecting persons as ends in themselves.

Kant's *Groundwork* appeared shortly after the American Revolution (1776) and just before the French Revolution (1789). In line with the spirit and moral thrust of those revolutions, it offers a powerful basis for what the eighteenth-century revolutionaries called the rights of man, and what we in the early twenty-first century call universal human rights.

Kant's philosophy is hard going. But don't let that scare you away. It is worth the effort, because the stakes are enormous. The *Groundwork* takes up a big question: What is the supreme principle of morality? And in the course of answering that question, it addresses another hugely important one: What is freedom?

Kant's answers to these questions have loomed over moral and political philosophy ever since. But his historical influence is not the only reason to pay attention to him. Daunting though Kant's philosophy may seem at first glance, it actually informs much contemporary thinking about morality and politics, even if we are unaware of it. So making sense of Kant is not only a philosophical exercise; it is also a way of examining some of the key assumptions implicit in our public life.

Kant's emphasis on human dignity informs present-day notions of universal human rights. More important, his account of freedom figures in many of our contemporary debates about justice. In the introduction to this book, I distinguished three approaches to justice. One approach, that of the utilitarians, says that the way to define justice and to determine the right thing to do is to ask what will maximize welfare, or the collective happiness of society as a whole. A second approach connects justice to freedom. Libertarians offer an example of this approach. They say the just distribution of income and wealth is whatever distribution arises from the free exchange of goods and services in an unfettered market. To regulate the market is unjust, they maintain, because it violates the individual's freedom of choice. A third approach says that justice means giving people what they morally deserve—allocating goods to reward and promote virtue. As we will see when we turn to Aristotle (in Chapter 8), the virtue-based approach connects justice to reflection about the good life.

Kant rejects approach one (maximizing welfare) and approach three (promoting virtue). Neither, he thinks, respects human freedom. So Kant is a powerful advocate for approach two—the one that connects justice and morality to freedom. But the idea of freedom he puts forth is demanding—more demanding than the freedom of choice we exercise when buying and selling goods on the market. What we commonly think of as market freedom or consumer choice is not true freedom, Kant argues, because it simply involves satisfying desires we haven't chosen in the first place.

In a moment, we'll come to Kant's more exalted idea of freedom. But before we do, let's see why he thinks the utilitarians are wrong to think of justice and morality as a matter of maximizing happiness.

The Trouble with Maximizing Happiness

Kant rejects utilitarianism. By resting rights on a calculation about what will produce the greatest happiness, he argues, utilitarianism leaves rights vulnerable. There is also a deeper problem: trying to derive moral principles from the desires we happen to have is the wrong way to think about morality. Just because something gives many people pleasure doesn't make it right. The mere fact that the majority, however big, favors a certain law, however intensely, does not make the law just.

Kant argues that morality can't be based on merely empirical considerations, such as the interests, wants, desires, and preferences people have at any given time. These factors are variable and contingent, he points out, so they could hardly serve as the basis for universal moral principles—such as universal human rights. But Kant's more fundamental point is that basing moral principles on preferences and desires—even the desire for happiness—misunderstands what morality is about. The utilitarian's happiness principle "contributes nothing whatever toward establishing morality, since making a man happy is quite different from making him good and making him prudent or astute in seeking his advantage quite different from making him virtuous."[2] Basing morality on interests and preferences destroys its dignity. It doesn't teach us how to distinguish right from wrong, but "only to become better at calculation."[3]

If our wants and desires can't serve as the basis of morality, what's left? One possibility is God. But that is not Kant's answer. Although he was a Christian, Kant did not base morality on divine authority. He argues instead that we can arrive at the supreme principle of morality through the exercise of what he calls "pure practical reason." To see how, according to Kant, we can reason our way to the moral law, let's now explore the close connection, as Kant sees it, between our capacity for reason and our capacity for freedom.

Kant argues that every person is worthy of respect, not because we own ourselves but because we are rational beings, capable of reason; we are also autonomous beings, capable of acting and choosing freely.

Kant doesn't mean that we always succeed in acting rationally, or in choosing autonomously. Sometimes we do and sometimes we don't. He means only that we have the capacity for reason, and for freedom, and that this capacity is common to human beings as such.

Kant readily concedes that our capacity for reason is not the only capacity we possess. We also have the capacity to feel pleasure and pain. Kant recognizes that we are sentient creatures as well as rational ones. By "sentient," Kant means that we respond to our senses, our feelings. So Bentham was right—but only half right. He was right to observe that we like pleasure and dislike pain. But he was wrong to insist that they are "our sovereign masters." Kant argues that reason can be sovereign, at least some of the time. When reason governs our will, we are not driven by the desire to seek pleasure and avoid pain.

Our capacity for reason is bound up with our capacity for freedom. Taken together, these capacities make us distinctive, and set us apart from mere animal existence. They make us more than mere creatures of appetite.

What Is Freedom?

To make sense of Kant's moral philosophy, we need to understand what he means by freedom. We often think of freedom as the absence of obstacles to doing what we want. Kant disagrees. He has a more stringent, demanding notion of freedom.

Kant reasons as follows: When we, like animals, seek pleasure or the avoidance of pain, we aren't really acting freely. We are acting as the slaves of our appetites and desires. Why? Because whenever we are seeking to satisfy our desires, everything we do is for the sake of some end given outside us. I go this way to assuage my hunger, that way to slake my thirst.

Suppose I'm trying to decide what flavor of ice cream to order: Should I go for chocolate, vanilla, or espresso toffee crunch? I may think of myself as exercising freedom of choice, but what I'm really doing is trying to figure out which flavor will best satisfy my preferences—preferences I didn't choose in the first place. Kant doesn't say it's wrong to satisfy our preferences. His point is that, when we do so, we are not acting freely, but acting according to a determination given outside us. After all, I didn't choose my desire for espresso toffee crunch rather than vanilla. I just have it.

Some years ago, Sprite had an advertising slogan: "Obey your thirst." Sprite's ad contained (inadvertently, no doubt) a Kantian insight. When I pick up a can of Sprite (or Pepsi or Coke), I act out of obedience, not freedom. I am responding to a desire I haven't chosen. I am obeying my thirst.

People often argue over the role of nature and nurture in shaping behavior. Is the desire for Sprite (or other sugary drinks) inscribed in the genes or induced by advertising? For Kant, this debate is beside the point. Whenever my behavior is biologically determined or socially conditioned, it is not truly free. To act freely, according to Kant, is to act autonomously. And to act autonomously is to act according to a law I give myself—not according to the dictates of nature or social convention.

One way of understanding what Kant means by acting autonomously is to contrast autonomy with its opposite. Kant invents a word to capture this contrast—*heteronomy*. When I act heteronomously, I act according to determinations given outside of me. Here is an illustration: When you drop a billiard ball, it falls to the ground. As it falls, the billiard ball is not acting freely; its movement is governed by the laws of nature—in this case, the law of gravity.

Suppose that I fall (or am pushed) from the Empire State Building. As I hurtle toward the earth, no one would say that I am acting freely; my movement is governed by the law of gravity, as with the billiard ball.

Now suppose I land on another person and kill that person. I would not be morally responsible for the unfortunate death, any more than the billiard ball would be morally responsible if it fell from a great height and hit someone on the head. In neither case is the falling object—me or the billiard ball—acting freely. In both cases, the falling object is governed by the law of gravity. Since there is no autonomy, there can be no moral responsibility.

Here, then, is the link between freedom as autonomy and Kant's idea of morality. To act freely is not to choose the best means to a given end; it is to choose the end itself, for its own sake—a choice that human beings can make and billiard balls (and most animals) cannot.

Persons and Things

It is 3:00 a.m., and your college roommate asks you why you are up late pondering moral dilemmas involving runaway trolleys.

"To write a good paper in Ethics 101," you reply.

"But why write a good paper?" your roommate asks.

"To get a good grade."

"But why care about grades?"

"To get a job in investment banking."

"But why get a job in investment banking?"

"To become a hedge fund manager someday."

"But why be a hedge fund manager?"

"To make a lot of money."

"But why make a lot of money?"

"To eat lobster often, which I like. I am, after all, a sentient crea-ture. *That's* why I'm up late thinking about runaway trolleys!"

This is an example of what Kant would call heteronomous determi-nation—doing something for the sake of something else, for the sake of something else, and so on. When we act heteronomously, we act for the sake of ends given outside us. We are instruments, not authors, of the purposes we pursue.

Kant's notion of autonomy stands in stark contrast to this. When we act autonomously, according to a law we give ourselves, we do something for its own sake, as an end in itself. We cease to be instru-ments of purposes given outside us. This capacity to act autonomously is what gives human life its special dignity. It marks out the difference between persons and things.

For Kant, respecting human dignity means treating persons as ends in themselves. This is why it is wrong to use people for the sake of the general welfare, as utilitarianism does. Pushing the heavy man onto the track to block the trolley uses him as a means, and so fails to respect him as an end in himself. An enlightened utilitarian (such as Mill) may refuse to push the man, out of concern for secondary effects that would diminish utility in the long run. (People would soon be afraid to stand on bridges, etc.) But Kant would maintain that this is the wrong reason to desist from pushing. It still treats the would-be victim as an instrument, an object, a mere means to the happiness of others. It lets him live, not for his own sake, but so that other people can cross bridges without a second thought.

This raises the question of what gives an action moral worth. It takes us from Kant's specially demanding idea of freedom to his equally demanding notion of morality.

What's Moral? Look for the Motive

According to Kant, the moral worth of an action consists not in the consequences that flow from it, but in the intention from which the act is done. What matters is the motive, and the motive must be of a certain kind. What matters is doing the right thing because it's right, not for some ulterior motive.

"A good will is not good because of what it effects or accomplishes," Kant writes. It is good in itself, whether or not it prevails. "Even if . . . this will is entirely lacking in power to carry out its intentions; if by its utmost effort it still accomplishes nothing . . . even then it would still shine like a jewel for its own sake as something which has its full value in itself."[4]

For any action to be morally good, "it is not enough that it should *conform* to the moral law—it must also be done for the sake of the moral law."[5] And the motive that confers moral worth on an action is the motive of duty, by which Kant means doing the right thing for the right reason.[6]

In saying that only the motive of duty confers moral worth on an action, Kant is not yet saying what particular duties we have. He is not yet telling us what the supreme principle of morality commands. He's simply observing that, when we assess the moral worth of an action, we assess the motive from which it's done, not the consequences it produces.[6]

If we act out of some motive other than duty, such as self-interest, for example, our action lacks moral worth. This is true, Kant maintains, not only for self-interest but for any and all attempts to satisfy our wants, desires, preferences, and appetites. Kant contrasts motives such as these—he calls them "motives of inclination"—with the motive of duty. And he insists that only actions done out of the motive of duty have moral worth.

The calculating shopkeeper and the Better Business Bureau

Kant offers several examples that bring out the difference between duty and inclination. The first involves a prudent shopkeeper. An inexperienced customer, say, a child, goes into a grocery store to buy a loaf of bread. The grocer could overcharge him—charge him more than the usual price for a loaf of bread—and the child would not know. But the grocer realizes that, if others discovered he took advantage of the child in this way, word might spread and hurt his business. For this reason, he decides not to overcharge the child. He charges him the usual price. So the shopkeeper does the right thing, but for the wrong reason. The only reason he deals honestly with the child is to protect his reputation. The shopkeeper acts honestly only for the sake of self-interest; the shopkeeper's action lacks moral worth.[7]

A modern-day parallel to Kant's prudent shopkeeper can be found in the recruiting campaign of the Better Business Bureau of New York. Seeking to enlist new members, the BBB sometimes runs a full-page ad in the *New York Times* with the headline "Honesty is the best policy. It's also the most profitable." The text of the ad leaves no mistake about the motive being appealed to.

Honesty. It's as important as any other asset. Because a business that deals in truth, openness, and fair value cannot help but do well. It is toward this end [that] we support the Better Business Bureau. Come join us. And profit from it.

Kant would not condemn the Better Business Bureau; promoting honest business dealing is commendable. But there is an important moral difference between honesty for its own sake and honesty for the sake of the bottom line. The first is a principled position, the second a prudential one. Kant argues that only the principled position is in line with the motive of duty, the only motive that confers moral worth on an action.

Or consider this example: Some years ago, the University of Maryland sought to combat a widespread cheating problem by asking students to sign pledges not to cheat. As an inducement, students who took the pledge were offered a discount card good for savings of 10 to 25 percent at local shops.[8] No one knows how many students promised not to cheat for the sake of a discount at the local pizza place. But most of us would agree that bought honesty lacks moral worth. (The discounts might or might not succeed in reducing the incidence of cheating; the moral question, however, is whether honesty motivated by the desire for a discount or a monetary reward has moral worth. Kant would say no.)

These cases bring out the plausibility of Kant's claim that only the motive of duty—doing something because it's right, not because it's useful or convenient—confers moral worth on an action. But two further examples bring out a complexity in Kant's claim.

Staying alive

The first involves the duty, as Kant sees it, to preserve one's own life. Since most people have a strong inclination to continue living, this duty rarely comes into play. Most of the precautions we take to preserve our lives therefore lack moral content. Buckling our seat belts and keeping our cholesterol in check are prudential acts, not moral ones.

Kant acknowledges that it is often difficult to know what motivates people to act as they do. And he recognizes that motives of duty and inclination may both be present. His point is that only the motive of duty—doing something because it's right, not because it's useful or pleasing or convenient—confers moral worth on an action. He illustrates this point with the example of suicide.

Most people go on living because they love life, not because they have a duty to do so. Kant offers a case where the motive of duty comes into view. He imagines a hopeless, miserable person so filled with despair that he has no desire to go on living. If such a person summons the will to preserve his life, not from inclination but from duty, then his action has moral worth.[9]

Kant does not maintain that only miserable people can fulfill the duty to preserve their lives. It is possible to love life and still preserve it for the right reason—namely, that one has a duty to do so. The desire to go on living doesn't undermine the moral worth of preserving one's life, provided the person recognizes the duty to preserve his or her own life, and does so with this reason in mind.

The moral misanthrope

Perhaps the hardest case for Kant's view involves what he takes to be the duty to help others. Some people are altruistic. They feel compassion for others and take pleasure in helping them. But for Kant, doing good deeds out of compassion, "however right and however amiable it may be," lacks moral worth. This may seem counterintuitive. Isn't it good to be the kind of person who takes pleasure in helping others? Kant would say yes. He certainly doesn't think there is anything wrong with acting out of compassion. But he distinguishes between this motive for helping others—that doing the good deed gives me pleasure—and the motive of duty. And he maintains that only the motive of duty confers moral worth on an action. The compassion of the altruist "deserves praise and encouragement, but not esteem."[10]

What, then, would it take for a good deed to have moral worth?

Kant offers a scenario: Imagine that our altruist suffers a misfortune that extinguishes his love of humanity. He becomes a misanthrope who lacks all sympathy and compassion. But this cold-hearted soul tears himself out of his indifference and comes to the aid of his fellow human beings. Lacking any inclination to help, he does so "for the sake of duty alone." Now, for the first time, his action has moral worth.[11]

This seems in some ways an odd judgment. Does Kant mean to valorize misanthropes as moral exemplars? No, not exactly. Taking pleasure in doing the right thing does not necessarily undermine its moral worth. What matters, Kant tells us, is that the good deed be done because it's the right thing to do—whether or not doing it gives us pleasure.

The spelling bee hero

Consider an episode that took place some years ago at the national spelling bee in Washington, D.C. A thirteen-year-old boy was asked to spell *echolalia*, a word that means a tendency to repeat whatever one hears. Although he misspelled the word, the judges misheard him, told him he had spelled the word right, and allowed him to advance. When the boy learned that he had misspelled the word, he went to the judges and told them. He was eliminated after all. Newspaper headlines the next day proclaimed the honest young man a "spelling bee hero," and his photo appeared in *The New York Times*. "The judges said I had a lot of integrity," the boy told reporters. He added that part of his motive was, "I didn't want to feel like a slime."[12]

When I read that quote from the spelling bee hero, I wondered what Kant would think. Not wanting to feel like a slime is an inclination, of course. So, if that was the boy's motive for telling the truth, it would seem to undermine the moral worth of his act. But this seems too harsh. It would mean that only unfeeling people could ever perform morally worthy acts. I don't think this is what Kant means.

If the only reason the boy told the truth was to avoid feeling guilty, or to avoid bad publicity should his error be discovered, then his truth-telling would lack moral worth. But if he told the truth because he knew it was the right thing to do, his act has moral worth regardless of the pleasure or satisfaction that might attend it. As long as he did the right thing for the right reason, feeling good about it doesn't undermine its moral worth.

The same is true of Kant's altruist. If he comes to the aid of other people simply for the pleasure it gives him, then his action lacks moral worth. But if he recognizes a duty to help one's fellow human beings and acts out of that duty, then the pleasure he derives from it is not morally disqualifying.

In practice, of course, duty and inclination often coexist. It is often hard to sort out one's own motives, let alone know for sure the motives of other people. Kant doesn't deny this. Nor does he think that only a hardhearted misanthrope can perform morally worthy acts. The point of his misanthrope example is to isolate the motive of duty—to see it unclouded by sympathy or compassion. And once we glimpse the motive of duty, we can identify the feature of our good deeds that gives them their moral worth—namely, their principle, not their consequences.

What Is the Supreme Principle of Morality?

If morality means acting from duty, it remains to be shown what duty requires. To know this, for Kant, is to know the supreme principle of morality. What is the supreme principle of morality? Kant's aim in the *Groundwork* is to answer this question.

We can approach Kant's answer by seeing how he connects three big ideas: morality, freedom, and reason. He explains these ideas through a series of contrasts or dualisms. They involve a bit of jargon, but if you notice the parallel among these contrasting terms, you are well on your way to understanding Kant's moral philosophy. Here are the contrasts to keep in mind:

Contrast 1 (morality):   duty v. inclination

Contrast 2 (freedom):   autonomy v. heteronomy

Contrast 3 (reason):   categorical v. hypothetical imperatives

We've already explored the first of these contrasts, between duty and inclination. Only the motive of duty can confer moral worth on an action. Let me see if I can explain the other two.

The second contrast describes two different ways that my will can be determined—autonomously and heteronomously. According to Kant, I'm free only when my will is determined autonomously, governed by a law I give myself. Again, we often think of freedom as being able to do what we want, to pursue our desires unimpeded. But Kant poses a powerful challenge to this way of thinking about freedom: If you didn't choose those desires freely in the first place, how can you think of yourself as free when you're pursuing them? Kant captures this challenge in this contrast between autonomy and heteronomy.

When my will is determined heteronomously, it is determined externally, from outside of me. But this raises a difficult question: If freedom means something more than following my desires and inclinations, how is it possible? Isn't everything I do motivated by some desire or inclination determined by outside influences?

The answer is far from obvious. Kant observes that "everything in nature works in accordance with laws," such as the laws of natural necessity, the laws of physics, the laws of cause and effect.[13] This includes us. We are, after all, natural beings. Human beings are not exempt from the laws of nature.

But if we are capable of freedom, we must be capable of acting according to some other kind of law, a law other than the laws of physics. Kant argues that all action is governed by laws of some kind or other.

And if our actions were governed solely by the laws of physics, then we would be no different from that billiard ball. So if we're capable of freedom, we must be capable of acting not according to a law that is given or imposed on us, but according to a law we give ourselves. But where could such a law come from?

Kant's answer: from reason. We're not only sentient beings, governed by the pleasure and pain delivered by our senses; we are also rational beings, capable of reason. If reason determines my will, then the will becomes the power to choose independent of the dictates of nature or inclination. (Notice that Kant isn't asserting that reason always does govern my will; he's only saying that, insofar as I'm capable of acting freely, according to a law I give myself, then it must be the case that reason can govern my will.)

Of course, Kant isn't the first philosopher to suggest that human beings are capable of reason. But his idea of reason, like his conceptions of freedom and morality, is especially demanding. For the empiricist philosophers, including the utilitarians, reason is wholly instrumental. It enables us to identify means for the pursuit of certain ends—ends that reason itself does not provide. Thomas Hobbes called reason the "scout for the desires." David Hume called reason the "slave of the passions."

The utilitarians viewed human beings as capable of reason, but only instrumental reason. Reason's work, for the utilitarians, is not to determine what ends are worth pursuing. Its job is to figure out how to maximize utility by satisfying the desires we happen to have.

Kant rejects this subordinate role for reason. For him, reason is not just the slave of the passions. If that were all reason amounted to, Kant says, we'd be better off with instinct.[14]

Kant's idea of reason—of practical reason, the kind involved in morality—is not instrumental reason but "pure practical reason, which legislates a priori, regardless of all empirical ends."[15]

Categorical Versus Hypothetical Imperatives

But how can reason do this? Kant distinguishes two ways that reason can command the will, two different kinds of imperative. One kind of imperative, perhaps the most familiar kind, is a hypothetical imperative. Hypothetical imperatives use instrumental reason: If you want X, then do Y. If you want a good business reputation, then treat your customers honestly.

Kant contrasts hypothetical imperatives, which are always conditional, with a kind of imperative that is unconditional: a categorical imperative. "If the action would be good solely as a means to something else," Kant writes, "the imperative is hypothetical. If the action is represented as good in itself, and therefore as necessary for a will which of itself accords with reason, then the imperative is categorical."[16] The term *categorical* may seem like jargon, but it's not that distant from our ordinary use of the term. By "categorical," Kant means unconditional. So, for example, when a politician issues a categorical denial of an alleged scandal, the denial is not merely emphatic; it's unconditional— without any loophole or exception. Similarly, a categorical duty or categorical right is one that applies regardless of the circumstances.

For Kant, a categorical imperative commands, well, categorically— without reference to or dependence on any further purpose. "It is concerned not with the matter of the action and its presumed results, but with its form, and with the principle from which it follows. And what is essentially good in the action consists in the mental disposition, let the consequences be what they may." Only a categorical imperative, Kant argues, can qualify as an imperative of morality.[17]

The connection among the three parallel contrasts now comes into view. To be free in the sense of autonomous requires that I act not out of a hypothetical imperative but out of a categorical imperative.

This leaves one big question: What *is* the categorical imperative, and what does it command of us? Kant says we can answer this question from the idea of "a practical law that by itself commands absolutely and without any further motives."[18] We can answer this question from the idea of a law that binds us as rational beings regardless of our particular ends. So what is it?

Kant offers several versions or formulations of the categorical imperative, which he believes all amount to the same thing.

Categorical imperative I: Universalize your maxim

The first version Kant calls the formula of the universal law: "Act only on that maxim whereby you can at the same time will that it should become a universal law."[19] By "maxim," Kant means a rule or principle that gives the reason for your action. He is saying, in effect, that we should act only on principles that we could universalize without contradiction. To see what Kant means by this admittedly abstract test, let's consider a concrete moral question: Is it ever right to make a promise you know you won't be able to keep?

Suppose I am in desperate need of money and so ask you for a loan. I know perfectly well that I won't be able to pay it back anytime soon. Would it be morally permissible to get the loan by making a false promise to repay the money promptly, a promise I know I can't keep? Would a false promise be consistent with the categorical imperative? Kant says no, obviously not. The way I can see that the false promise is at odds with the categorical imperative is by trying to universalize the maxim upon which I'm about to act.[20]

What is the maxim in this case? Something like this: "Whenever someone needs money badly, he should ask for a loan and promise to repay, even though he knows he won't be able to do so." If you tried to universalize this maxim and at the same time to act on it, Kant says, you would discover a contradiction: If everybody made false promises when they needed money, nobody would believe such promises. In fact, there would be no such thing as promises; universalizing the false promise would undermine the institution of promise-keeping. But then it would be futile, even irrational, for you to try to get money by promising. This shows that making a false promise is morally wrong, at odds with the categorical imperative.

Some people find this version of Kant's categorical imperative unpersuasive. The formula of the universal law bears a certain resemblance to the moral bromide grown-ups use to chastise children who cut in line or speak out of turn: "What if everybody did that?" If everyone lied, then no one could rely on anybody's word, and we'd all be worse off. If this is what Kant is saying, he is making a consequentialist argument after all—rejecting the false promise not in principle, but for its possibly harmful effects or consequences.

No less a thinker than John Stuart Mill leveled this criticism against Kant. But Mill misunderstood Kant's point. For Kant, seeing whether I could universalize the maxim of my action and continue acting on it is not a way of speculating about possible consequences. It is a test to see whether my maxim accords with the categorical imperative. A false promise is not morally wrong because, writ large, it would undermine social trust (though it might well do so). It is wrong because, in making it, I privilege my needs and desires (in this case, for money) over everybody else's. The universalizing test points to a powerful moral claim: it's a way of checking to see if the action I am about to undertake puts my interests and special circumstances ahead of everyone else's.

Categorical imperative II: Treat persons as ends

The moral force of the categorical imperative becomes clearer in Kant's second formulation of it, the formula of humanity as an end. Kant introduces the second version of the categorical imperative as follows: We can't base the moral law on any particular interests, purposes, or ends, because then it would be only relative to the person whose ends they were. "But suppose there were something whose existence has in itself an absolute value," as an end in itself. "Then in it, and in it alone, would there be the ground of a possible categorical imperative."[21]

What could possibly have an absolute value, as an end in itself? Kant's answer: humanity. "I say that man, and in general every rational being, exists as an end in himself, not merely as a means for arbitrary use by this or that will."[22] This is the fundamental difference, Kant reminds us, between persons and things. Persons are rational beings. They don't just have a relative value, but if anything has, they have an absolute value, an intrinsic value. That is, rational beings have dignity.

This line of reasoning leads Kant to the second formulation of the categorical imperative: "Act in such a way that you always treat humanity, whether in your own person or in the person of any other, never simply as a means, but always at the same time as an end."[23] This is the formula of humanity as an end.

Consider again the false promise. The second formulation of the categorical imperative helps us see, from a slightly different angle, why it's wrong. When I promise to repay you the money I hope to borrow, knowing that I won't be able to, I'm manipulating you. I'm using you as a means to my financial solvency, not treating you as an end, worthy of respect.

Now consider the case of suicide. What's interesting to notice is that both murder and suicide are at odds with the categorical imperative, and for the same reason. We often think of murder and suicide as radically different acts, morally speaking. Killing someone else deprives him of his life against his will, while suicide is the choice of the person who commits it. But Kant's notion of treating humanity as an end puts murder and suicide on the same footing. If I commit murder, I take someone's life for the sake of some interest of my own—robbing a bank, or consolidating my political power, or giving vent to my anger. I use the victim as a means, and fail to respect his or her humanity as an end. This is why murder violates the categorical imperative.

For Kant, suicide violates the categorical imperative in the same way. If I end my life to escape a painful condition, I use myself as a means for the relief of my own suffering. But as Kant reminds us, a person is not a thing, "not something to be used merely as a means." I have no more right to dispose of humanity in my own person than in someone else. For Kant, suicide is wrong for the same reason that murder is wrong. Both treat persons as things, and fail to respect humanity as an end in itself.[24]

The suicide example brings out a distinctive feature of what Kant considers the duty to respect our fellow human beings. For Kant, self-respect and respect for other persons flow from one and the same principle. The duty of respect is a duty we owe to persons as rational beings, as bearers of humanity. It has nothing to do with who in particular the person may be.

There is a difference between respect and other forms of human attachment. Love, sympathy, solidarity, and fellow feeling are moral sentiments that draw us closer to some people than to others. But the reason we must respect the dignity of persons has nothing to do with anything particular about them. Kantian respect is unlike love. It's unlike sympathy. It's unlike solidarity or fellow feeling. These reasons for caring about other people have to do with who they are in particular. We love our spouses and the members of our family. We feel sympathy for people with whom we can identify. We feel solidarity with our friends and comrades.

But Kantian respect is respect for humanity as such, for a rational capacity that resides, undifferentiated, in all of us. This explains why violating it in my own case is as objectionable as violating it in the case of someone else. It also explains why the Kantian principle of respect lends itself to doctrines of universal human rights. For Kant, justice requires us to uphold the human rights of all persons, regardless of where they live or how well we know them, simply because they are human beings, capable of reason, and therefore worthy of respect.

Morality and Freedom

We can now see the link, as Kant conceives it, between morality and freedom. Acting morally means acting out of duty—for the sake of the moral law. The moral law consists of a categorical imperative, a principle that requires us to treat persons with respect, as ends in themselves. Only when I act in accordance with the categorical imperative am I acting freely. For whenever I act according to a hypothetical imperative, I act for the sake of some interest or end given outside of me. But in that case, I'm not really free; my will is determined not by me, but by outside forces—by the necessities of my circumstance or by the wants and desires I happen to have.

I can escape the dictates of nature and circumstance only by acting autonomously, according to a law I give myself. Such a law must be unconditioned by my particular wants and desires. So Kant's demanding notions of freedom and morality are connected. Acting freely, that is, autonomously, and acting morally, according to the categorical imperative, are one and the same.

This way of thinking about morality and freedom leads Kant to his devastating critique of utilitarianism. The effort to base morality on some particular interest or desire (such as happiness or utility) was bound to fail. "For what they discovered was never duty, but only the necessity of acting from a certain interest." But any principle based on interest "was bound to be always a conditioned one and could not possibly serve as a moral law."[25]

Questions for Kant

Kant's moral philosophy is powerful and compelling. But it can be difficult to grasp, especially at first. If you have followed along so far, several questions may have occurred to you. Here are four especially important ones.

QUESTION 1: *Kant's categorical imperative tells us to treat everyone with respect, as an end in itself. Isn't this pretty much the same as the Golden Rule? ("Do unto others as you would have them do unto you.")*

ANSWER: No. The Golden Rule depends on contingent facts about how people would like to be treated. The categorical imperative requires that we abstract from such contingencies and respect persons as rational beings, regardless of what they might want in a particular situation.

Suppose you learn that your brother has died in a car accident. Your elderly mother, in frail condition in a nursing home, asks for news of him. You are torn between telling her the truth and sparing her the shock and agony of it. What is the right thing to do? The Golden Rule would ask, "How would you like to be treated in a similar circumstance?" The answer, of course, is highly contingent. Some people would rather be spared harsh truths at vulnerable moments, while others want the truth, however painful. You might well conclude that, if you found yourself in your mother's condition, you would rather not be told.

For Kant, however, this is the wrong question to ask. What matters is not how you (or your mother) would feel under these circumstances, but what it means to treat persons as rational beings, worthy of respect. Here is a case where compassion might point one way and Kantian respect another. From the standpoint of the categorical imperative, lying to your mother out of concern for her feelings would arguably use her as a means to her own contentment rather than respect her as a rational being.

QUESTION 2: *Kant seems to suggest that answering to duty and acting autonomously are one and the same. But how can this be? Acting according to duty means having to obey a law. How can subservience to a law be compatible with freedom?*

ANSWER: Duty and autonomy go together only in a special case— when I am the author of the law I have a duty to obey. My dignity as a free person does not consist in being subject to the moral law, but in being the author of "this very same law . . . and subordinated to it only on this ground." When we abide by the categorical imperative, we abide by a law we have chosen. "The dignity of man consists precisely in his capacity to make universal law,

although only on condition of being himself also subject to the law
he makes."[26]

QUESTION 3: *If autonomy means acting according to a law I give myself, what
guarantees that everyone will choose the same moral law? If the categorical
imperative is the product of my will, isn't it likely that different people will come
up with different categorical imperatives? Kant seems to think that we will all
agree on the same moral law. But how can he be sure that different people won't
reason differently, and arrive at various moral laws?*

ANSWER: When we will the moral law, we don't choose as you and
me, particular persons that we are, but as rational beings, as participants in what Kant calls "pure practical reason." So it's a mistake
to think that the moral law is up to us as individuals. Of course, if
we reason from our particular interests, desires, and ends, we may be
led to any number of principles. But these are not moral principles,
only prudential ones. Insofar as we exercise pure practical reason, we
abstract from our particular interests. This means that everyone who
exercises pure practical reason will reach the same conclusion—will
arrive at a single (universal) categorical imperative. "Thus a free will
and a will under moral laws are one and the same."[27]

QUESTION 4: *Kant argues that if morality is more than a matter of prudential
calculation, it must take the form of a categorical imperative. But how can we
know that morality exists apart from the play of power and interests? Can we ever
be sure that we are capable of acting autonomously, with a free will? What if scientists discover (through brain-imaging, for example, or cognitive neuroscience)
that we have no free will after all: Would that disprove Kant's moral philosophy?*

ANSWER: Freedom of the will is not the kind of thing that science
can prove or disprove. Neither is morality. It's true that human beings inhabit the realm of nature. Everything we do can be described
from a physical or biological point of view. When I raise my hand to
cast a vote, my action can be explained in terms of muscles, neu-
rons, synapses, and cells. But it can also be explained in terms of

ideas and beliefs. Kant says we can't help but understand ourselves from both standpoints—the empirical realm of physics and biology, and an "intelligible" realm of free human agency.

To answer this question more fully, I need to say a bit more about these two standpoints. They are two perspectives we can take on human agency, and on the laws that govern our actions. Here is how Kant describes the two standpoints:

> A rational being . . . has two points of view from which he can regard himself and from which he can know laws governing . . . all his actions. He can consider himself *first*—so far as he belongs to the sensible world—to be under laws of nature (heteronomy); and *secondly*—so far as he belongs to the intelligible world—to be under laws which, being independent of nature, are not empirical but have their ground in reason alone."[28]

The contrast between these two perspectives lines up with the three contrasts we have already discussed:

Contrast 1 (morality):	duty v. inclination
Contrast 2 (freedom):	autonomy v. heteronomy
Contrast 3 (reason):	categorical v. hypothetical imperatives
Contrast 4 (standpoints):	intelligible v. sensible realms

As a natural being, I belong to the sensible world. My actions are determined by the laws of nature and the regularities of cause and effect. This is the aspect of human action that physics, biology, and neuroscience can describe. As a rational being, I inhabit an intelligible world. Here, being independent of the laws of nature, I am capable of autonomy, capable of acting according to a law I give myself.

Kant argues that only from this second (intelligible) standpoint can I regard myself as free, "for to be independent of determination by causes in the sensible world (and this is what reason must always attribute to itself) is to be free."[29]

If I were only an empirical being, I would not be capable of freedom; every exercise of will would be conditioned by some interest or desire. All choice would be heteronomous choice, governed by the pursuit of some end. My will could never be a first cause, only the effect of some prior cause, the instrument of one or another impulse or inclination.

Insofar as we think of ourselves as free, we cannot think of ourselves as merely empirical beings. "When we think of ourselves as free, we transfer ourselves into the intelligible world as members and recognize the autonomy of the will together with its consequence—morality."[30]

So—to return to the question—how are categorical imperatives possible? Only because "the idea of freedom makes me a member of the intelligible world."[31] The idea that we can act freely, take moral responsibility for our actions, and hold other people morally responsible for their actions requires that we see ourselves from this perspective—from the standpoint of an agent, not merely an object. If you really want to resist this notion, and claim that human freedom and moral responsibility are utter illusions, then Kant's account can't prove you wrong. But it would be difficult if not impossible to understand ourselves, to make sense of our lives, without some conception of freedom and morality. And any such conception, Kant thinks, commits us to the two standpoints—the standpoints of the agent and of the object. And once you see the force of this picture, you will see why science can never prove or disprove the possibility of freedom.

Remember, Kant admits that we aren't only rational beings. We don't only inhabit the intelligible world. If we were only rational beings, not subject to the laws and necessities of nature, then all of our actions "would invariably accord with the autonomy of the will."[32] Because we inhabit, simultaneously, both standpoints—the realm of necessity and the realm of freedom—there is always potentially a gap between what we do and what we ought to do, between the way things are and the way they ought to be.

Another way of putting this point is to say that morality is not empirical. It stands at a certain distance from the world. It passes judgment on the world. Science can't, for all its power and insight, reach moral questions, because it operates within the sensible realm.

"To argue freedom away," Kant writes, "is as impossible for the most abstruse philosophy as it is for the most ordinary human reason."[33] It's also impossible, Kant might have added, for cognitive neuroscience, however sophisticated. Science can investigate nature and inquire into the empirical world, but it cannot answer moral questions or disprove free will. That is because morality and freedom are not empirical concepts. We can't prove that they exist, but neither can we make sense of our moral lives without presupposing them.

Sex, Lies, and Politics

One way of exploring Kant's moral philosophy is to see how he applied it to some concrete questions. I would like to consider three applications—sex, lies, and politics. Philosophers are not always the best authorities on how to apply their theories in practice. But Kant's applications are interesting in their own right and also shed some light on his philosophy as a whole.

Kant's case against casual sex

Kant's views on sexual morality are traditional and conservative. He opposes every conceivable sexual practice except sexual intercourse between husband and wife. Whether all of Kant's views on sex actually follow from his moral philosophy is less important than the underlying idea they reflect—that we do not own ourselves and are not at our own disposal. He objects to casual sex (by which he means sex outside of marriage), however consensual, on the grounds that it is degrading and objectifying to both partners. Casual sex is objectionable, he thinks, because it is all about the satisfaction of sexual desire, not about respect for the humanity of one's partner.

> The desire which a man has for a woman is not directed toward her because she is a human being, but because she is a woman; that she is a human being is of no concern to the man; only her sex is the object of his desires.[34]

Even when casual sex involves the mutual satisfaction of the partners, "each of them dishonours the human nature of the other. They make of humanity an instrument for the satisfaction of their lusts and inclinations."[35] (For reasons we'll come to in a moment, Kant thinks marriage elevates sex by taking it beyond physical gratification and connecting it with human dignity.)

Turning to the question of whether prostitution is moral or immoral, Kant asks under what conditions the use of our sexual faculties is in keeping with morality. His answer, in this as in other situations, is that we should not treat others—or ourselves—merely as objects. We are not at our own disposal. In stark contrast to libertarian notions of self-possession, Kant insists that we do not own ourselves. The moral requirement that we treat persons as ends rather than as mere means limits the way we may treat our bodies and ourselves. "Man cannot dispose over himself because he is not a thing; he is not his own property."[36]

In contemporary debates about sexual morality, those who invoke autonomy rights argue that individuals should be free to choose for themselves what use to make of their own bodies. But this isn't what Kant means by autonomy. Paradoxically, Kant's conception of autonomy imposes certain limits on the way we may treat ourselves. For, recall: To be autonomous is to be governed by a law I give myself—the categorical imperative. And the categorical imperative requires that I treat all persons (including myself) with respect—as an end, not merely as a means. So, for Kant, acting autonomously requires that we treat ourselves with respect, and not objectify ourselves. We can't use our bodies any way we please.

Markets in kidneys were not prevalent in Kant's day, but the rich did buy teeth for implantation from the poor. (*Transplanting of Teeth*, a drawing by the eighteenth-century English caricaturist Thomas Rowlandson, shows a scene in a dentist's office in which a surgeon extracts teeth from a chimney sweep while wealthy women wait for their implants.) Kant considered this practice a violation of human dignity. A person "is not entitled to sell a limb, not even one of his teeth."[37] To do so is to treat oneself as an object, a mere means, an instrument of profit.

Kant found prostitution objectionable on the same grounds. "To allow one's person for profit to be used by another for the satisfaction of sexual desire, to make of oneself an object of demand, is to . . . make of oneself a thing on which another satisfies his appetite, just as he satisfies his hunger upon a steak." Human beings are "not entitled to offer themselves, for profit, as things for the use of others in the satisfaction of their sexual propensities." To do so is to treat one's person as a mere thing, an object of use. "The underlying moral principle is that man is not his own property and cannot do with his body what he will."[38]

Kant's opposition to prostitution and casual sex brings out the contrast between autonomy as he conceives it—the free will of a rational being—and individual acts of consent. The moral law we arrive at through the exercise of our will requires that we treat humanity—in our own person and in others—never only as a means but as an end in itself. Although this moral requirement is based on autonomy, it rules out certain acts among consenting adults, namely those that are at odds with human dignity and self-respect.

Kant concludes that only sex within marriage can avoid "degrading humanity." Only when two persons give each other the whole of themselves, and not merely the use of their sexual capacities, can sex be other than objectifying. Only when both partners share with each other their "person, body and soul, for good and ill and in every respect," can their sexuality lead to "a union of human beings."[39] Kant does not say that every marriage actually brings about a union of this kind. And he may be wrong to think that no such unions can ever occur outside of marriage, or that sexual relations outside of marriage involve nothing more than sexual gratification. But his views about sex highlight the difference between two ideas that are often confused in contemporary debate—between an ethic of unfettered consent and an ethic of respect for the autonomy and dignity of persons.

Is it wrong to lie to a murderer?

Kant takes a hard line against lying. In the *Groundwork*, it serves as a prime example of immoral behavior. But suppose a friend was hiding in your house, and a murderer came to the door looking for him. Wouldn't it be right to lie to the murderer? Kant says no. The duty to tell the truth holds regardless of the consequences.

Benjamin Constant, a French philosopher and contemporary of Kant, took issue with this uncompromising stance. The duty to tell the truth applies, Constant argued, only to those who deserve the truth, as surely the murderer does not. Kant replied that lying to the murderer is wrong, not because it harms him, but because it violates the principle of right: "Truthfulness in statements that cannot be avoided is the formal duty of man to everyone, however great the disadvantage that may arise therefrom for him or for any other."[40]

Admittedly, helping a murderer carry out his evil deed is a pretty heavy "disadvantage." But remember, for Kant, morality is not about consequences; it's about principle. You can't control the consequences of your action—in this case, telling the truth—since consequences are bound up with contingency. For all you know, your friend, fearing that the murderer is on his way, has already slipped out the back door. The reason you must tell the truth, Kant states, is not that the murderer is entitled to the truth, or that a lie would harm him. It's that a lie—any lie—"vitiates the very source of right . . . To be truthful (honest) in all declarations is, therefore, a sacred and unconditionally commanding law of reason that admits of no expediency whatsoever."[41]

This seems a strange and extreme position. Surely we don't have a moral duty to tell a Nazi storm trooper that Anne Frank and her family are hiding in the attic. It would seem that Kant's insistence on telling the truth to the murderer at the door either misapplies the categorical imperative or proves its folly.

Implausible though Kant's claim may seem, I would like to offer a certain defense of it. Although my defense differs from the one that Kant offers, it is nonetheless in the spirit of his philosophy, and, I hope, sheds some light on it.

Imagine yourself in the predicament with a friend hiding in the closet and the murderer at the door. Of course you don't want to help the murderer carry out his evil plan. That is a given. You don't want to say anything that will lead the murderer to your friend. The question is, what do you say? You have two choices. You could tell an outright lie: "No, she's not here." Or you could offer a true but misleading statement: "An hour ago, I saw her down the road, at the grocery store."

From Kant's point of view, the second strategy is morally permissible, but the first is not. You might consider this caviling. What, morally speaking, is the difference between a technically true but misleading statement and an outright lie? In both cases, you are hoping to mislead the murderer into believing that your friend is not hiding in the house.

Kant believes a great deal is at stake in the distinction. Consider "white lies," the small untruths we sometimes tell out of politeness, to avoid hurt feelings. Suppose a friend presents you with a gift. You open the box and find a hideous tie, something you would never wear. What do you say? You might say, "It's beautiful!" This would be a white lie. Or you might say, "You shouldn't have!" Or, "I've never seen a tie like this. Thank you." Like the white lie, these statements might give your friend the false impression that you like the tie. But they would nonetheless be true.

Kant would reject the white lie, because it makes an exception to the moral law on consequentialist grounds. Sparing someone's feelings is an admirable end, but it must be pursued in a way that is consistent with the categorical imperative, which requires that we be willing to universalize the principle on which we act. If we can carve out exceptions whenever we think our ends are sufficiently compelling, then the categorical character of the moral law unravels. The true but misleading statement, by contrast, does not threaten the categorical imperative in the same way. In fact, Kant once invoked this distinction when faced with a dilemma of his own.

Would Kant have defended Bill Clinton?

A few years before his exchange with Constant, Kant found himself in trouble with King Friedrich Wilhelm II. The king and his censors considered Kant's writings on religion disparaging to Christianity, and demanded that he pledge to refrain from any further pronouncements on the topic. Kant responded with a carefully worded statement: "As your Majesty's faithful subject, I shall in the future completely desist from all public lectures or papers concerning religion."[42]

Kant was aware, when he made his statement, that the king was not likely to live much longer. When the king died a few years later, Kant considered himself absolved of the promise, which bound him only "as your Majesty's faithful subject." Kant later explained that he had chosen his words "most carefully, so that I should not be deprived of my freedom . . . forever, but only so long as His Majesty was alive."[43] By this clever evasion, the paragon of Prussian probity succeeded in misleading the censors without lying to them.

Hairsplitting? Perhaps. But something of moral significance does seem to be at stake in the distinction between a bald-faced lie and an artful dodge. Consider former president Bill Clinton. No American public figure in recent memory chose his words or crafted his denials more carefully. When asked, during his first presidential campaign, whether he had ever used recreational drugs, Clinton replied that he had never broken the antidrug laws of his country or state. He later conceded that he had tried marijuana while a student at Oxford in England.

His most memorable such denial came in response to reports that he had had sex in the White House with a twenty-two-year-old intern, Monica Lewinsky: "I want to say one thing to the American people. I want you to listen to me . . . I did not have sexual relations with that woman, Ms. Lewinsky."

It later came out that the president did have sexual encounters with Monica Lewinsky, and the scandal led to impeachment proceedings. During the impeachment hearings, a Republican congressman argued with a Clinton attorney, Gregory Craig, over whether the president's denial of "sexual relations" was a lie:

REP. BOB INGLIS (R-S.C.): Now, Mr. Craig, did he lie to the American people when he said, "I never had sex with that woman"? Did he lie?

CRAIG: He certainly misled and deceived—

INGLIS: Wait a minute, now. Did he lie?

CRAIG: To the American people—he misled them and did not tell them the truth at that moment.

INGLIS: OK, so you're not going to rely—and the President has personally insisted . . . that no legalities or technicalities should be allowed to obscure the simple moral truth. Did he lie to the American people when he said, "I never had sex with that woman"?

CRAIG: He doesn't believe he did and because of the way—let me explain that—explain, Congressman.

INGLIS: He doesn't believe that he lied?

CRAIG: No, he does not believe that he lied, because his notion of what sex is, is what the dictionary definition is. It is in fact something you may not agree with, but in his own mind, his definition was not—

INGLIS: OK, I understand that argument.

CRAIG: OK.

INGLIS: This is an amazing thing, that you now sit before us and you're taking back all of his—all of his apologies.

CRAIG: No.

INGLIS: You're taking them all back, aren't you?

CRAIG: No, I'm not.

INGLIS: Because now you're back to the argument—there are many arguments you can make here. One of them is he didn't have sex with her. It was oral sex, it wasn't real sex. Now is that what you're here to say to us today, that he did not have sex with Monica Lewinsky?

CRAIG: What he said was, to the American people, that he did not have sexual relations. And I understand you're not going to like this, Congressman, because it—you will see it as a technical defense or a hairsplitting, evasive answer. But sexual relations is defined in every dictionary in a certain way, and he did not have that kind of sexual contact with Monica Lewinsky . . . So, did he deceive the American people? Yes. Was it wrong? Yes. Was it blameworthy? Yes.[44]

The president's attorney conceded, as Clinton had already done, that the relationship with the intern was wrong, inappropriate, and blameworthy, and that the president's statements about it "misled and deceived" the public. The only thing he refused to concede was that the president had lied.

What was at stake in that refusal? The explanation can't simply be the legalistic one that lying under oath, in a deposition or in court, is a basis for perjury charges. The statement at issue was not made under oath, but in a televised statement to the American public. And yet both the Republican inquisitor and the Clinton defender believed that something important was at stake in establishing whether Clinton had lied or merely misled and deceived. Their spirited colloquy over the *L* word—"Did he lie?"—supports the Kantian thought that there is a morally relevant difference between a lie and a misleading truth.

But what could that difference be? The intention is arguably the same in both cases. Whether I lie to the murderer at the door or offer him a clever evasion, my intention is to mislead him into thinking that my friend is not hiding in my house. And on Kant's moral theory, it's the intention, or motive, that matters.

The difference, I think, is this: A carefully crafted evasion pays homage to the duty of truth-telling in a way that an outright lie does not. Anyone who goes to the bother of concocting a misleading but technically true statement when a simple lie would do expresses, however obliquely, respect for the moral law.

A misleading truth includes two motives, not one. If I simply lie to the murderer, I act out of one motive—to protect my friend from harm. If I tell the murderer that I recently saw my friend at the grocery store, I act out of two motives—to protect my friend and at the same time to uphold the duty to tell the truth. In both cases, I am pursuing an admirable goal, that of protecting my friend. But only in the second case do I pursue this goal in a way that accords with the motive of duty.

Some might object that, like a lie, a technically true but misleading statement could not be universalized without contradiction. But consider the difference: If everyone lied when faced with a murderer at the door or an embarrassing sex scandal, then no one would believe such statements, and they wouldn't work. The same cannot be said of misleading truths. If everyone who found himself in a dangerous or embarrassing situation resorted to carefully crafted evasions, people would not necessarily cease to believe them. Instead, people would learn to listen like lawyers and parse such statements with an eye to their literal meaning. This is exactly what happened when the press and the public became familiar with Clinton's carefully worded denials.

Kant's point is not that this state of affairs, in which people parse politicians' denials for their literal meaning, is somehow better than one in which nobody believes politicians at all. That would be a consequentialist argument. Kant's point is rather that a misleading statement that is nonetheless true does not coerce or manipulate the listener in

the same way as an outright lie. It's always possible that a careful listener could figure it out.

So there is reason to conclude that, on Kant's moral theory, true
but misleading statements—to a murderer at the door, the Prussian
censors, or the special prosecutor—are morally permissible in a way
that bald-faced lies are not. You may think that I've worked too hard to
save Kant from an implausible position. Kant's claim that it's wrong to
lie to the murderer at the door may not ultimately be defensible. But
the distinction between an outright lie and a misleading truth helps illustrate Kant's moral theory. And it brings out a surprising similarity
between Bill Clinton and the austere moralist from Konigsberg.

Kant and justice

Unlike Aristotle, Bentham, and Mill, Kant wrote no major work of
political theory, only some essays. And yet, the account of morality and
freedom that emerges from his ethical writings carries powerful implications for justice. Although Kant does not work out the implications
in detail, the political theory he favors rejects utilitarianism in favor of
a theory of justice based on a social contract.

First, Kant rejects utilitarianism, not only as a basis for personal
morality but also as a basis for law. As he sees it, a just constitution aims
at harmonizing each individual's freedom with that of everyone else. It
has nothing to do with maximizing utility, which "must on no account
interfere" with the determination of basic rights. Since people "have
different views on the empirical end of happiness and what it consists
of," utility can't be the basis of justice and rights. Why not? Because
resting rights on utility would require the society to affirm or endorse
one conception of happiness over others. To base the constitution on
one particular conception of happiness (such as that of the majority)
would impose on some the values of others; it would fail to respect the
right of each person to pursue his or her own ends. "No one can compel me to be happy in accordance with his conception of the welfare of

others," Kant writes, "for each may seek his happiness in whatever way he sees fit, so long as he does not infringe upon the freedom of others" to do the same.[45]

A second distinctive feature of Kant's political theory is that it derives justice and rights from a social contract—but a social contract with a puzzling twist. Earlier contract thinkers, including Locke, argued that legitimate government arises from a social contract among men and women who, at one time or another, decide among themselves on the principles that will govern their collective life. Kant sees the contract differently. Although legitimate government must be based on an original contract, "we need by no means assume that this contract . . . actually exists as a *fact*, for it cannot possibly be so." Kant maintains that the original contract is not actual but imaginary.[46]

Why derive a just constitution from an imaginary contract rather than a real one? One reason is practical: It's often hard to prove historically, in the distant history of nations, that any social contract ever took place. A second reason is philosophical: Moral principles can't be derived from empirical facts alone. Just as the moral law can't rest on the interests or desires of individuals, principles of justice can't rest on the interests or desires of a community. The mere fact that a group of people in the past agreed to a constitution is not enough to make that constitution just.

What kind of imaginary contract could possibly avoid this problem? Kant simply calls it "an *idea* of reason, which nonetheless has undoubted practical reality; for it can oblige every legislator to frame his laws in such a way that they could have been produced by the united will of a whole nation," and obligate each citizen "as if he had consented." Kant concludes that this imaginary act of collective consent "is the test of the rightfulness of every public law."[47]

Kant didn't tell us what this imaginary contract would look like or what principles of justice it would produce. Almost two centuries later, an American political philosopher, John Rawls, would try to answer these questions.

6. THE CASE FOR EQUALITY / JOHN RAWLS

Most of us Americans never signed a social contract. In fact, the only people in the United States who have actually agreed to abide by the Constitution (public officials aside) are naturalized citizens—immigrants who have taken an oath of allegiance as a condition of their citizenship. The rest of us are never required, or even asked, to give our consent. So why are we obligated to obey the law? And how can we say that our government rests on the consent of the governed?

John Locke says we've given tacit consent. Anyone who enjoys the benefits of a government, even by traveling on the highway, implicitly consents to the law, and is bound by it.[1] But tacit consent is a pale form of the real thing. It is hard to see how just passing through town is morally akin to ratifying the Constitution.

Immanuel Kant appeals to hypothetical consent. A law is just if it could have been agreed to by the public as a whole. But this, too, is a puzzling alternative to an actual social contract. How can a hypothetical agreement do the moral work of a real one?

John Rawls (1921–2002), an American political philosopher, offers an illuminating answer to this question. In *A Theory of Justice* (1971), he argues that the way to think about justice is to ask what principles we would agree to in an initial situation of equality.[2]

Rawls reasons as follows: Suppose we gathered, just as we are, to choose the principles to govern our collective life—to write a social contract. What principles would we choose? We would probably find it difficult to agree. Different people would favor different principles, reflecting their various interests, moral and religious beliefs, and social positions. Some people are rich and some are poor; some are powerful and well connected; others, less so. Some are members of racial, ethnic, or religious minorities; others, not. We might settle on a compromise. But even the compromise would likely reflect the superior bargaining power of some over others. There is no reason to assume that a social contract arrived at in this way would be a just arrangement.

Now consider a thought experiment: Suppose that when we gather to choose the principles, we don't know where we will wind up in society. Imagine that we choose behind a "veil of ignorance" that temporarily prevents us from knowing anything about who in particular we are. We don't know our class or gender, our race or ethnicity, our political opinions or religious convictions. Nor do we know our advantages and disadvantages—whether we are healthy or frail, highly educated or a high-school dropout, born to a supportive family or a broken one. If no one knew any of these things, we would choose, in effect, from an original position of equality. Since no one would have a superior bargaining position, the principles we would agree to would be just.

This is Rawls's idea of the social contract—a hypothetical agreement in an original position of equality. Rawls invites us to ask what principles we—as rational, self-interested persons—would choose if we found ourselves in that position. He doesn't assume that we are all motivated by self-interest in real life; only that we set aside our moral and religious convictions for purposes of the thought experiment. What principles would we choose?

First of all, he reasons, we would not choose utilitarianism. Behind the veil of ignorance, each of us would think, "For all I know, I might wind up being a member of an oppressed minority." And no one would want to risk being the Christian thrown to the lions for the pleasure of the crowd. Nor would we choose a purely laissez-faire, libertarian principle that would give people a right to keep all the money they made in a market economy. "I might wind up being Bill Gates," each person would reason, "but then again, I might turn out to be a homeless person. So I'd better avoid a system that could leave me destitute and without help."

Rawls believes that two principles of justice would emerge from the hypothetical contract. The first provides equal basic liberties for all citizens, such as freedom of speech and religion. This principle takes priority over considerations of social utility and the general welfare. The second principle concerns social and economic equality. Although it does not require an equal distribution of income and wealth, it permits only those social and economic inequalities that work to the advantage of the least well off members of society.

Philosophers argue about whether or not the parties to Rawls's hypothetical social contract would choose the principles he says they would. In a moment, we'll see why Rawls thinks these two principles would be chosen. But before turning to the principles, let's take up a prior question: Is Rawls's thought experiment the right way to think about justice? How can principles of justice possibly be derived from an agreement that never actually took place?

The Moral Limits of Contracts

To appreciate the moral force of Rawls's hypothetical contract, it helps to notice the moral limits of actual contracts. We sometimes assume that, when two people make a deal, the terms of their agreement must be fair. We assume, in other words, that contracts justify the terms that they produce. But they don't—at least not on their own. Actual contracts are not self-sufficient moral instruments. The mere fact that you and I make a deal is not enough to make it fair. Of any actual contract, it can always be asked, "Is it fair, what they agreed to?" To answer this question, we can't simply point to the agreement itself; we need some independent standard of fairness.

Where could such a standard come from? Perhaps, you might think, from a bigger, prior contract—a constitution, for example. But constitutions are open to the same challenge as other agreements. The fact that a constitution is ratified by the people does not prove that its provisions are just. Consider the U.S. Constitution of 1787. Despite its many virtues, it was marred by its acceptance of slavery, a defect that persisted until after the Civil War. The fact that the Constitution was agreed to—by the delegates in Philadelphia and then by the states—was not enough to make it just.

It might be argued that this defect can be traced to a flaw in the consent. African American slaves were not included in the Constitutional Convention, nor were women, who didn't win the right to vote until more than a century later. It is certainly possible that a more representative convention would have produced a more just constitution. But that is a matter of speculation. No actual social contract or constitutional convention, however representative, is guaranteed to produce fair terms of social cooperation.

To those who believe that morality begins and ends with consent, this may seem a jarring claim. But it is not all that controversial. We often question the fairness of the deals people make. And we are familiar with the contingencies that can lead to bad deals: one of the parties may be a better negotiator, or have a stronger bargaining position, or know more about the value of the things being exchanged. The famous words of Don Corleone in *The Godfather*, "I'm gonna make him an offer he can't refuse," suggest (in extreme form) the pressure that hovers, to some degree, over most negotiations.

To recognize that contracts do not confer fairness on the terms they produce doesn't mean we should violate our agreements whenever we please. We may be obligated to fulfill even an unfair bargain, at least up to a point. Consent matters, even if it's not all there is to justice. But it is less decisive than we sometimes think. We often confuse the moral work of consent with other sources of obligation.

Suppose we make a deal: You will bring me a hundred lobsters, and I will pay you $1,000. You harvest and deliver the lobsters, I eat them and enjoy them, but refuse to pay. You say I owe you the money. Why, I ask? You might point to our agreement, but you might also point to the benefit I've enjoyed. You could very well say that I have an obligation to repay the benefit that, thanks to you, I've enjoyed.

Now suppose we make the same deal, but this time, after you've gone to the work of catching the lobsters and bringing them to my doorstep, I change my mind. I don't want them after all. You still try to collect. I say, "I don't owe you anything. This time, I haven't benefited." At this point, you might point to our agreement, but you might also point to the hard work you've done to trap the lobsters while relying on the expectation that I would buy them. You could say I'm obligated to pay by virtue of the efforts you've made on my behalf.

Now let's see if we can imagine a case where the obligation rests on consent alone—without the added moral weight of repaying a benefit or compensating you for the work you did on my behalf. This time, we make the same deal, but moments later, before you've spent any time gathering lobsters, I call you back and say, "I've changed my mind. I don't want any lobsters." Do I still owe you the $1,000? Do you say, "A deal is a deal," and insist that my act of consent creates an obligation even without any benefit or reliance?

Legal thinkers have debated this question for a long time. Can consent create an obligation on its own, or is some element of benefit or reliance also required?[3] This debate tells us something about the morality of contracts that we often overlook: actual contracts carry moral weight insofar as they realize two ideals—autonomy and reciprocity.

As voluntary acts, contracts express our autonomy; the obligations they create carry weight because they are self-imposed—we take them freely upon ourselves. As instruments of mutual benefit, contracts draw on the ideal of reciprocity; the obligation to fulfill them arises from the obligation to repay others for the benefits they provide us.

In practice, these ideals—autonomy and reciprocity—are imperfectly realized. Some agreements, though voluntary, are not mutually beneficial. And sometimes we can be obligated to repay a benefit simply on grounds of reciprocity, even in the absence of a contract. This points to the moral limits of consent: In some cases, consent may not be enough to create a morally binding obligation; in others, it may not be necessary.

When Consent Is Not Enough: Baseball Cards and the Leaky Toilet

Consider two cases that show that consent alone is not enough: When my two sons were young, they collected baseball cards and traded them with each other. The older son knew more about the players and the value of the cards. He sometimes offered his younger brother trades that were unfair—two utility infielders, say, for Ken Griffey, Jr. So I instituted a rule that no trade was complete until I had approved it. You may think this was paternalistic, which it was. (That's what paternalism is for.) In circumstances like this one, voluntary exchanges can clearly be unfair.

Some years ago, I read a newspaper article about a more extreme case: An elderly widow in Chicago had a leaky toilet in her apartment. She hired a contractor to fix it—for $50,000. She signed a contract that required her to pay $25,000 as a down payment, and the remainder in installments. The scheme was discovered when she went to the bank to withdraw the $25,000. The teller asked why she needed such a large withdrawal, and the woman replied that she had to pay the plumber. The teller contacted the police, who arrested the unscrupulous contractor for fraud.[4]

All but the most ardent contractarians would concede that the $50,000 toilet repair was egregiously unfair—despite the fact that two willing parties agreed to it. This case illustrates two points about the moral limits of contracts: First, the fact of an agreement does not guarantee the fairness of the agreement. Second, consent is not enough to create a binding moral claim. Far from an instrument of mutual benefit, this contract mocks the ideal of reciprocity. This explains, I think, why few people would say that the elderly woman was morally obliged to pay the outrageous sum.

It might be replied that the toilet repair scam was not a truly voluntary contract, but a kind of exploitation, in which an unscrupulous plumber took advantage of an elderly woman who didn't know any better. I don't know the details of the case, but let's assume for the sake of argument that the plumber did not coerce the woman, and that she was of sound mind (though ill informed about the price of plumbing) when she agreed to the deal. The fact that the agreement was voluntary by no means ensures that it involves the exchange of equal or comparable benefits.

I've argued so far that consent is not a sufficient condition of moral obligation; a lopsided deal may fall so far short of mutual benefit that even its voluntary character can't redeem it. I'd now like to offer a further, more provocative claim: Consent is not a necessary condition of moral obligation. If the mutual benefit is clear enough, the moral claims of reciprocity may hold even without an act of consent.

When Consent Is Not Essential: Hume's House and the Squeegee Men

The kind of case I have in mind once confronted David Hume, the eighteenth-century Scottish moral philosopher. When he was young, Hume wrote a scathing critique of Locke's idea of a social contract. He called it a "philosophical fiction which never had and never could have any reality,"[5] and "one of the most mysterious and incomprehensible operations that can possibly be imagined."[6] Years later, Hume had an experience that put to the test his rejection of consent as the basis of obligation.[7]

Hume owned a house in Edinburgh. He rented it to his friend James Boswell, who in turn sublet it to a subtenant. The subtenant decided that the house needed some repairs. He hired a contractor to do the work, without consulting Hume. The contractor made the repairs and sent the bill to Hume. Hume refused to pay on the grounds that he hadn't consented. He hadn't hired the contractor. The case went to court. The contractor acknowledged that Hume hadn't consented. But the house needed the repairs, and he performed them.

Hume thought this was a bad argument. The contractor's claim was simply "that the work was necessary to be done," Hume told the court. But this is "no good answer, because by the same rule he may go through every house in Edinburgh, and do what he thinks proper to be done, without the landlord's consent . . . and give the same reason for what he did, that the work was necessary and that the house was the better of it." But this, Hume maintained, was "a doctrine quite new and . . . altogether untenable."[8]

When it came to his house repairs, Hume didn't like a purely benefit-based theory of obligation. But his defense failed, and the court ordered him to pay.

The idea that an obligation to repay a benefit can arise without consent is morally plausible in the case of Hume's house. But it can easily slide into high-pressure sales tactics and other abuses. In the 1980s and early '90s, "squeegee men" became an intimidating presence on New York City streets. Equipped with a squeegee and a bucket of water, they would descend upon a car stopped at a red light, wash the windshield (often without asking the driver's permission), and then ask for payment. They operated on the benefit-based theory of obligation invoked by Hume's contractor. But in the absence of consent, the line between performing a service and panhandling often blurred. Mayor Rudolph Giuliani decided to crack down on the squeegee men and ordered the police to arrest them.[9]

Benefit or Consent? Sam's Mobile Auto Repair

Here is another example of the confusion that can arise when the consent-based and benefit-based aspects of obligation are not clearly distinguished. Many years ago, when I was a graduate student, I drove across the country with some friends. We stopped at a rest stop in Hammond, Indiana, and went into a convenience store. When we returned to our car, it wouldn't start. None of us knew much about car repair. As we wondered what to do, a van pulled up beside us. On the side was a sign that said, "Sam's Mobile Repair Van." Out of the van came a man, presumably Sam.

He approached us and asked if he could help. "Here's how I work," he explained. "I charge fifty dollars an hour. If I fix your car in five minutes, you will owe me fifty dollars. If I work on your car for an hour and can't fix it, you will still owe me fifty dollars."

"What are the odds you'll be able to fix the car?" I asked. He didn't answer me directly, but starting poking around under the steering column. I was unsure what to do. I looked to my friends to see what they thought. After a short time, the man emerged from under the steering column and said, "Well, there's nothing wrong with the ignition system, but you still have forty-five minutes left. Do you want me to look under the hood?"

"Wait a minute," I said. "I haven't hired you. We haven't made any agreement." The man became very angry and said, "Do you mean to say that if I had fixed your car just now while I was looking under the steering column you wouldn't have paid me?"

I said, "That's a different question."

I didn't go into the distinction between consent-based and benefit-based obligations. Somehow I don't think it would have helped. But the contretemps with Sam the repairman highlights a common confusion about consent. Sam believed that if he had fixed my car while he was poking around, I would have owed him the fifty dollars. I agree. But the reason I would have owed him the money is that he would have performed a benefit—namely, fixing my car. He inferred that, because I would have owed him, I must (implicitly) have agreed to hire him. But this inference is a mistake. It wrongly assumes that wherever there is an obligation, there must have been an agreement—some act of consent. It overlooks the possibility that obligation can arise without consent. If Sam had fixed my car, I would have owed him in the name of reciprocity. Simply thanking him and driving off would have been unfair. But this doesn't imply that I had hired him.

When I tell this story to my students, most agree that, under the circumstances, I didn't owe Sam the fifty dollars. But many hold this view for reasons different from mine. They argue that, since I didn't explicitly hire Sam, I owed him nothing—and would have owed him nothing even if he had fixed my car. Any payment would have been an act of generosity—a gratuity, not a duty. So they come to my defense, not by embracing my expansive view of obligation, but by asserting a stringent view of consent.

Despite our tendency to read consent into every moral claim, it is hard to make sense of our moral lives without acknowledging the independent weight of reciprocity. Consider a marriage contract. Suppose I discover, after twenty years of faithfulness on my part, that my wife has been seeing another man. I would have two different grounds for moral outrage. One invokes consent: "But we had an agreement. You made a vow. You broke your promise." The second would invoke reciprocity: "But I've been so faithful for my part. Surely I deserve better than this. This is no way to repay my loyalty." And so on. The second complaint makes no reference to consent, and does not require it. It would be morally plausible even if we never exchanged marital vows, but lived together as partners for all those years.

Imagining the Perfect Contract

What do these various misadventures tell us about the morality of contracts? Contracts derive their moral force from two different ideals, autonomy and reciprocity. But most actual contracts fall short of these ideals. If I'm up against someone with a superior bargaining position, my agreement may not be wholly voluntary, but pressured or, in the extreme case, coerced. If I'm negotiating with someone with greater knowledge of the things we are exchanging, the deal may not be mutually beneficial. In the extreme case, I may be defrauded or deceived.

In real life, persons are situated differently. This means that differences in bargaining power and knowledge are always possible. And as long as this is true, the fact of an agreement does not, by itself, guarantee the fairness of an agreement. This is why actual contracts are not self-sufficient moral instruments. It always makes sense to ask, "But is it fair, what they have agreed to?"

But imagine a contract among parties who were equal in power and knowledge, rather than unequal; who were identically situated, not differently situated. And imagine that the object of this contract was not plumbing or any ordinary deal, but the principles to govern our lives together, to assign our rights and duties as citizens. A contract like this, among parties like these, would leave no room for coercion or deception or other unfair advantages. Its terms would be just, whatever they were, by virtue of their agreement alone.

If you can imagine a contract like this, you have arrived at Rawls's idea of a hypothetical agreement in an initial situation of equality. The veil of ignorance ensures the equality of power and knowledge that the original position requires. By ensuring that no one knows his or her place in society, his strengths or weaknesses, his values or ends, the veil of ignorance ensures that no one can take advantage, even unwittingly, of a favorable bargaining position.

> If a knowledge of particulars is allowed, then the outcome is biased by arbitrary contingencies . . . If the original position is to yield agreements that are just, the parties must be fairly situated and treated equally as moral persons. The arbitrariness of the world must be corrected for by adjusting the circumstances of the initial contract situation.[10]

The irony is that a hypothetical agreement behind a veil of ignorance is not a pale form of an actual contract and so a morally weaker thing; it's a pure form of an actual contract, and so a morally more powerful thing.

Two Principles of Justice

Suppose Rawls is right: The way to think about justice is to ask what principles we would choose in an original position of equality, behind a veil of ignorance. What principles would emerge?

According to Rawls, we wouldn't choose utilitarianism. Behind the veil of ignorance, we don't know where we will wind up in society, but we do know that we will want to pursue our ends and be treated with respect. In case we turn out to be a member of an ethnic or religious minority, we don't want to be oppressed, even if this gives pleasure to the majority. Once the veil of ignorance rises and real life begins, we don't want to find ourselves as victims of religious persecution or racial discrimination. In order to protect against these dangers, we would reject utilitarianism and agree to a principle of equal basic liberties for all citizens, including the right to liberty of conscience and freedom of thought. And we would insist that this principle take priority over attempts to maximize the general welfare. We would not sacrifice our fundamental rights and liberties for social and economic benefits.

What principle would we choose to govern social and economic inequalities? To guard against the risk of finding ourselves in crushing poverty, we might at first thought favor an equal distribution of income and wealth. But then it would occur to us that we could do better, even for those on the bottom. Suppose that by permitting certain inequalities, such as higher pay for doctors than for bus drivers, we could improve the situation of those who have the least—by increasing access to health care for the poor. Allowing for this possibility, we would adopt what Rawls calls "the difference principle": only those social and economic inequalities are permitted that work to the benefit of the least advantaged members of society.

Exactly how egalitarian is the difference principle? It's hard to say, because the effect of pay differences depends on social and economic circumstances. Suppose higher pay for doctors led to more and better medical care in impoverished rural areas. In that case, the wage difference could be consistent with Rawls's principle. But suppose paying doctors more had no impact on health services in Appalachia, and simply produced more cosmetic surgeons in Beverly Hills. In that case, the wage difference would be hard to justify from Rawls's point of view.

What about the big earnings of Michael Jordan or the vast fortune of Bill Gates? Could these inequalities be consistent with the difference principle? Of course, Rawls's theory is not meant to assess the fairness of this or that person's salary; it is concerned with the basic structure of society, and the way it allocates rights and duties, income and wealth, power and opportunities. For Rawls, the question to ask is whether Gates's wealth arose as part of a system that, taken as a whole, works to the benefit of the least well off. For example, was it subject to a progressive tax system that taxed the rich to provide for the health, education, and welfare of the poor? If so, and if this system made the poor better off than they would have been under a more strictly equal arrangement, then such inequalities could be consistent with the difference principle.

Some people question whether the parties to the original position would choose the difference principle. How does Rawls know that, behind the veil of ignorance, people wouldn't be gamblers, willing to take their chances on a highly unequal society in hopes of landing on top? Maybe some would even opt for a feudal society, willing to risk being a landless serf in the hopes of being a king.

Rawls doesn't believe that people choosing principles to govern their fundamental life prospects would take such chances. Unless they knew themselves to be lovers of risk (a quality blocked from view by the veil of ignorance), people would not make risky bets at high stakes.

But Rawls's case for the difference principle doesn't rest entirely on the assumption that people in the original position would be risk averse. Underlying the device of the veil of ignorance is a moral argument that can be presented independent of the thought experiment. Its main idea is that the distribution of income and opportunity should not be based on factors that are arbitrary from a moral point of view.

The Argument from Moral Arbitrariness

Rawls presents this argument by comparing several rival theories of justice, beginning with feudal aristocracy. These days, no one defends the justice of feudal aristocracies or caste systems. These systems are unfair, Rawls observes, because they distribute income, wealth, opportunity, and power according to the accident of birth. If you are born into nobility, you have rights and powers denied those born into serfdom. But the circumstances of your birth are no doing of yours. So it's unjust to make your life prospects depend on this arbitrary fact.

Market societies remedy this arbitrariness, at least to some degree. They open careers to those with the requisite talents and provide equality before the law. Citizens are assured equal basic liberties, and the distribution of income and wealth is determined by the free market. This system—a free market with formal equality of opportunity—corresponds to the libertarian theory of justice. It represents an improvement over feudal and caste societies, since it rejects fixed hierarchies of birth. Legally, it allows everyone to strive and to compete. In practice, however, opportunities may be far from equal.

Those who have supportive families and a good education have obvious advantages over those who do not. Allowing everyone to enter the race is a good thing. But if the runners start from different starting points, the race is hardly fair. That is why, Rawls argues, the distribution of income and wealth that results from a free market with formal equality of opportunity cannot be considered just. The most obvious injustice of the libertarian system "is that it permits distributive shares to be improperly influenced by these factors so arbitrary from a moral point of view."[11]

One way of remedying this unfairness is to correct for social and economic disadvantage. A fair meritocracy attempts to do so by going beyond merely formal equality of opportunity. It removes obstacles to achievement by providing equal educational opportunities, so that those from poor families can compete on an equal basis with those from more privileged backgrounds. It institutes Head Start programs, childhood nutrition and health care programs, education and job training programs—whatever is needed to bring everyone, regardless of class or family background, to the same starting point. According to the meritocratic conception, the distribution of income and wealth that results from a free market is just, but only if everyone has the same opportunity to develop his or her talents. Only if everyone begins at the same starting line can it be said that the winners of the race deserve their rewards.

Rawls believes that the meritocratic conception corrects for certain morally arbitrary advantages, but still falls short of justice. For, even if you manage to bring everyone up to the same starting point, it is more or less predictable who will win the race—the fastest runners. But being a fast runner is not wholly my own doing. It is morally contingent in the same way that coming from an affluent family is contingent. "Even if it works to perfection in eliminating the influence of social contingencies," Rawls writes, the meritocratic system "still permits the distribution of wealth and income to be determined by the natural distribution of abilities and talents."[12]

If Rawls is right, even a free market operating in a society with equal educational opportunities does not produce a just distribution of income and wealth. The reason: "Distributive shares are decided by the outcome of the natural lottery; and this outcome is arbitrary from a moral perspective. There is no more reason to permit the distribution of income and wealth to be settled by the distribution of natural assets than by historical and social fortune."[13]

Rawls concludes that the meritocratic conception of justice is flawed for the same reason (though to a lesser degree) as the libertarian conception; both base distributive shares on factors that are morally arbitrary. "Once we are troubled by the influence of either social contingencies or natural chance on the determination of the distributive shares, we are bound, on reflection, to be bothered by the influence of the other. From a moral standpoint the two seem equally arbitrary."[14]

Once we notice the moral arbitrariness that taints both libertarian and the meritocratic theories of justice, Rawls argues, we can't be satisfied short of a more egalitarian conception. But what could this conception be? It is one thing to remedy unequal educational opportunities, but quite another to remedy unequal native endowments. If we are bothered by the fact that some runners are faster than others, don't we have to make the gifted runners wear lead shoes? Some critics of egalitarianism believe that the only alternative to a meritocratic market society is a leveling equality that imposes handicaps on the talented.

An Egalitarian Nightmare

"Harrison Bergeron," a short story by Kurt Vonnegut, Jr., plays out this worry as dystopian science fiction. "The year was 2081," the story begins, "and everybody was finally equal . . . Nobody was smarter than anybody else. Nobody was better looking than anybody else. Nobody was stronger or quicker than anybody else." This thoroughgoing equality was enforced by agents of the United States Handicapper General. Citizens of above average intelligence were required to wear mental handicap radios in their ears. Every twenty seconds or so, a government transmitter would send out a sharp noise to prevent them "from taking unfair advantage of their brains."[15]

Harrison Bergeron, age fourteen, is unusually smart, handsome, and gifted, and so has to be fitted with heavier handicaps than most. Instead of the little ear radio, "he wore a tremendous pair of earphones, and spectacles with thick wavy lenses." To disguise his good looks,

Harrison is required to wear "a red rubber ball for a nose, keep his eyebrows shaved off, and cover his even white teeth with black caps at snaggle-tooth random." And to offset his physical strength, he has to walk around wearing heavy scrap metal. "In the race of life, Harrison carried three hundred pounds."[16]

One day, Harrison sheds his handicaps in an act of heroic defiance against the egalitarian tyranny. I won't spoil the story by revealing the conclusion. It should already be clear how Vonnegut's story makes vivid a familiar complaint against egalitarian theories of justice.

Rawls's theory of justice, however, is not open to that objection. He shows that a leveling equality is not the only alternative to a meritocratic market society. Rawls's alternative, which he calls the difference principle, corrects for the unequal distribution of talents and endowments without handicapping the talented. How? Encourage the gifted to develop and exercise their talents, but with the understanding that the rewards these talents reap in the market belong to the community as a whole. Don't handicap the best runners; let them run and do their best. Simply acknowledge in advance that the winnings don't belong to them alone, but should be shared with those who lack similar gifts.

Although the difference principle does not require an equal distribution of income and wealth, its underlying idea expresses a powerful, even inspiring vision of equality:

> The difference principle represents, in effect, an agreement to regard the distribution of natural talents as a common asset and to share in the benefits of this distribution whatever it turns out to be. Those who have been favored by nature, whoever they are, may gain from their good fortune only on terms that improve the situation of those who have lost out. The naturally advantaged are not to gain merely because they are more gifted, but only to cover the costs of training and education and for using their endowments in ways that help the less fortunate as well. No one deserves his greater natural capacity nor merits a more favorable starting place in society. But it does not follow

that one should eliminate these distinctions. There is another way to deal with them. The basic structure of society can be arranged so that these contingencies work for the good of the least fortunate.[17]

Consider, then, four rival theories of distribution justice:

1. Feudal or caste system: fixed hierarchy based on birth.
2. Libertarian: free market with formal equality of opportunity.
3. Meritocratic: free market with fair equality of opportunity.
4. Egalitarian: Rawls's difference principle.

Rawls argues that each of the first three theories bases distributive shares on factors that are arbitrary from a moral point of view—whether accident of birth, or social and economic advantage, or natural talents and abilities. Only the difference principle avoids basing the distribution of income and wealth on these contingencies.

Although the argument from moral arbitrariness does not rely on the argument from the original position, it is similar in this respect: Both maintain that, in thinking about justice, we should abstract from, or set aside, contingent facts about persons and their social positions.

Objection 1: Incentives

Rawls's case for the difference principle invites two main objections. First, what about incentives? If the talented can benefit from their talents only on terms that help the least well off, what if they decide to work less, or not to develop their skills in the first place? If tax rates are high or pay differentials small, won't talented people who might have been surgeons go into less demanding lines of work? Won't Michael Jordan work less hard on his jump shot, or retire sooner than he otherwise might?

Rawls's reply is that the difference principle permits income inequalities for the sake of incentives, provided the incentives are needed to improve the lot of the least advantaged. Paying CEOs more or cutting taxes on the wealthy simply to increase the gross domestic product would not be enough. But if the incentives generate economic growth that makes those at the bottom better off than they would be with a more equal arrangement, then the difference principle permits them.

It is important to notice that allowing wage differences for the sake of incentives is different from saying that the successful have a privileged moral claim to the fruits of their labor. If Rawls is right, income inequalities are just only insofar as they call forth efforts that ultimately help the disadvantaged, not because CEOs or sports stars deserve to make more money than factory workers.

Objection 2: Effort

This brings us to a second, more challenging objection to Rawls's theory of justice: What about effort? Rawls rejects the meritocratic theory of justice on the grounds that people's natural talents are not their own doing. But what about the hard work people devote to cultivating their talents? Bill Gates worked long and hard to develop Microsoft. Michael Jordan put in endless hours honing his basketball skills. Notwithstanding their talents and gifts, don't they deserve the rewards their efforts bring?

Rawls replies that even effort may be the product of a favorable upbringing. "Even the willingness to make an effort, to try, and so to be deserving in the ordinary sense is itself dependent upon happy family and social circumstances."[18] Like other factors in our success, effort is influenced by contingencies for which we can claim no credit. "It seems clear that the effort a person is willing to make is influenced by his natural abilities and skills and the alternatives open to him. The better endowed are more likely, other things equal, to strive conscientiously . . ."[19]

When my students encounter Rawls's argument about effort, many strenuously object. They argue that their achievements, including their admission to Harvard, reflect their own hard work, not morally arbitrary factors beyond their control. Many view with suspicion any theory of justice that suggests we don't morally deserve the rewards our efforts bring.

After we debate Rawls's claim about effort, I conduct an unscientific survey. I point out that psychologists say that birth order has an influence on effort and striving—such as the effort the students associate with getting into Harvard. The first-born reportedly have a stronger work ethic, make more money, and achieve more conventional success than their younger siblings. These studies are controversial, and I don't know if their findings are true. But just for the fun of it, I ask my students how many are first in birth order. About 75 to 80 percent raise their hands. The result has been the same every time I have taken the poll.

No one claims that being first in birth order is one's own doing. If something as morally arbitrary as birth order can influence our tendency to work hard and strive conscientiously, then Rawls may have a point. Even effort can't be the basis of moral desert.

The claim that people deserve the rewards that come from effort and hard work is questionable for a further reason: although proponents of meritocracy often invoke the virtues of effort, they don't really believe that effort alone should be the basis of income and wealth. Consider two construction workers. One is strong and brawny, and can build four walls in a day without breaking a sweat. The other is weak and scrawny, and can't carry more than two bricks at a time. Although he works very hard, it takes him a week to do what his muscular co-worker achieves, more or less effortlessly, in a day. No defender of meritocracy would say the weak but hardworking worker deserves to be paid more, in virtue of his superior effort, than the strong one.

Or consider Michael Jordan. It's true, he practiced hard. But some lesser basketball players practice even harder. No one would say they deserve a bigger contract than Jordan's as a reward for all the hours they put in. So, despite the talk about effort, it's really contribution, or achievement, that the meritocrat believes is worthy of reward. Whether or not our work ethic is our own doing, our contribution depends, at least in part, on natural talents for which we can claim no credit.

Rejecting Moral Desert

If Rawls's argument about the moral arbitrariness of talents is right, it leads to a surprising conclusion: Distributive justice is not a matter of rewarding moral desert.

He recognizes that this conclusion is at odds with our ordinary way of thinking about justice: "There is a tendency for common sense to suppose that income and wealth, and the good things in life generally, should be distributed according to moral desert. Justice is happiness according to virtue . . . Now justice as fairness rejects this conception."[20]

Rawls undermines the meritocratic view by calling into question its basic premise, namely, that once we remove social and economic barriers to success, people can be said to deserve the rewards their talents bring:

> We do not deserve our place in the distribution of native endowments, any more than we deserve our initial starting point in society. That we deserve the superior character than enables us to make the effort to cultivate our abilities is also problematic; for such character depends in good part upon fortunate family and social circumstances in early life for which can claim no credit. The notion of desert does not apply here.[21]

If distributive justice is not about rewarding moral desert, does this mean that people who work hard and play by the rules have no claim whatsoever on the rewards they get for their efforts? No, not exactly. Here Rawls makes an important but subtle distinction—between moral desert and what he calls "entitlements to legitimate expectations." The difference is this: Unlike a desert claim, an entitlement can arise only once certain rules of the game are in place. It can't tell us how to set up the rules in the first place.

The conflict between moral desert and entitlements underlies many of our most heated debates about justice: Some say that increasing tax rates on the wealthy deprives them of something they morally deserve; or that considering racial and ethnic diversity as a factor in college admissions deprives applicants with high SAT scores of an advantage they morally deserve. Others say no—people don't morally deserve these advantages; we first have to decide what the rules of the game (the tax rates, the admissions criteria) should be. Only then can we say who is entitled to what.

Consider the difference between a game of chance and a game of skill. Suppose I play the state lottery. If my number comes up, I am entitled to my winnings. But I can't say that I deserved to win, because a lottery is a game of chance. My winning or losing has nothing to do with my virtue or skill in playing the game.

Now imagine the Boston Red Sox winning the World Series. Having done so, they are entitled to the trophy. Whether or not they deserved to win would be a further question. The answer would depend on how they played the game. Did they win by a fluke (a bad call by the umpire at a decisive moment, for example) or because they actually played better than their opponents, displaying the excellences and virtues (good pitching, timely hitting, sparkling defense, etc.) that define baseball at its best?

With a game of skill, unlike a game of chance, there can be a difference between who is entitled to the winnings and who deserved to win. This is because games of skill reward the exercise and display of certain virtues.

Rawls argues that distributive justice is not about rewarding virtue or moral desert. Instead, it's about meeting the legitimate expectations that arise once the rules of the game are in place. Once the principles of justice set the terms of social cooperation, people are entitled to the benefits they earn under the rules. But if the tax system requires them to hand over some portion of their income to help the disadvantaged, they can't complain that this deprives them of something they morally deserve.

A just scheme, then, answers to what men are entitled to; it satisfies their legitimate expectations as founded upon social institutions. But what they are entitled to is not proportional to nor dependent upon their intrinsic worth. The principles of justice that regulate the basic structure of society . . . do not mention moral desert, and there is no tendency for distributive shares to correspond to it.[22]

Rawls rejects moral desert as the basis for distributive justice on two grounds. First, as we've already seen, my having the talents that enable me to compete more successfully than others is not entirely my own doing. But a second contingency is equally decisive: the qualities that a society happens to value at any given time also morally arbitrary. Even if I had sole, unproblematic claim to my talents, it would still be the case that the rewards these talents reap will depend on the contingencies of supply and demand. In medieval Tuscany, fresco painters were highly valued; in twenty-first-century California, computer programmers are, and so on. Whether my skills yield a lot or a little depends on what the society happens to want. What counts as contributing depends on the qualities a given society happens to prize.

Consider these wage differentials:

• The average schoolteacher in the United States makes about $43,000 per year. David Letterman, the late-night talk show host, earns $31 million a year.
• John Roberts, chief justice of the U.S. Supreme Court, is paid $217,400 a year. Judge Judy, who has a reality television show, makes $25 million a year.

Are these pay differentials fair? The answer, for Rawls, would depend on whether they arose within a system of taxation and redistribution that worked to the benefit of the least well off. If so, Letterman and Judge Judy would be entitled to their earnings. But it can't be said that Judge Judy deserves to make one hundred times more than Chief Justice Roberts, or that Letterman deserves to make seven hundred times as much as a schoolteacher. The fact that they happen to live in a society that lavishes huge sums on television stars is their good luck, not something they deserve.

The successful often overlook this contingent aspect of their success. Many of us are fortunate to possess, at least in some measure, the qualities our society happens to prize. In a capitalist society, it helps to have entrepreneurial drive. In a bureaucratic society, it helps to get on easily and smoothly with superiors. In a mass democratic society, it helps to look good on television, and to speak in short, superficial sound bites. In a litigious society, it helps to go to law school, and to have the logical and reasoning skills that will allow you to score well on the LSATs.

That our society values these things is not our doing. Suppose that we, with our talents, inhabited not a technologically advanced, highly litigious society like ours, but a hunting society, or a warrior society, or a society that conferred its highest rewards and prestige on those who displayed physical strength, or religious piety. What would become of our talents then? Clearly, they wouldn't get us very far. And no doubt some of us would develop others. But would we be less worthy or less virtuous than we are now?

Rawls's answer is no. We might receive less, and properly so. But while we would be entitled to less, we would be no less worthy, no less deserving than others. The same is true of those in our society who lack prestigious positions, and who possess fewer of the talents that our society happens to reward.

So, while we are entitled to the benefits that the rules of the game promise for the exercise of our talents, it is a mistake and a conceit to suppose that we deserve in the first place a society that values the qualities we have in abundance.

Woody Allen makes a similar point in his movie *Stardust Memories*.

Allen, playing a character akin to himself, a celebrity comedian named Sandy, meets up with Jerry, a friend from his old neighborhood who is chagrined at being a taxi driver.

> **SANDY:** So what are you doing? What are you up to?
>
> **JERRY:** You know what I do? I drive a cab.
>
> **SANDY:** Well, you look good. You—There's nothing wrong with that.
>
> **JERRY:** Yeah. But look at me compared to you . . .
>
> **SANDY:** What do you want me to say? I was the kid in the neighborhood who told the jokes, right?
>
> **JERRY:** Yeah.
>
> **SANDY:** So, so—we, you know, we live in a—in a society that puts a big value on jokes, you know? If you think of it this way—(*clearing his throat*) if I had been an Apache Indian, those guys didn't need comedians at all, right? So I'd be out of work.
>
> **JERRY:** So? Oh, come on, that doesn't help me feel any better.[23]

The taxi driver was not moved by the comedian's riff on the moral arbitrariness of fame and fortune. Viewing his meager lot as a matter of bad luck didn't lessen the sting. Perhaps that's because, in a meritocratic society, most people think that worldly success reflects what we deserve; the idea is not easy to dislodge. Whether distributive justice can be detached altogether from moral desert is a question we explore in the pages to come.

Is Life Unfair?

In 1980, as Ronald Reagan ran for president, the economist Milton Friedman published a bestselling book, co-authored with his wife, Rose, called *Free to Choose*. It was a spirited, unapologetic defense of the free-market economy, and it became a textbook—even an anthem—for the Reagan years. In defending laissez-faire principles against egalitarian objections, Friedman made a surprising concession. He acknowledged that those who grow up in wealthy families and attend elite schools have an unfair advantage over those from less privileged backgrounds. He also conceded that those who, through no doing of their own, inherit talents and gifts have an unfair advantage over others. Unlike Rawls, however, Friedman insisted that we should not try to remedy this unfairness. Instead, we should learn to live with it, and enjoy the benefits it brings:

> Life is not fair. It is tempting to believe that government can rectify what nature has spawned. But it is also important to recognize how much we benefit from the very unfairness we deplore. There's nothing fair . . . about Muhammad Ali's having been born with the skill that made him a great fighter . . . It is certainly not fair that Muhammad Ali should be able to earn millions of dollars in one night. But wouldn't it have been even more unfair to the people who enjoyed watching him if, in the pursuit of some abstract ideal of equality, Muhammad Ali had not been permitted to earn more for one night's fight . . . than the lowest man on the totem pole could get for a day's unskilled work on the docks?[24]

In *A Theory of Justice*, Rawls rejects the counsel of complacence that Friedman's view reflects. In a stirring passage, Rawls states a familiar truth that we often forget: The way things are does not determine the way they ought to be.

> We should reject the contention that the ordering of institutions is always defective because the distribution of natural talents and the contingencies of social circumstance are unjust, and this injustice must inevitably carry over to human arrangements. Occasionally this reflection is offered as an excuse for ignoring injustice, as if the refusal to acquiesce in injustice is on a par with being unable to accept death. The natural distribution is neither just nor unjust; nor is it unjust that persons are born into society at some particular position. These are

simply natural facts. What is just and unjust is the way that institutions deal with these facts.[25]

Rawls proposes that we deal with these facts by agreeing "to share one another's fate," and "to avail [ourselves] of the accidents of nature and social circumstance only when doing so is for the common benefit."[26] Whether or not his theory of justice ultimately succeeds, it represents the most compelling case for a more equal society that American political philosophy has yet produced.

7. ARGUING AFFIRMATIVE ACTION

Cheryl Hopwood did not come from an affluent family. Raised by a single mother, she worked her way through high school, community college, and California State University at Sacramento. She then moved to Texas and applied to the University of Texas Law School, the best law school in the state and one of the leading law schools in the country. Although Hopwood had compiled a grade point average of 3.8 and did reasonably well on the law school admissions test (scoring in the 83rd percentile), she was not admitted.[1]

Hopwood, who is white, thought her rejection was unfair. Some of the applicants admitted instead of her were African American and Mexican American students who had lower college grades and test scores than she did. The school had an affirmative action policy that gave preference to minority applicants. In fact, all of the minority students with grades and test scores comparable to Hopwood's had been admitted.

Hopwood took her case to federal court, arguing that she was a victim of discrimination. The university replied that part of the law school's mission was to increase the racial and ethnic diversity of the Texas legal profession, including not only law firms, but also the state legislature and the courts. "Law in a civil society depends overwhelmingly on the willingness of society to accept its judgment," said Michael Sharlot, dean of the law school. "It becomes harder to achieve that if we don't see members of all groups playing roles in the administration of justice."[2] In Texas, African Americans and Mexican Americans comprise 40 percent of the population, but a far smaller proportion of the legal profession. When Hopwood applied, the University of Texas law school used an affirmative action admissions policy that aimed at enrolling about 15 percent of the class from among minority applicants.[3]

In order to achieve this goal, the university set lower admissions standards for minority applicants than for nonminority applicants. University officials argued, however, that all of the minority students who were admitted were qualified to do the work, and almost all succeed in graduating from law school and passing the bar exam. But that was small comfort to Hopwood, who believed she'd been treated unfairly, and should have been admitted.

Hopwood's challenge to affirmative action was not the first to find its way to court, nor would it be the last. For over three decades, the courts have wrestled with the hard moral and legal questions posed by affirmative action. In 1978, in the *Bakke* case, the U.S. Supreme Court narrowly upheld an affirmative action admissions policy of the medical school at University of California at Davis.[4] In 2003, a closely divided Supreme Court ruled that race could be used as a factor in admissions in a case involving the University of Michigan Law School.[5] Meanwhile, voters in California, Washington, and Michigan have recently enacted ballot initiatives to ban racial preferences in public education and employment.

The question for the courts is whether affirmative action hiring and admissions policies violate the U.S. Constitution's guarantee of equal protection of the laws. But let's set aside the constitutional question and focus directly on the moral question: Is it unjust to consider race and ethnicity as factors in hiring or university admissions?

To answer this question, let's consider three reasons that proponents of affirmative action offer for taking race and ethnicity into account: correcting for bias in standardized tests, compensating for past wrongs, and promoting diversity.

Correcting for the Testing Gap

One reason for taking race and ethnicity into account is to correct for possible bias in standardized tests. The ability of the SAT (Scholastic Aptitude Test) and other such tests to predict academic and career success has long been disputed. In 1951, an applicant to the doctoral program in the School of Religion at Boston University presented mediocre scores on the GRE (Graduate Record Exam). The young Martin Luther King, Jr., who would become one of the greatest orators in American history, scored below average in verbal aptitude.[6] Fortunately, he was admitted anyway.

Some studies show that black and Hispanic students on the whole score lower than white students on standardized tests, even adjusting for economic class. But whatever the cause of the testing gap, using standardized tests to predict academic success requires interpreting the scores in light of students' family, social, cultural, and educational backgrounds. A 700 SAT score from a student who attended poor public schools in the South Bronx means more than the same score for a graduate of an elite private school on the Upper East Side of Manhattan. But assessing test scores in light of students' racial, ethnic, and economic backgrounds does not challenge the notion that colleges and universities should admit those students with the greatest academic promise; it is simply an attempt to find the most accurate measure of each individual's academic promise.

The real affirmative action debate is about two other rationales—the compensatory argument and the diversity argument.

Compensating for Past Wrongs

The compensatory argument views affirmative action as a remedy for past wrongs. It says minority students should be given preference to make up for a history of discrimination that has placed them at an unfair disadvantage. This argument treats admission primarily as a benefit to the recipient and seeks to distribute the benefit in a way that compensates for past injustice and its lingering effects.

But the compensatory argument runs into a tough challenge: critics point out that those who benefit are not necessarily those who have suffered, and those who pay the compensation are seldom those responsible for the wrongs being rectified. Many beneficiaries of affirmative action are middle-class minority students who did not suffer the hardships that afflict young African Americans and Hispanics from the inner city. Why should an African American student from an affluent Houston suburb get an edge over Cheryl Hopwood, who may actually have faced a tougher economic struggle?

If the point is to help the disadvantaged, critics argue, affirmative action should be based on class, not race. And if racial preferences are intended to compensate for the historic injustice of slavery and segregation, how can it be fair to exact that compensation from people such as Hopwood, who played no part in perpetrating the injustice?

Whether the compensatory case for affirmative action can answer this objection depends on the difficult concept of collective responsibility: Can we ever have a moral responsibility to redress wrongs committed by a previous generation? To answer this question, we need to know more about how moral obligations arise. Do we incur obligations only as individuals, or do some obligations claim us as members of communities with historic identities? Since we will come to this question later in the book, let's set it aside for the moment and turn to the diversity argument.

Promoting Diversity

The diversity argument for affirmative action does not depend on controversial notions of collective responsibility. Nor does it depend on showing that the minority student given preference in admission has personally suffered discrimination or disadvantage. It treats admission less as a reward to the recipient than as a means of advancing a socially worthy aim.

The diversity rationale is an argument in the name of the common good—the common good of the school itself and also of the wider society. First, it holds that a racially mixed student body is desirable because it enables students to learn more from one another than they would if all of them came from similar backgrounds. Just as a student body drawn from one part of the country would limit the range of intellectual and cultural perspectives, so would one that reflected homogeneity of race, ethnicity, and class. Second, the diversity argument maintains that equipping disadvantaged minorities to assume positions of leadership in key public and professional roles advances the university's civic purpose and contributes to the common good.

The diversity argument is the one most frequently advanced by colleges and universities. When faced with Hopwood's challenge, the dean of the University of Texas Law School cited the civic purpose served by his school's affirmative action policy. Part of the law school's mission was to help increase the diversity of the Texas legal profession and to enable African Americans and Hispanics to assume leadership roles in government and law. By this measure, he said, the law school's affirmative action program was a success: "We see minority graduates of ours as elected officials, working in prominent law firms, as members of the Texas legislature and the federal bench. To the extent that there are minorities in important offices in Texas, they are often our graduates."[7]

When the U.S. Supreme Court heard the *Bakke* case, Harvard College submitted a friend-of-the-court brief defending affirmative action on educational grounds.[8] It stated that grades and test scores had never been the only standard of admission. "If scholarly excellence were the sole or even predominant criterion, Harvard College would lose a great deal of its vitality and intellectual excellence . . . [T]he quality of the educational experience offered to all students would suffer." In the past, diversity had meant "students from California, New York, and Massachusetts; city dwellers and farm boys; violinists, painters and football players; biologists, historians and classicists; potential stockbrokers, academics and politicians." Now, the college also cared about racial and ethnic diversity.

> A farm boy from Idaho can bring something to Harvard College that a Bostonian cannot offer. Similarly, a black student can usually bring something that a white student cannot offer. The quality of the educational experience of all the students in Harvard College depends in part on these differences in the background and outlook that students bring with them.[9]

Critics of the diversity argument offer two kinds of objection— one practical, the other principled. The practical objection questions the effectiveness of affirmative action policies. It argues that the use of racial preferences will not bring about a more pluralistic society or reduce prejudice and inequalities but will damage the self-esteem of minority students, increase racial consciousness on all sides, heighten racial tensions, and provoke resentment among white ethnic groups who feel they, too, should get a break. The practical objection does not claim that affirmative action is unjust, but rather that it is unlikely to achieve its aims, and may do more harm than good.

Do Racial Preferences Violate Rights?

The principled objection claims that, however worthy the goal of a more diverse classroom or a more equal society, and however successful affirmative action policies may be in achieving it, using race or ethnicity as a factor in admissions is unfair. The reason: doing so violates the rights of applicants such as Cheryl Hopwood, who, through no fault of their own, are put at a competitive disadvantage.

For a utilitarian, this objection would not carry much weight. The case for affirmative action would simply depend on weighing the educational and civic benefits it produces against the disappointment it causes Hopwood and other white applicants at the margin who lose out. But many proponents of affirmative action are not utilitarians; they are Kantian or Rawlsian liberals who believe that even desirable ends must not override individual rights. For them, if using race as a factor in admissions violates Hopwood's rights, then doing so is unjust.

Ronald Dworkin, a rights-oriented legal philosopher, addresses this objection by arguing that the use of race in affirmative action policies doesn't violate anybody's rights.[10] What right, he asks, has Hopwood been denied? Perhaps she believes that people have a right not to be judged according to factors, such as race, that are beyond their control. But most traditional criteria for university admission involve factors beyond one's control. It's not my fault that I come from Massachusetts rather than Idaho, or that I'm a lousy football player, or that I can't carry a tune. Nor is it my fault if I lack the aptitude to do well on the SAT.

Perhaps the right at stake is the right to be considered according to academic criteria alone—not being good at football, or coming from Idaho, or having volunteered in a soup kitchen. On this view, if my grades, test scores, and other measures of academic promise land me in the top group of applicants, then I deserve to be admitted. I deserve, in other words, to be considered according to my academic merit alone.

But as Dworkin points out, there is no such right. Some universities may admit students solely on the basis of academic qualifications, but most do not. Universities define their missions in various ways. Dworkin argues that no applicant has a right that the university define its mission and design its admissions policy in a way that prizes above all any particular set of qualities—whether academic skills, athletic abilities, or anything else. Once the university defines its mission and sets its admissions standards, you have a legitimate expectation to admission insofar as you meet those standards better than other applicants. Those who finish in the top group of candidates—counting academic promise, ethnic and geographical diversity, athletic prowess, extracurricular activities, community service, and so on—are entitled to be admitted; it would be unfair to exclude them. But no one has a right to be considered according to any particular set of criteria in the first place.[11]

Here lies the deep though contested claim at the heart of the diversity argument for affirmative action: Admission is not an honor bestowed to reward superior merit or virtue. Neither the student with high test scores nor the student who comes from a disadvantaged minority group morally deserves to be admitted. Her Admission is justified insofar as it contributes to the social purpose the university serves, not because it rewards the student for her merit or virtue, independently defined. Dworkin's point is that justice in admissions is not a matter of rewarding merit or virtue; we can know what counts as a fair way of allocating seats in the freshman class only once the university defines its mission. The mission defines the relevant merits, not the other way around. Dworkin's account of justice in university admissions runs parallel to Rawls's account of justice in income distribution: It is not a matter of moral desert.

Racial Segregation and Anti-Jewish Quotas

Does this mean that colleges and universities are free to define their missions however they please, and that any admissions policy that fits the declared mission is fair? If so, what about the racially segregated campuses of the American South not long ago? As it happens, the University of Texas Law School had been at the center of an earlier constitutional challenge. In 1946, when the school was segregated, it denied admission to Heman Marion Sweatt on the grounds that the school did not admit blacks. His challenge led to a landmark U.S. Supreme Court case, *Sweatt v. Painter* (1950), which dealt a blow to segregation in higher education.

But if the only test of the fairness of an admissions policy is its fit with the school's mission, then what was wrong with the argument the Texas Law School presented at the time? Its mission was to train lawyers for Texas law firms. Since Texas law firms did not hire blacks, the law school argued, its mission would not be served by admitting them.

You might argue that the University of Texas Law School, as a public institution, is constrained in its choice of mission to a greater extent than private universities. It is certainly true that the notable constitutional challenges to affirmative action in higher education have involved state universities—the University of California at Davis (in the *Bakke* case), the University of Texas (*Hopwood*), and the University of Michigan (*Grutter*). But since we are trying to determine the justice or injustice of using race—not its legality—the distinction between public and private universities is not decisive.

Private associations as well as public institutions can be criticized for injustice. Recall the sit-ins at lunch counters protesting racial discrimination in the segregated American South. The lunch counters were privately owned, but the racial discrimination they practiced was unjust nonetheless. (In fact, the 1964 Civil Rights Act made such discrimination illegal.)

Or consider the anti-Jewish quotas employed, formally or infor-
mally, by some Ivy League universities in the 1920s and '30s. Were
these quotas morally defensible simply because the universities were
private, not public? In 1922, Harvard's president, A. Lawrence Lowell,
proposed a 12 percent limit on Jewish enrollment, in the name of reducing anti-Semitism. "The anti-Semitic feeling among students is increasing," he said, "and it grows in proportion to the increase in the
number of Jews."[12] In the 1930s, the director of admissions at Dartmouth wrote to an alumnus who had complained about the growing
number of Jews on campus. "I am glad to have your comments on the
Jewish problem," the official wrote. "If we go beyond the 5 per cent or
6 per cent in the Class of 1938, I shall be grieved beyond words." In
1945, the president of Dartmouth justified limits on Jewish enrollment by invoking the mission of the school: "Dartmouth is a Christian
College founded for the Christianization of its students."[13]

If, as the diversity rationale for affirmative action assumes, universities may set any admissions criteria that advance their mission as they
define it, is it possible to condemn racist exclusion and anti-Semitic
restrictions? Is there a principled distinction between the use of race to
exclude people in the segregationist South and the use of race to include people in present-day affirmative action? The most obvious answer is that, in its segregationist days, the Texas law school used race as
a badge of inferiority, whereas today's racial preferences do not insult
or stigmatize anyone. Hopwood considered her rejection unfair, but
she cannot claim that it expresses hatred or contempt.

This is Dworkin's answer. Segregation-era racial exclusion de-
pended on "the despicable idea that one race may be inherently more
worthy than another," whereas affirmative action involves no such prejudice. It simply asserts that, given the importance of promoting diversity in key professions, being black or Hispanic "may be a socially useful
trait."[14]

Rejected applicants such as Hopwood might not find this distinction satisfying, but it does have a certain moral force. The law school is

not saying that Hopwood is inferior or that the minority students admitted instead of her deserve an advantage that she does not. It is simply saying that racial and ethnic diversity in the classroom and the courtroom serves the law school's educational purposes. And unless the pursuit of those purposes somehow violates the rights of those who lose out, disappointed applicants can't legitimately claim that they've been treated unfairly.

Affirmative Action for Whites?

Here is a test for the diversity argument: Can it sometimes justify racial preferences for whites? Consider the case of Starrett City. This apartment complex in Brooklyn, New York, with twenty thousand residents, is the largest federally subsidized middle-income housing project in the United States. It opened in the mid-1970s, with the goal of being a racially integrated community. It achieved this goal through the use of "occupancy controls" that sought to balance the ethnic and racial composition of the community, limiting the African American and Hispanic population to about 40 percent of the total. In short, it used a quota system. The quotas were based not on prejudice or contempt, but on a theory about racial "tipping points" drawn from the urban experience. The managers of the project wanted to avoid the tipping point that had triggered "white flight" in other neighborhoods and undermined integration. By maintaining racial and ethnic balance, they hoped to sustain a stable, racially diverse community.[15]

It worked. The community became highly desirable, many families wanted to move in, and Starrett City established a waiting list. Due in part to the quota system, which allocated fewer apartments for African Americans than for whites, black families had to wait longer than white families. By the mid-1980s, a white family had to wait three to four months for an apartment, while a black family had to wait as long as two years.

Here, then, was a quota system favoring white applicants—based not on racial prejudice but on the goal of sustaining an integrated community. Some black applicants found the race-conscious policy unfair, and filed a discrimination suit. The NAACP, which favored affirmative action in other contexts, represented them. In the end, a settlement was reached that allowed Starrett City to keep its quota system but required the state to expand minority access to other housing projects.

Was Starrett City's race-conscious way of allocating apartments unjust? No, not if you accept the diversity rationale for affirmative action. Racial and ethnic diversity play out differently in housing projects and college classrooms, and the goods at stake are not the same. But from the standpoint of fairness, the two cases stand or fall together. If diversity serves the common good, and if no one is discriminated against based on hatred or contempt, then racial preferences do not violate anyone's rights. Why not? Because, following Rawls's point about moral desert, no one deserves to be considered for an apartment or a seat in the freshman class according to his or her merits, independently defined. What counts as merit can be determined only once the housing authority or the college officials define their mission.

Can Justice Be Detached from Moral Desert?

The renunciation of moral desert as the basis of distributive justice is morally attractive but also disquieting. It's attractive because it undermines the smug assumption, familiar in meritocratic societies, that success is the crown of virtue, that the rich are rich because they are more deserving than the poor. As Rawls reminds us, "no one deserves his greater natural capacity nor merits a more favorable starting place in society." Nor is it our doing that we live in a society that happens to prize our particular strengths. That is a measure of our good fortune, not our virtue.

What's disquieting about severing justice from moral desert is less easy to describe. The belief that jobs and opportunities are rewards for those who deserve them runs deep, perhaps more so in the United States than in other societies. Politicians constantly proclaim that those who "work hard and play by the rules" deserve to get ahead, and encourage people who realize the American dream to view their success as a reflection of their virtue. This conviction is at best a mixed blessing. Its persistence is an obstacle to social solidarity; the more we regard our success as our own doing, the less responsibility we feel for those who fall behind.

It may be that this persisting belief—that success should be seen as a reward for virtue—is simply a mistake, a myth whose hold we should try to dissolve. Rawls's point about the moral arbitrariness of fortune puts it powerfully in doubt. And yet it may not be possible, politically or philosophically, to detach arguments about justice from debates about desert as decisively as Rawls and Dworkin suggest. Let me try to explain why.

First, justice often has an honorific aspect. Debates about distributive justice are about not only who gets what but also what qualities are worthy of honor and reward. Second, the idea that merit arises only once social institutions define their mission is subject to a complication: the social institutions that figure most prominently in debates about justice—schools, universities, occupations, professions, public offices—are not free to define their mission just any way they please. These institutions are defined, at least in part, by the distinctive goods they promote. While there is room for argument about what, at any moment, the mission of a law school or an army or an orchestra should be, it's not the case that just anything goes. Certain goods are appropriate to certain social institutions, and to ignore these goods in allocating roles can be a kind of corruption.

We can see the way justice is entangled with honor by recalling Hopwood's case. Suppose Dworkin is right that moral desert has nothing to do with who should be admitted. Here is the letter of rejection the law school should have sent Hopwood:[16]

Dear Ms. Hopwood,

We regret to inform you that your application for admission has been rejected. Please understand that we intend no offense by our decision. We do not hold you in contempt. In fact, we don't even regard you as less deserving than those who were admitted.

It is not your fault that when you came along society happened not to need the qualities you had to offer. Those admitted instead of you are not deserving of a place, nor worthy of praise for the factors that led to their admission. We are only using them—and you—as instruments of a wider social purpose.

We realize you will find this news disappointing. But your disappointment should not be exaggerated by the thought that this rejection reflects in any way on your intrinsic moral worth. You have our sympathy in the sense that it is too bad you did not happen to have the traits society happened to want when you applied. Better luck next time.

Sincerely yours . . .

And here is the letter of acceptance, shorn of honorific implications, that a philosophically frank law school should send those it admits:

Dear successful applicant,

We are pleased to inform you that your application for admission has been accepted. It turns out that you happen to have the traits that society needs at the moment, so we propose to exploit your assets for society's advantage by admitting you to the study of law.

You are to be congratulated, not in the sense that you deserve credit for having the qualities that led to your admission—you do not—but only in the sense that the winner of a lottery is to be congratulated. You are lucky to have come along with the right traits at the right moment. If you choose to accept our offer, you will ultimately be entitled to the benefits that attach to being used in this way. For this, you may properly celebrate.

You, or more likely your parents, may be tempted to celebrate in the further sense that you take this admission to reflect favorably, if not on your native endowments, then at least on the conscientious effort you have made to cultivate your abilities. But the notion that you deserve even the superior character necessary to your effort is equally problematic, for your character depends on fortunate circumstances of various kinds for which you can claim no credit. The notion of desert does not apply here.

We look forward nonetheless to seeing you in the fall.

Sincerely yours . . .

Such letters might lessen the sting for those who are rejected, and dampen the hubris of those who are accepted. So why do colleges continue to send (and applicants to expect) letters replete with congratulatory, honorific rhetoric? Perhaps because colleges can't entirely dispense with the idea that their role is not only to advance certain ends but also to honor and reward certain virtues.

Why Not Auction College Admission?

This leads us to the second question, about whether colleges and universities may define their mission however they please. Put ethnic and racial preferences aside for the moment and consider another affirmative action controversy—the debate over "legacy preferences." Many colleges give children of alumni an edge in admission. One rationale for doing so is to build community and school spirit over time. Another is the hope that grateful alumni parents will provide their alma mater with generous financial support.

In order to isolate the financial rationale, consider what universities call "development admits"—applicants who are not children of alumni but who have wealthy parents able to make a sizeable financial contribution to the school. Many universities admit such students even if their grades and test scores are not as high as would otherwise be required. To take this idea to the extreme, imagine that a university decided to auction 10 percent of the seats in the freshman class to the highest bidders.

Would this system of admission be fair? If you believe that *merit* simply means the ability to contribute, in one way or another, to the mission of the university, the answer may be yes. Whatever their mission, all universities need money to achieve it.

By Dworkin's expansive definition of merit, a student admitted to a school for the sake of a $10 million gift for the new campus library is meritorious; her admission serves the good of the university as a whole. Students rejected in favor of the philanthropist's child might complain they've been treated unfairly. But Dworkin's reply to Hopwood applies equally to them. All fairness requires is that no one be rejected out of prejudice or contempt, and that applicants be judged by criteria related to the mission the university sets for itself. In this case, those conditions are met. The students who lose out aren't the victims of prejudice; it's just their bad luck to lack parents willing and able to donate a new library.

But this standard is too weak. It still seems unfair for wealthy parents to be able to buy their child a ticket to the Ivy League. But what does the injustice consist in? It can't be the fact that applicants from poor or middle-class families are put at a disadvantage beyond their control. As Dworkin points out, many factors beyond our control are legitimate factors in admission.

Perhaps what's troubling about the auction has less to do with the opportunity of the applicants than the integrity of the university. Selling seats to the highest bidder is more appropriate for a rock concert or a sporting event than for an educational institution. The just way of allocating access to a good may have something to do with the nature of that good, with its purpose. The affirmative action debate reflects competing notions of what colleges are for: To what extent should they pursue scholarly ·excellence, to what extent civic goods, and how should these purposes be balanced? Though a college education also serves the good of preparing students for successful careers, its primary purpose is not commercial. So selling education as if it were merely a consumer good is a kind of corruption.

What, then, is the university's purpose? Harvard is not Wal-Mart—or even Bloomingdales. Its purpose is not to maximize revenue but to serve the common good through teaching and research. It is true that teaching and research are expensive, and universities devote much effort to fund-raising. But when the goal of money-making predominates to the point of governing admission, the university has strayed far from the scholarly and civic goods that are its primary reason for being.

The idea that justice in allocating access to a university has something to do with the goods that universities properly pursue explains why selling admission is unjust. It also explains why it's hard to separate questions of justice and rights from questions of honor and virtue. Universities give honorary degrees to celebrate those who display the virtues universities exist to promote. But in a way, every degree a university confers is an honorary degree.

Tying debates about justice to arguments about honor, virtue, and the meaning of goods may seem a recipe for hopeless disagreement. People hold different conceptions of honor and virtue. The proper mission of social institutions—whether universities, corporations, the military, the professions, or the political community generally—is contested and fraught. So it is tempting to seek a basis for justice and rights that keeps its distance from those controversies.

Much modern political philosophy tries to do just that. As we've seen, the philosophies of Kant and Rawls are bold attempts to find a basis for justice and rights that is neutral with respect to competing visions of the good life. It is now time to see if their project succeeds.

8. WHO DESERVES WHAT? / ARISTOTLE

Callie Smartt was a popular freshman cheerleader at Andrews High School in West Texas. The fact that she had cerebral palsy and moved about in a wheelchair didn't dampen the enthusiasm she inspired among the football players and fans by her spirited presence on the sidelines at junior varsity games. But at the end of the season, Callie was kicked off the squad.[1]

At the urging of some other cheerleaders and their parents, school officials told Callie that, to make the squad the next year, she would have to try out like everyone else, in a rigorous gymnastic routine involving splits and tumbles. The head cheerleader's father led the opposition to Callie's inclusion on the cheerleading team. He claimed he was concerned for her safety. But Callie's mother suspected the opposition was motivated by resentment of the acclaim Callie received.

Callie's story raises two questions. One is a question of fairness. Should she be required to do gymnastics in order to qualify as a cheerleader, or is this requirement unfair, given her disability? One way of answering this question would be to invoke the principle of nondiscrimination: Provided she can perform well in the role, Callie should not be excluded from cheerleading simply because, through no fault of her own, she lacks the physical ability to perform gymnastic routines.

But the nondiscrimination principle isn't much help, because it begs the question at the heart of the controversy: What does it mean to perform well in the role of cheerleader? Callie's opponents claim that to be a good cheerleader you must be able to do tumbles and splits. That, after all, is how cheerleaders traditionally excite the crowd. Callie's supporters would say this confuses the purpose of cheerleading with one way of achieving it. The real point of cheerleading is to inspire school spirit and energize the fans. When Callie roars up and down the sidelines in her wheelchair, waving her pom-poms and flashing her smile, she does well what cheerleaders are supposed to do—fire up the crowd. So in order to decide what the qualifications should be, we have to decide what's essential to cheerleading, and what's merely incidental.

The second question raised by Callie's story is about resentment. What kind of resentment might motivate the head cheerleader's father? Why is he bothered by the presence of Callie on the squad? It can't be fear that Callie's inclusion deprives his daughter of a place; she's already on the team. Nor is it the simple envy he might feel toward a girl who outshines his daughter at gymnastic routines, which Callie, of course, does not.

Here is my hunch: his resentment probably reflects a sense that Callie is being accorded an honor she doesn't deserve, in a way that mocks the pride he takes in his daughter's cheerleading prowess. If great cheerleading is something that can be done from a wheelchair, then the honor accorded those who excel at tumbles and splits is depreciated to some degree.

If Callie should be a cheerleader because she displays, despite her disability, the virtues appropriate to the role, her claim does pose a certain threat to the honor accorded the other cheerleaders. The gymnastic skills they display no longer appear essential to excellence in cheerleading, only one way among others of rousing the crowd. Ungenerous though he was, the father of the head cheerleader correctly grasped what was at stake. A social practice once taken as fixed in its purpose and in the honors it bestowed was now, thanks to Callie, redefined. She had shown that there's more than one way to be a cheerleader.

Notice the connection between the first question, about fairness, and the second, about honor and resentment. In order to determine a fair way to allocate cheerleading positions, we need to determine the nature and purpose of cheerleading. Otherwise, we have no way of saying what qualities are essential to it. But determining the essence of cheerleading can be controversial, because it embroils us in arguments about what qualities are worthy of honor. What counts as the purpose of cheerleading depends partly on what virtues you think deserve recognition and reward.

As this episode shows, social practices such as cheerleading have not only an instrumental purpose (cheering on the team) but also an honorific, or exemplary, purpose (celebrating certain excellences and virtues). In choosing its cheerleaders, the high school not only promotes school spirit but also makes a statement about the qualities it hopes students will admire and emulate. This explains why the dispute was so intense. It also explains what is otherwise puzzling—how those already on the team (and their parents) could feel they had a personal stake in the debate over Callie's eligibility. These parents wanted cheerleading to honor the traditional cheerleader virtues their daughters possessed.

Justice, Telos, and Honor

Seen in this way, the dustup over cheerleaders in West Texas is a short course in Aristotle's theory of justice. Central to Aristotle's political philosophy are two ideas, both present in the argument over Callie:

1. Justice is teleological. Defining rights requires us to figure out the *telos* (the purpose, end, or essential nature) of the social practice in question.
2. Justice is honorific. To reason about the telos of a practice—or to argue about it—is, at least in part, to reason or argue about what virtues it should honor and reward.

The key to understanding Aristotle's ethics and politics is to see the force of these two considerations, and the relation between them.

Modern theories of justice try to separate questions of fairness and rights from arguments about honor, virtue, and moral desert. They seek principles of justice that are neutral among ends, and enable people to choose and pursue their ends for themselves. Aristotle (384–322 B.C.) does not think justice can be neutral in this way. He believes that debates about justice are, unavoidably, debates about honor, virtue, and the nature of the good life.

Seeing why Aristotle thinks justice and the good life must be connected will help us see what's at stake in the effort to separate them.

For Aristotle, justice means giving people what they deserve, giving each person his or her due. But what is a person due? What are the relevant grounds of merit or desert? That depends on what's being distributed. Justice involves two factors: "things, and the persons to whom things are assigned." And in general we say that "persons who are equal should have assigned to them equal things."[2]

But here there arises a difficult question: Equals in what respect? That depends on what we're distributing—and on the virtues relevant to those things.

Suppose we're distributing flutes. Who should get the best ones? Aristotle's answer: the best flute players.

Justice discriminates according to merit, according to the relevant excellence. And in the case of flute playing, the relevant merit is the ability to play well. It would be unjust to discriminate on any other basis, such as wealth, or nobility of birth, or physical beauty, or chance (a lottery).

> Birth and beauty may be greater goods than ability to play the flute, and those who possess them may, upon balance, surpass the flute-player more in these qualities than he surpasses them in his flute-playing; but the fact remains that *he* is the man who ought to get the better supply of flutes.[3]

There is something funny about comparing excellences across vastly disparate dimensions. It may not even make sense to ask, "Am I more handsome than she is a good lacrosse player?" Or, "Was Babe Ruth a greater baseball player than Shakespeare was a playwright?" Questions such as these may make sense only as parlor games. Aristotle's point is that, in distributing flutes, we should not look for the richest or best-looking or even the best person overall. We should look for the best flute player.

This idea is perfectly familiar. Many orchestras conduct auditions behind a screen, so that the quality of the music can be judged without bias or distraction. Less familiar is Aristotle's reason. The most obvious reason for giving the best flutes to the best flute players is that doing so will produce the best music, making us listeners better off. But this is not Aristotle's reason. He thinks the best flutes should go to the best flute players because that's what flutes are *for*—to be played well.

The purpose of flutes is to produce excellent music. Those who can best realize this purpose ought to have the best ones.

Now it's also true that giving the best instruments to the best musicians will have the welcome effect of producing the best music, which everyone will enjoy—producing the greatest happiness for the greatest number. But it's important to see that Aristotle's reason goes beyond this utilitarian consideration.

His way of reasoning from the purpose of a good to the proper allocation of the good is an instance of teleological reasoning. (*Teleological* comes from the Greek word telos, which means purpose, end, or goal.) Aristotle claims that in order to determine the just distribution of a good, we have to inquire into the telos, or purpose, of the good being distributed.

Teleological Thinking: Tennis Courts and *Winnie-the-Pooh*

Teleological reasoning may seem a strange way to think about justice, but it does have a certain plausibility. Suppose you have to decide how to allocate use of the best tennis courts on a college campus. You might give priority to those who can pay the most for them, by setting a high fee. Or you might give priority to campus big shots—the president of the college, say, or the Nobel Prize–winning scientists. But suppose two renowned scientists were playing a rather indifferent tennis game, barely getting the ball over the net, and the varsity tennis team came along, wanting to use the court. Wouldn't you say that the scientists should move to a lesser court so that the varsity players could use the best one? And wouldn't your reason be that excellent tennis players can make the best use of the best courts, which are wasted on mediocre players?

Or suppose a Stradivarius violin is for up sale, and a wealthy collector outbids Itzhak Perlman for it. The collector wants to display the violin in his living room. Wouldn't we regard this as something of a loss, perhaps even an injustice—not because we think the auction is unfair, but because the outcome is unfitting? Lying behind this reaction may be the (teleological) thought that a Stradivarius is meant to be played, not displayed.

In the ancient world, teleological thinking was more prevalent than it is today. Plato and Aristotle thought that fire rose because it was reaching for the sky, its natural home, and that stones fell because they were striving to get closer to the earth, where they belonged. Nature was seen as having a meaningful order. To understand nature, and our place in it, was to grasp its purpose, its essential meaning.

With the advent of modern science, nature ceased to be seen as a meaningful order. Instead, it came to be understood mechanistically, governed by the laws of physics. To explain natural phenomena in terms of purposes, meanings, and ends was now considered naïve and anthropomorphic. Despite this shift, the temptation to see the world as teleologically ordered, as a purposeful whole, is not wholly absent. It persists, especially in children, who have to be educated out of seeing the world in this way. I noticed this when my children were very young, and I read them the book *Winnie-the-Pooh*, by A. A. Milne. The story evokes a childlike view of nature as enchanted, animated by meaning and purpose.

Early in the book, Winnie-the-Pooh is walking in the forest and comes to a large oak tree. From the top of the tree, "there came a loud buzzing-noise."

> Winnie-the-Pooh sat down at the foot of the tree, put his head between his paws and began to think.
>
> First of all he said to himself: "That buzzing-noise means something. You don't get a buzzing-noise like that, just buzzing and buzzing, without its meaning something. If there's a buzzing-noise, somebody's making a buzzing-noise, and the only reason for making a buzzing-noise that *I* know of is because you're a bee."
>
> Then he thought another long time, and said: "And the only reason for being a bee that *I* know of is making honey."
>
> And then he got up, and said: "And the only reason for making honey is so as *I* can eat it." So he began to climb the tree.[4]

Pooh's childlike line of thought about the bees is a good example of teleological reasoning. By the time we are adults, most of us outgrow this way of viewing the natural world, seeing it as charming but quaint. And having rejected teleological thinking in science, we are also inclined to reject it in politics and morals. But it is not easy to dispense with teleological reasoning in thinking about social institutions and political practices. Today, no scientist reads Aristotle's works on biology or physics and takes them seriously. But students of ethics and politics continue to read and ponder Aristotle's moral and political philosophy.

What's the Telos of a University?

The debate over affirmative action can be recast in terms that echo Aristotle's account of flutes. We begin by seeking just criteria of distribution: Who has a right to be admitted? In addressing this question, we find ourselves asking (at least implicitly), "What is the purpose, or te-los, of a university?"

As is often the case, the telos is not obvious but contestable. Some say universities are for the sake of promoting scholarly excellence, and that academic promise should be the sole criterion of admission. Others say universities also exist to serve certain civic purposes, and that the ability to become a leader in a diverse society, for example, should be among the criteria of admission. Sorting out the telos of a university seems essential to determining the proper criteria of admission. This brings out the teleological aspect of justice in university admissions.

Closely connected to the debate about a university's purpose is a question about honor: What virtues or excellences do universities properly honor and reward? Those who believe that universities exist to celebrate and reward scholarly excellence alone are likely to reject affirmative action, whereas those who believe universities also exist to promote certain civic ideals may well embrace it.

That arguments about universities—and cheerleaders and flutes—naturally proceed in this way bears out Aristotle's point: Arguments about justice and rights are often arguments about the purpose, or te-los, of a social institution, which in turn reflect competing notions of the virtues the institution should honor and reward.

What can we do if people disagree about the telos, or purpose, of the activity in question? Is it possible to reason about the telos of a so-cial institution, or is the purpose of a university, say, simply whatever the founding authority or governing board declared it to be?

Aristotle believes that it is possible to reason about the purpose of social institutions. Their essential nature is not fixed once and for all, but neither is it simply a matter of opinion. (If the purpose of Harvard College were simply determined by the intention of its founders, then its primary purpose would still be the training of Congregationalist ministers.)

How, then, can we reason about the purpose of a social practice in the face of disagreement? And how do notions of honor and virtue come into play? Aristotle offers his most sustained answer to these questions in his discussion of politics.

What's the Purpose of Politics?

When we discuss distributive justice these days, we are concerned mainly with the distribution of income, wealth, and opportunities. For Aristotle, distributive justice was not mainly about money but about offices and honors. Who should have the right to rule? How should political authority be distributed?

At first glance, the answer seems obvious—equally, of course. One person, one vote. Any other way would be discriminatory. But Aristotle reminds us that all theories of distributive justice discriminate. The question is: Which discriminations are just? And the answer depends on the purpose of the activity in question.

So, before we can say how political rights and authority should be distributed, we have to inquire into the purpose, or telos, of politics. We have to ask, "What is political association *for?*"

This may seem an unanswerable question. Different political communities care about different things. It's one thing to argue about the purpose of a flute, or a university. Notwithstanding the room for disagreement at the margins, their purposes are more or less circumscribed. The purpose of a flute has something to do with making music; the purpose of a university has something to do with education. But can we really determine the purpose or goal of political activity as such?

These days, we don't think of politics as such as having some particular, substantive end, but as being open to the various ends that citizens may espouse. Isn't that why we have elections—so that people can choose, at any given moment, what purposes and ends they want collectively to pursue? To attribute some purpose or end to political community in advance would seem to preempt the right of citizens to decide for themselves. It would also risk imposing values not everyone shares. Our reluctance to invest politics with a determinate telos, or end, reflects a concern for individual freedom. We view politics as a procedure that enables persons to choose their ends for themselves.

Aristotle doesn't see it this way. For Aristotle, the purpose of politics is not to set up a framework of rights that is neutral among ends. It is to form good citizens and to cultivate good character.

> [A]ny polis which is truly so called, and is not merely one in name, must devote itself to the end of encouraging goodness. Otherwise, a political association sinks into a mere alliance . . . Otherwise, too, law becomes a mere covenant . . . "a guarantor of men's rights against one another"—instead of being, as it should be, a rule of life such as will make the members of a polis good and just.[5]

Aristotle criticizes what he takes to be the two major claimants to political authority—oligarchs and democrats. Each has a claim, he says, but only a partial claim. The oligarchs maintain that they, the wealthy, should rule. The democrats maintain that free birth should be the sole criterion of citizenship and political authority. But both groups exaggerate their claims, because both misconstrue the purpose of political community.

The oligarchs are wrong because political community isn't only about protecting property or promoting economic prosperity. If it were only about those things, then property owners would deserve the greatest share of political authority. For their part, the democrats are wrong because political community isn't only about giving the majority its way. By *democrats*, Aristotle means what we would call majoritarians. He rejects the notion that the purpose of politics is to satisfy the preferences of the majority.

Both sides overlook the highest end of political association, which for Aristotle is to cultivate the virtue of citizens. The end of the state is not "to provide an alliance for mutual defence . . . or to ease economic exchange and promote economic intercourse."[6] For Aristotle, politics is about something higher. It's about learning how to live a good life.

The purpose of politics is nothing less than to enable people to develop their distinctive human capacities and virtues—to deliberate about the common good, to acquire practical judgment, to share in self-government, to care for the fate of the community as a whole.

Aristotle acknowledges the usefulness of other, lesser forms of association, such as defense pacts and free trade agreements. But he insists that associations of this kind don't amount to true political communities. Why not? Because their ends are limited. Organizations such as NATO and NAFTA and the WTO are concerned only with security or economic exchange; they don't constitute a shared way of life that shapes the character of the participants. And the same can be said of a city or a state concerned only with security and trade and that is indifferent to the moral and civic education of its members. "If the spirit of their intercourse were still the same after their coming together as it had been when they were living apart," Aristotle writes, their association can't really be considered a polis, or political community.[7]

"A polis is not an association for residence on a common site, or for the sake of preventing mutual injustice and easing exchange." While these conditions are necessary to a polis, they are not sufficient. "The end and purpose of a polis is the good life, and the institutions of social life are means to that end."[8]

If the political community exists to promote the good life, what are the implications for the distribution of offices and honors? As with flutes, so with politics: Aristotle reasons from the purpose of the good to the appropriate way of distributing it. "Those who contribute most to an association of this character" are those who excel in civic virtue, those who are best at deliberating about the common good. Those who are greatest in civic excellence—not the wealthiest, or the most numerous, or the most handsome—are the ones who merit the greatest share of political recognition and influence.[9]

Since the end of politics is the good life, the highest offices and honors should go to people, such as Pericles, who are greatest in civic virtue and best at identifying the common good. Property holders should have their say. Majoritarian considerations should matter some. But the greatest influence should go to those with the qualities of character and judgment to decide if and when and how to go to war with Sparta.

The reason people such as Pericles (and Abraham Lincoln) should hold the highest offices and honors is not simply that they will enact wise policies, making everyone better off. It is also that political community exists, at least in part, to honor and reward civic virtue. According public recognition to those who display civic excellence serves the educative role of the good city. Here again, we see how the teleological and honorific aspects of justice go together.

Can You Be a Good Person If You Don't Participate in Politics?

If Aristotle is right that the end of politics is the good life, it's easy to conclude that those who display the greatest civic virtue merit the highest offices and honors. But is he right that politics is for the sake of the good life? This is, at best, a controversial claim. These days, we generally view politics as a necessary evil, not an essential feature of the good life. When we think of politics, we think of compromise, posturing, special interests, corruption. Even idealistic uses of politics—as an instrument of social justice, as a way to make the world a better place—cast politics as a means to an end, one calling among others, not as an essential aspect of the human good.

Why, then, does Aristotle think that participating in politics is somehow essential to living a good life? Why can't we live perfectly good, virtuous lives without politics?

The answer lies in our nature. Only by living in a polis and participating in politics do we fully realize our nature as human beings. Aristotle sees us as beings "meant for political association, in a higher degree than bees or other gregarious animals." The reason he gives is this: Nature makes nothing in vain, and human beings, unlike other animals, are furnished with the faculty of language. Other animals can make sounds, and sounds can indicate pleasure and pain. But language, a distinctly human capacity, isn't just for registering pleasure and pain. It's about declaring what is just and what is unjust, and distinguishing right from wrong. We don't grasp these things silently, and then put words to them; language is the medium through which we discern and deliberate about the good.[10]

Only in political association, Aristotle claims, can we exercise our distinctly human capacity for language, for only in a polis do we deliberate with others about justice and injustice and the nature of the good life. "We thus see that the polis exists by nature and that it is prior to the individual," he writes in Book I of *The Politics*.[11] By *prior*, he means prior in function, or purpose, not chronologically prior. Individuals, families, and clans existed before cities did; but only in the polis are we able to realize our nature. We are not self-sufficient when we are isolated, because we can't yet develop our capacity for language and moral deliberation.

The man who is isolated—who is unable to share in the benefits of political association, or has no need to share because he is already self-sufficient—is no part of the polis, and must therefore be either a beast or a god.[12]

So we only fulfill our nature when we exercise our faculty of language, which requires in turn that we deliberate with others about right and wrong, good and evil, justice and injustice.

But why, you might wonder, can we exercise this capacity for language and deliberation only in politics? Why can't we do it in families, clans, or clubs? To answer this question, we need to consider the account of virtue and the good life that Aristotle presents in the *Nicomachean Ethics*. Although this work is primarily about moral philosophy, it shows how acquiring virtue is bound up with being a citizen.

The moral life aims at happiness, but by *happiness* Aristotle doesn't mean what the utilitarians mean—maximizing the balance of pleasure over pain. The virtuous person is someone who takes pleasure and pain in the right things. If someone takes pleasure in watching dog fights, for example, we consider this a vice to be overcome, not a true source of happiness. Moral excellence does not consist in aggregating pleasures and pains but in aligning them, so that we delight in noble things and take pain in base ones. Happiness is not a state of mind but a way of being, "an activity of the soul in accordance with virtue."[13]

But why is it necessary to live in a polis to live a virtuous life? Why can't we learn sound moral principles at home, or in a philosophy class, or by reading a book about ethics—and then apply them as needed? Aristotle says we don't become virtuous that way. "Moral virtue comes about as a result of habit." It's the kind of thing we learn by doing. "The virtues we get by first exercising them, as also happens in the case of the arts as well."[14]

Learning by Doing

In this respect, becoming virtuous is like learning to play the flute. No one learns how to play a musical instrument by reading a book or listening to a lecture. You have to practice. And it helps to listen to accomplished musicians, and hear how they play. You can't become a violinist without fiddling. So it is with moral virtue: "we become just by doing just acts, temperate by doing temperate acts, brave by doing brave acts."[15]

It is similar with other practices and skills, such as cooking. Many cookbooks are published, but no one becomes a great chef simply by reading them. You have to do lots of cooking. Joke telling is another example. You don't become a comedian by reading joke books and collecting funny stories. Nor could you simply learn the principles of comedy. You have to practice—the pacing, timing, gestures, and tone—and watch Jack Benny, or Johnny Carson, or Eddie Murphy, or Robin Williams.

If moral virtue is something we learn by doing, we have somehow to develop the right habits in the first place. For Aristotle, this is the primary purpose of law—to cultivate the habits that lead to good character. "Legislators make the citizens good by forming habits in them, and this is the wish of every legislator, and those who do not effect it miss their mark, and it is in this that a good constitution differs from a bad one." Moral education is less about promulgating rules than forming habits and shaping character. "It makes no small difference . . . whether we form habits of one kind or of another from our very youth; it makes a very great difference, or rather *all* the difference."[16]

Aristotle's emphasis on habit does not mean he considers moral virtue a form of rote behavior. Habit is the first step in moral education. But if all goes well, the habit eventually takes, and we come to see the point of it. The etiquette columnist Judith Martin (aka "Miss Manners") once bemoaned the lost habit of writing thank-you letters. Nowadays we assume that feelings trump manners, she observed; as long as you feel grateful, you don't need to bother with such formalities. Miss Manners disagrees: "I think, to the contrary, that it is safer to hope that practicing proper behavior eventually encourages virtuous feeling; that if you write enough thank-you letters, you may actually feel a flicker of gratitude."[17]

That's how Aristotle conceives moral virtue. Being steeped in virtuous behavior helps us acquire the disposition to act virtuously.

It is common to think that acting morally means acting according to a precept or a rule. But Aristotle thinks this misses a distinctive feature of moral virtue. You could be equipped with the right rule and still not know how or when to apply it. Moral education is about learning to discern the particular features of situations that call for this rule rather than that one. "Matters concerned with conduct and questions of what is good for us have no fixity, any more than matters of health . . . The agents themselves must in each case consider what is appropriate to the occasion, as happens also in the art of medicine or of navigation."[18]

The only general thing that can be said about moral virtue, Aristotle tells us, is that it consists of a mean between extremes. But he readily concedes that this generality doesn't get us very far, because discerning the mean in any given situation is not easy. The challenge is to do the right thing "to the right person, to the right extent, at the right time, with the right motive, and in the right way."[19]

This means that habit, however essential, can't be the whole of moral virtue. New situations always arise, and we need to know which habit is appropriate under the circumstances. Moral virtue therefore requires judgment, a kind of knowledge Aristotle calls "practical wisdom." Unlike scientific knowledge, which concerns "things that are universal and necessary,"[20] practical wisdom is about how to act. It must "recognize the particulars; for it is practical, and practice is concerned with particulars."[21] Aristotle defines practical wisdom as "a reasoned and true state of capacity to act with regard to the human good."[22]

Practical wisdom is a moral virtue with political implications. People with practical wisdom can deliberate well about what is good, not only for themselves but for their fellow citizens, and for human beings in general. Deliberation is not philosophizing, because it attends to what is changeable and particular. It is oriented to action in the here and now. But it is more than calculation. It seeks to identify the highest human good attainable under the circumstances.[23]

Politics and the Good Life

We can now see more clearly why, for Aristotle, politics is not one calling among others, but is essential to the good life. First, the laws of the polis inculcate good habits, form good character, and set us on the way to civic virtue. Second, the life of the citizen enables us to exercise capacities for deliberation and practical wisdom that would otherwise lie dormant. This is not the kind of thing we can do at home. We can sit on the sidelines and wonder what policies we would favor if we had to decide. But this is not the same as sharing in significant action and bearing responsibility for the fate of the community as a whole. We become good at deliberating only by entering the arena, weighing the alternatives, arguing our case, ruling and being ruled—in short, by being citizens.

Aristotle's vision of citizenship is more elevated and strenuous than ours. For him, politics is not economics by other means. Its purpose is higher than maximizing utility or providing fair rules for the pursuit of individual interests. It is, instead, an expression of our nature, an occasion for the unfolding of our human capacities, an essential aspect of the good life.

Aristotle's Defense of Slavery

Not everyone was included in the citizenship Aristotle celebrated. Women were ineligible, as were slaves. According to Aristotle, their natures did not suit them to be citizens. We now see such exclusion as an obvious injustice. It's worth recalling that these injustices persisted for more than two thousand years after Aristotle wrote. Slavery was not abolished in the United States until 1865, and women won the right to vote only in 1920. Still, the historic persistence of these injustices does not exonerate Aristotle for accepting them.

In the case of slavery, Aristotle not only accepted it but offered a philosophical justification. It's worth examining his defense of slavery to see what light it sheds on his political theory as a whole. Some see in Aristotle's argument for slavery a defect in teleological thinking as such; others see it as misguided application of such thinking, beclouded by the prejudices of his time.

I don't think Aristotle's defense of slavery reveals a flaw that condemns his political theory as a whole. But it's important to see the force of that thoroughgoing claim.

For Aristotle, justice is a matter of fit. To allocate rights is to look for the telos of social institutions, and to fit persons to the roles that suit them, the roles that enable them to realize their nature. Giving persons their due means giving them the offices and honors they deserve and the social roles that accord with their nature.

Modern political theories are uneasy with the notion of fit. Liberal theories of justice, from Kant to Rawls, worry that teleological conceptions are at odds with freedom. For them, justice is not about fit but about choice. To allocate rights is not to fit people to roles that suit their nature; it is to let people choose their roles for themselves.

From this point of view, the notions of telos and fit are suspect, even dangerous. Who is to say what role is fitting for me, or appropriate to my nature? If I'm not free to choose my social role for myself, I might well be forced into a role against my will. So the notion of fit can easily slide into slavery, if those in power decide that a certain group is somehow suited for a subordinate role.

Prompted by this worry, liberal political theory argues that social roles should be allocated by choice, not fit. Rather than fit people to roles we think will suit their nature, we should enable people to choose their roles for themselves. Slavery is wrong, in this view, because it coerces people into roles they have not chosen. The solution is to reject an ethic of telos and fit in favor of an ethic of choice and consent.

But this conclusion is too quick. Aristotle's defense of slavery is no proof against teleological thinking. On the contrary, Aristotle's own theory of justice provides ample resources for a critique of his views on slavery. In fact, his notion of justice as fit is more morally demanding, and potentially more critical of existing allocations of work, than theories based on choice and consent. To see how this is so, let's examine Aristotle's argument.

For slavery to be just, according to Aristotle, two conditions must be met: it must be necessary, and it must be natural. Slavery is necessary, Aristotle argues, because someone must look after the household chores if citizens are to spend time in the assembly deliberating about the common good. The polis requires a division of labor. Unless we invent machines that could take care of all menial tasks, some people have to attend to the necessities of life so that others can be free to participate in politics.

So Aristotle concludes that slavery is necessary. But necessity is not enough. For slavery to be just, it must also be the case that certain persons are suited by their nature to perform this role.[24] So Aristotle

asks if there are "persons for whom slavery is the better and just condition, or whether the reverse is the case and all slavery is contrary to
nature."[25] Unless there are such people, the political and economic
need for slaves is not enough to justify slavery.

Aristotle concludes that such people exist. Some people are born
to be slaves. They differ from ordinary people in the same way that the
body differs from the soul. Such people "are by nature slaves, and it is
better for them . . . to be ruled by a master."[26]

"A man is thus by nature a slave if he is capable of becoming (and
this is the reason why he also actually becomes) the property of another, and if he participates in reason to the extent of apprehending it
in another, though destitute of it himself.[27]

"[J]ust as some are by nature free, so others are by nature slaves,
and for these latter the condition of slavery is both beneficial and
just."[28]

Aristotle seems to sense something questionable in the claim he is
making, because he quickly qualifies it: "But it is easy to see that those
who hold an opposite view are also in a way correct."[29] Looking at
slavery as it existed in the Athens of his day, Aristotle had to admit that
the critics had a point. Many slaves found themselves in that condition
for a purely contingent reason: they were formerly free people who
had been captured in war. Their status as slaves had nothing to do with
their being fit for the role. For them, slavery was not natural, but the
result of bad luck. By Aristotle's own standard, their slavery is unjust:
"Not all those who are actually slaves, or actually freemen, are natural
slaves or natural freemen."[30]

How can you tell who is fit to be a slave? Aristotle asks. In principle,
you would have to see who, if anyone, flourishes as a slave, and who
chafes in the role or tries to flee. The need for force is a good indica-
tion that the slave in question is not suited to the role.[31] For Aristotle,
coercion is a sign of injustice, not because consent legitimates all roles,
but because the need for force suggests an unnatural fit. Those who are
cast in a role consistent with their nature don't need to be forced.

For liberal political theory, slavery is unjust because it is coercive. For teleological theories, slavery is unjust because it is at odds with our nature; coercion is a symptom of the injustice, not the source of it. It is perfectly possible to explain, within the ethic of telos and fit, the injustice of slavery, and Aristotle goes some way (though not all the way) toward doing so.

The ethic of telos and fit actually sets a more demanding moral standard for justice in the workplace than does the liberal ethic of choice and consent.[32] Consider a repetitive, dangerous job, such as working long hours on an assembly line in a chicken processing plant. Is this form of labor just or unjust?

For the libertarian, the answer would depend on whether the workers had freely exchanged their labor for a wage: if they did, the work is just. For Rawls, the arrangement would be just only if the free exchange of labor took place against fair background conditions. For Aristotle, even consent against fair background conditions is not sufficient; for the work to be just, it has to be suited to the nature of the workers who perform it. Some jobs fail this test. They are so dangerous, repetitive, and deadening as to be unfit for human beings. In those cases, justice requires that the work be reorganized to accord with our nature. Otherwise, the job is unjust in the same way that slavery is.

Casey Martin's Golf Cart

Casey Martin was a professional golfer with a bad leg. Due to a circulatory disorder, walking the course caused Martin considerable pain and posed a serious risk of hemorrhaging and fracture. Despite his disability, Martin had always excelled at the sport. He played on Stanford's championship team while in college, then turned pro.

Martin asked the PGA (Professional Golfers' Association) for permission to use a golf cart during tournaments. The PGA turned him down, citing its rule prohibiting carts in top professional tournaments.

Martin took his case to court. He argued that the Americans with Disabilities Act (1990) required reasonable accommodations for people with disabilities, provided the change did not "fundamentally alter the nature" of the activity.[33]

Some of the biggest names in golf testified in the case. Arnold Palmer, Jack Nicklaus, and Ken Venturi all defended the ban on carts. They argued that fatigue is an important factor in tournament golf, and that riding rather than walking would give Martin an unfair advantage.

The case went to the United States Supreme Court, where the justices found themselves wrestling with what seemed to one a silly question, at once beneath their dignity and beyond their expertise: "Is someone riding around a golf course from shot to shot *really* a golfer?"[34]

In fact, however, the case raised a question of justice in classic Aristotelian form: In order to decide whether Martin had a right to a golf cart, the Court had to determine the essential nature of the activity in question. Was walking the course essential to golf, or merely incidental? If, as the PGA claimed, walking was an essential aspect of the sport, then to let Martin ride in a cart would "fundamentally alter the nature" of the game. To resolve the question about rights, the court had to determine the telos, or essential nature, of the game.

The Court ruled 7–2 that Martin had a right to use a golf cart. Justice John Paul Stevens, writing for the majority, analyzed the history of golf and concluded that the use of carts was not inconsistent with the fundamental character of the game. "From early on, the essence of the game has been shot-making—using clubs to cause a ball to progress from the teeing ground to a hole some distance away with as few strokes as possible."[35] As for the claim that walking tests the physical stamina of golfers, Stevens cited testimony by a physiology professor who calculated that only about five hundred calories were expended in walking eighteen holes, "nutritionally less than a Big Mac."[36] Because golf is "a low intensity activity, fatigue from the game is primarily a psychological phenomenon in which stress and motivation are the key ingredients."[37] The Court concluded that accommodating Martin's disability by letting him ride in a cart would not fundamentally alter the game or give him an unfair advantage.

Justice Antonin Scalia disagreed. In a spirited dissent, he rejected the notion that the Court could determine the essential nature of golf. His point was not simply that judges lack the authority or competence to decide the question. He challenged the Aristotelian premise underlying the Court's opinion—that it is possible to reason about the telos, or essential nature of a game:

> To say that something is "essential" is ordinarily to say that it is necessary to the achievement of a certain object. But since it is the very nature of a game to have no object except amusement (that is what distinguishes games from productive activity), it is quite impossible to say that any of a game's arbitrary rules is "essential."[38]

Since the rules of golf "are (as in all games) entirely arbitrary," Scalia wrote, there is no basis for critically assessing the rules laid down by the PGA. If the fans don't like them, "they can withdraw their patronage." But no one can say that this or that rule is irrelevant to the skills that golf is meant to test.

Scalia's argument is questionable on several grounds. First, it disparages sports. No real fan would speak of sports that way—as governed by totally arbitrary rules and having no real object or point. If people really believed that the rules of their favorite sport were arbitrary rather than designed to call forth and celebrate certain skills and talents worth admiring, it would be hard for them to care about the outcome of the game. Sport would fade into spectacle, a source of amusement rather than a subject of appreciation.

Second, it's perfectly possible to argue the merits of different rules, and to ask whether they improve or corrupt the game. These arguments take place all the time—on radio call-in shows and among those who govern the game. Consider the debate over the designated-hitter rule in baseball. Some say it improves the game by enabling the best hitters to bat, sparing weak-hitting pitchers the ordeal. Others say it damages the game by overemphasizing hitting and removing complex elements of strategy. Each position rests on a certain conception of what baseball at its best is all about: What skills does it test, what talents and virtues does it celebrate and reward? The debate over the designated-hitter rule is ultimately a debate about the telos of baseball—just as the debate over affirmative action is a debate about the purpose of the university.

Finally, Scalia, by denying that golf has a telos, misses altogether the honorific aspect of the dispute. What, after all, was the four-year saga over the golf cart really about? On the surface, it was an argument about fairness. The PGA and the golfing greats claimed that allowing Martin to ride would give him an unfair advantage; Martin replied that, given his disability, the cart would simply level the playing field.

If fairness were the only thing at stake, however, there is an easy and obvious solution: let all golfers use carts in the tournaments. If everyone can ride, the fairness objection disappears. But this solution was anathema to professional golf, even more unthinkable than making an exception for Casey Martin. Why? Because the dispute was less about fairness than about honor and recognition—specifically the desire of the PGA and top golfers that their sport be recognized and respected as an athletic event.

Let me put the point as delicately as possible: Golfers are somewhat sensitive about the status of their game. It involves no running or jumping, and the ball stands still. No one doubts that golf is a demanding game of skill. But the honor and recognition accorded great golfers depends on their sport being seen as a physically demanding athletic competition. If the game at which they excel can be played while riding in a cart, their recognition as athletes could be questioned or diminished. This may explain the vehemence with which some professional golfers opposed Casey Martin's bid for a cart. Here is Tom Kite, a twenty-five-year veteran of the PGA Tour, in an op-ed piece in *The New York Times*:

> It seems to me that those who support Casey Martin's right to use a cart are ignoring the fact that we are talking about a competitive sport. . . . We are talking about an athletic event. And anyone who doesn't think professional golf is an athletic sport simply hasn't been there or done that.[39]

Whoever is right about the essential nature of golf, the federal case over Casey Martin's cart offers a vivid illustration of Aristotle's theory of justice. Debates about justice and rights are often, unavoidably, debates about the purpose of social institutions, the goods they allocate, and the virtues they honor and reward. Despite our best attempts to make law neutral on such questions, it may not be possible to say what's just without arguing about the nature of the good life.

9. WHAT DO WE OWE ONE ANOTHER? / DILEMMAS OF LOYALTY

It's never easy to say, "I'm sorry." But saying so in public, on behalf of one's nation, can be especially difficult. Recent decades have brought a spate of anguished arguments over public apologies for historic injustices.

Apologies and Reparations

Much of the fraught politics of apology involves historic wrongs committed during World War II. Germany has paid the equivalent of billions of dollars in reparations for the Holocaust, in the form of payments to individual survivors and to the state of Israel.[1] Over the years, German political leaders have offered statements of apology, accepting responsibility for the Nazi past in varying degrees. In a speech to the Bundestag in 1951, German chancellor Konrad Adenauer claimed that "the overwhelming majority of the German people abominated the crimes committed against the Jews and did not participate in them." But he acknowledged that "unspeakable crimes have been committed in the name of the German people, calling for moral and material indemnity."[2] In 2000, German president Johannes Rau apologized for the Holocaust in a speech to the Israeli Knesset, asking "forgiveness for what Germans have done."[3]

Japan has been more reluctant to apologize for its wartime atroci-
ties. During the 1930s and '40s, tens of thousands of Korean and other
Asian women and girls were forced into brothels and abused as sex
slaves by Japanese soldiers.[4] Since the 1990s, Japan has faced growing
international pressure for a formal apology and restitution to the so-
called "comfort women." In the 1990s, a private fund offered payments
to the victims, and Japanese leaders made limited apologies.[5] But as
recently as 2007, Japanese prime minister Shinzo Abe insisted that the
Japanese military was not responsible for coercing the women into
sexual slavery. The U.S. Congress responded by passing a resolution
urging the Japanese government to formally acknowledge and apologize for its military's role in enslaving the comfort women.[6]

Other apology controversies involve historic injustices to indigenous peoples. In Australia, debate has raged in recent years over the
government's obligation to the aboriginal people. From the 1910s
to the early 1970s, aboriginal children of mixed race were forcibly
separated from their mothers and placed in white foster homes or settlement camps. (In most of these cases, the mothers were aborigines
and the fathers white.) The policy sought to assimilate the children to
white society and speed the disappearance of aboriginal culture.[7] The
government-sanctioned kidnappings are portrayed in *Rabbit-Proof Fence*
(2002), a movie that tells the story of three young girls who, in 1931,
escape from a settlement camp and set out on a 1,200-mile journey to
return to their mothers.

In 1997, an Australian human rights commission documented the
cruelties inflicted on the "stolen generation" of aborigines, and recom-
mended an annual day of national apology.[8] John Howard, the prime
minister at the time, opposed an official apology. The apology question
became a contentious issue in Australian politics. In 2008, newly
elected prime minister Kevin Rudd issued an official apology to the
aboriginal people. Although he did not offer individual compensation,
he promised measures to overcome the social and economic disadvantages suffered by Australia's indigenous population.[9]

In the United States, debates over public apologies and reparations have also gained prominence in recent decades. In 1988, President Ronald Reagan signed into law an official apology to Japanese Americans for their confinement in internment camps on the West Coast during World War II.[10] In addition to an apology, the legislation provided compensation of $20,000 to each survivor of the camps, and funds to promote Japanese American culture and history. In 1993, Congress apologized for a more distant historic wrong—the overthrow, a century earlier, of the independent kingdom of Hawaii.[11]

Perhaps the biggest looming apology question in the United States involves the legacy of slavery. The Civil War promise of "forty acres and a mule" for freed slaves never came to be. In the 1990s, the movement for black reparations gained new attention.[12] Every year since 1989, Congressman John Conyers has proposed legislation to create a commission to study reparations for African Americans.[13] Although the reparations idea has won support from many African American organizations and civil rights groups, it has not caught on with the general public.[14] Polls show that while a majority of African Americans favor reparations, only 4 percent of whites do.[15]

Although the reparations movement may have stalled, recent years have brought a wave of official apologies. In 2007, Virginia, which had been the largest slaveholding state, became the first to apologize for slavery.[16] A number of other states, including Alabama, Maryland, North Carolina, New Jersey, and Florida, followed.[17] And in 2008, the U.S. House of Representatives passed a resolution apologizing to African Americans for slavery and for the Jim Crow era of racial segregation that extended into the mid-twentieth century.[18]

Should nations apologize for historic wrongs? To answer this question, we need to think through some hard questions about collective responsibility and the claims of community.

The main justifications for public apologies are to honor the memory of those who have suffered injustice at the hands (or in the name) of the political community, to recognize the persisting effects of injustice on victims and their descendants, and to atone for the wrongs committed by those who inflicted the injustice or failed to prevent it. As public gestures, official apologies can help bind up the wounds of the past and provide a basis for moral and political reconciliation. Reparations and other forms of financial restitution can be justified on similar grounds, as tangible expressions of apology and atonement. They can also help alleviate the effects of the injustice on the victims or their heirs.

Whether these considerations are strong enough to justify an apology depends on the circumstances. In some cases, attempts to bring about public apologies or reparations may do more harm than good—by inflaming old animosities, hardening historic enmities, entrenching a sense of victimhood, or generating resentment. Opponents of public apologies often voice worries such as these. Whether, all things considered, an act of apology or restitution is more likely to heal or damage a political community is a complex matter of political judgment. The answer will vary from case to case.

Should We Atone for the Sins of our Predecessors?

But I would like to focus on another argument often raised by opponents of apologies for historic injustices—a principled argument that does not depend on the contingencies of the situation. This is the argument that people in the present generation should not—in fact, cannot—apologize for wrongs committed by previous generations.[19] To apologize for an injustice is, after all, to take some responsibility for it. You can't apologize for something you didn't do. So, how can you apologize for something that was done before you were born?

John Howard, the Australian prime minister, gave this reason for rejecting an official apology to the aborigines: "I do not believe that the current generation of Australians should formally apologize and accept responsibility for the deeds of an earlier generation."[20]

A similar argument was made in the U.S. debate over reparations for slavery. Henry Hyde, a Republican congressman, criticized the idea of reparations on these grounds: "I never owned a slave. I never oppressed anybody. I don't know that I should have to pay for someone who did [own slaves] generations before I was born."[21] Walter E. Williams, an African American economist who opposes reparations, voiced a similar view: "If the government got the money from the tooth fairy or Santa Claus, that'd be great. But the government has to take the money from citizens, and there are no citizens alive today who were responsible for slavery."[22]

Taxing today's citizens to pay reparations for a past wrong may seem to raise a special problem. But the same issue arises in debates over apologies that involve no financial compensation.

With apologies, it's the thought that counts. The thought at stake is the acknowledgment of responsibility. Anyone can deplore an injustice. But only someone who is somehow implicated in the injustice can apologize for it. Critics of apologies correctly grasp the moral stakes. And they reject the idea that the current generation can be morally responsible for the sins of their forebears.

When the New Jersey state legislature debated the apology question in 2008, a Republican assemblyman asked, "Who living today is guilty of slaveholding and thus capable of apologizing for the offense?" The obvious answer, he thought, was no one: "Today's residents of New Jersey, even those who can trace their ancestry back to . . . slaveholders, bear no collective guilt or responsibility for unjust events in which they personally played no role."[23]

As the U.S. House of Representatives prepared to vote an apology for slavery and segregation, a Republican critic of the measure compared it to apologizing for deeds carried out by your "great-great-great-grandfather."[24]

Moral Individualism

The principled objection to official apologies is not easy to dismiss. It rests on the notion that we are responsible only for what we ourselves do, not for the actions of other people, or for events beyond our control. We are not answerable for the sins of our parents or our grand-parents or, for that matter, our compatriots.

But this puts the matter negatively. The principled objection to official apologies carries weight because it draws on a powerful and attractive moral idea. We might call it the idea of "moral individualism." The doctrine of moral individualism does not assume that people are selfish. It is rather a claim about what it means to be free. For the moral individualist, to be free is to be subject only to obligations I voluntarily incur; whatever I owe others, I owe by virtue of some act of consent—a choice or a promise or an agreement I have made, be it tacit or explicit.

The notion that my responsibilities are limited to the ones I take upon myself is a liberating one. It assumes that we are, as moral agents, free and independent selves, unbound by prior moral ties, capable of choosing our ends for ourselves. Not custom or tradition or inherited status, but the free choice of each individual is the source of the only moral obligations that constrain us.

You can see how this vision of freedom leaves little room for collective responsibility, or for a duty to bear the moral burden of historic injustices perpetrated by our predecessors. If I promised my grandfather to pay his debts or apologize for his sins, that would be one thing. My duty to carry out the recompense would be an obligation founded on consent, not an obligation arising from a collective identity extending across generations. Absent some such promise, the moral individualist can make no sense of a responsibility to atone for the sins of my predecessors. The sins, after all, were theirs, not mine.

If the moral individualist vision of freedom is right, then the critics of official apologies have a point; we bear no moral burden for the wrongs of our predecessors. But far more than apologies and collective responsibility are at stake. The individualist view of freedom figures in many of the theories of justice most familiar in contemporary politics. If that conception of freedom is flawed, as I believe it is, then we need to rethink some of the fundamental features of our public life.

As we have seen, the notions of consent and free choice loom large, not only in contemporary politics, but also in modern theories of justice. Let's look back and see how various notions of choice and consent have come to inform our present-day assumptions.

An early version of the choosing self comes to us from John Locke. He argued that legitimate government must be based on consent. Why? Because we are free and independent beings, not subject to paternal authority or the divine right of kings. Since we are "by nature, all free, equal and independent, no one can be put out of this estate, and subjected to the political power of another, without his own consent."[25]

A century later, Immanuel Kant offered a more powerful version of the choosing self. Against the utilitarian and empiricist philosophers, Kant argued that we must think of ourselves as more than a bundle of preferences and desires. To be free is to be autonomous, and to be autonomous is to be governed by a law I give myself. Kantian autonomy is more demanding than consent. When I will the moral law, I don't simply choose according to my contingent desires or allegiances. Instead, I step back from my particular interests and attachments, and will as a participant in pure practical reason.

In the twentieth century, John Rawls adapted Kant's conception of the autonomous self and drew upon it in his theory of justice. Like Kant, Rawls observed that the choices we make often reflect morally arbitrary contingencies. Someone's choice to work in a sweatshop, for example, might reflect dire economic necessity, not free choice in any meaningful sense. So if we want society to be a voluntary arrangement, we can't base it on actual consent; we should ask instead what principles of justice we would agree to if we set aside our particular interests and advantages, and chose behind a veil of ignorance.

Kant's idea of an autonomous will and Rawls's idea of a hypothetical agreement behind a veil of ignorance have this in common: both conceive the moral agent as independent of his or her particular aims and attachments. When we will the moral law (Kant) or choose the principles of justice (Rawls), we do so without reference to the roles and identities that situate us in the world and make us the particular people we are.

If, in thinking about justice, we must abstract from our particular identities, it is hard to make the case that present-day Germans bear a special responsibility to make recompense for the Holocaust, or that Americans of this generation have a special responsibility to remedy the injustice of slavery and segregation. Why? Because once I set aside my identity as a German or an American and conceive myself as a free and independent self, there is no basis for saying my obligation to remedy these historic injustices is greater than anyone else's.

Conceiving persons as free and independent selves doesn't only make a difference for questions of collective responsibility across generations. It also has a more far-reaching implication: Thinking of the moral agent in this way carries consequences for the way we think about justice more generally. The notion that we are freely choosing, independent selves supports the idea that the principles of justice that define our rights should not rest on any particular moral or religious conception; instead, they should try to be neutral among competing visions of the good life.

Should Government Be Morally Neutral?

The idea that government should try to be neutral on the meaning of the good life represents a departure from ancient conceptions of politics. For Aristotle, the purpose of politics is not only to ease economic exchange and provide for the common defense; it is also to cultivate good character and form good citizens. Arguments about justice are therefore, unavoidably, arguments about the good life. "Before we can [investigate] the nature of an ideal constitution," Aristotle wrote, "it is necessary for us first to determine the nature of the most desirable way of life. As long as that is obscure, the nature of the ideal constitution must also remain obscure."[26]

These days, the notion that politics is about cultivating virtue strikes many as strange, even dangerous. Who is to say what virtue consists in? And what if people disagree? If the law seeks to promote certain moral and religious ideals, doesn't this open the way to intolerance and coercion? When we think of states that try to promote virtue, we don't think first of the Athenian polis; we think rather of religious fundamentalism, past and present—stonings for adultery, mandatory burkas, Salem witch trials, and so on.

For Kant and Rawls, theories of justice that rest on a certain conception of the good life, whether religious or secular, are at odds with freedom. By imposing on some the values of others, such theories fail to respect persons as free and independent selves, capable of choosing their own purposes and ends. So the freely choosing self and the neutral state go hand in hand: It is precisely because we are free and independent selves that we need a framework of rights that is neutral among ends, that refuses to take sides in moral and religious controversies, that leaves citizens free to choose their values for themselves.

Some might object that no theory of justice and rights can be morally neutral. On one level, this is obviously true. Kant and Rawls are not moral relativists. The idea that persons should be free to choose their ends for themselves is itself a powerful moral idea. But it does not tell you how to live your life. It only requires that, whatever ends you pursue, you do so in a way that respects other people's rights to do the same. The appeal of a neutral framework lies precisely in its refusal to affirm a preferred way of life or conception of the good.

Kant and Rawls do not deny they are advancing certain moral ideals. Their quarrel is with theories of justice that derive rights from some conception of the good. Utilitarianism is one such theory. It takes the good to consist in maximizing pleasure or welfare, and asks what system of rights is likely to achieve it. Aristotle offers a very different theory of the good. It is not about maximizing pleasure but about realizing our nature and developing our distinctly human capacities. Aristotle's reasoning is teleological in that he reasons from a certain conception of the human good.

This is the mode of reasoning that Kant and Rawls reject. They argue that the right is prior to the good. The principles that specify our duties and rights should not be based on any particular conception of the good life. Kant writes of "the confusion of the philosophers concerning the supreme principle of morals." The ancient philosophers made the mistake of "devoting their ethical investigations entirely to the definition of the concept of the highest good," and then trying to make this good "the determining ground of the moral law."[27] But according to Kant, this has things backward. It is also at odds with freedom. If we are to think of ourselves as autonomous beings, we must first will the moral law. Only then, after we've arrived at the principle that defines our duties and rights, can we ask what conceptions of the good are compatible with it.

Rawls makes a similar point with respect to principles of justice: "The liberties of equal citizenship are insecure when founded upon teleological principles."[28] It is easy to see how resting rights on utilitarian calculations leaves rights vulnerable. If the only reason to respect my right to religious liberty is to promote the general happiness, what happens if someday a large majority despises my religion and wants to ban it?

But utilitarian theories of justice are not the only targets of Rawls and Kant. If the right is prior to the good, then Aristotle's way of thinking about justice is also mistaken. For Aristotle, to reason about justice is to reason from the telos, or nature, of the good in question. To think about a just political order, we have to reason from the nature of the good life. We can't frame a just constitution until we first figure out the best way to live. Rawls disagrees: "[T]he structure of teleological doctrines is radically misconceived: from the start they relate the right and the good in the wrong way. We should not attempt to give form to our life by first looking to the good independently defined."[29]

Justice and Freedom

At stake in this debate is more than the abstract question of how we should reason about justice. The debate over the priority of the right over the good is ultimately a debate about the meaning of human freedom. Kant and Rawls reject Aristotle's teleology because it doesn't seem to leave us room to choose our good for ourselves. It is easy to see how Aristotle's theory gives rise to this worry. He sees justice as a matter of fit between persons and the ends or goods appropriate to their nature. But we are inclined to see justice as a matter of choice, not fit.

Rawls's case for the priority of the right over the good reflects the conviction that a "moral person is a subject with ends he has chosen."[30] As moral agents, we are defined not by our ends but by our capacity for choice. "It is not our aims that primarily reveal our nature" but rather the framework of rights we would choose if we could abstract from our aims. "For the self is prior to the ends which are affirmed by it; even a dominant end must be chosen from among numerous possibilities . . . We should therefore reverse the relation between the right and the good proposed by teleological doctrines and view the right as prior."[31]

The notion that justice should be neutral toward conceptions of the good life reflects a conception of persons as freely choosing selves, unbound by prior moral ties. These ideas, taken together, are characteristic of modern liberal political thought. By *liberal*, I don't mean the opposite of *conservative*, as these terms are used in American political debate. In fact, one of the distinctive features of American political debate is that the ideals of the neutral state and the freely choosing self can be found across the political spectrum. Much of the argument over the role of government and markets is a debate about how best to enable individuals to pursue their ends for themselves.

Egalitarian liberals favor civil liberties and basic social and economic rights—rights to health care, education, employment, income security, and so on. They argue that enabling individuals to pursue their own ends requires that government ensure the material conditions of truly free choice. Since the time of the New Deal, proponents of America's welfare state have argued less in the name of social solidarity and communal obligation than in the name of individual rights and freedom of choice. When Franklin D. Roosevelt launched Social Security in 1935, he did not present it as expressing the mutual obligation of citizens to one another. Instead, he designed it to resemble a private insurance scheme, funded by payroll "contributions" rather than general tax revenues.[32] And when, in 1944, he laid out an agenda for the American welfare state, he called it an "economic bill of rights." Rather than offer a communal rationale, FDR argued that such rights were essential to "true individual freedom," adding, "necessitous men are not free men."[33]

For their part, libertarians (usually called conservatives in contemporary politics, at least on economic issues) also argue for a neutral state that respects individual choice. (Libertarian philosopher Robert Nozick writes that government must be "scrupulously . . . neutral between its citizens."[34]) But they disagree with egalitarian liberals about what policies these ideals require. As laissez-faire critics of the welfare state, libertarians defend free markets and argue that people are entitled to keep the money they make. "How can a man be truly free," asked Barry Goldwater, a libertarian conservative and 1964 Republican presidential candidate, "if the fruits of his labor are not his to dispose of, but are treated, instead, as part of a common pool of public wealth?"[35] For libertarians, a neutral state requires civil liberties and a strict regime of private property rights. The welfare state, they argue, does not enable individuals to choose their own ends, but coerces some for the good of others.

Whether egalitarian or libertarian, theories of justice that aspire to neutrality have a powerful appeal. They offer hope that politics and law can avoid becoming entangled in the moral and religious controversies that abound in pluralist societies. And they express a heady conception of human freedom that casts us as the authors of the only moral obligations that constrain us.

Despite its appeal, however, this vision of freedom is flawed. So is the aspiration to find principles of justice that are neutral among competing conceptions of the good life.

This is at least the conclusion to which I'm drawn. Having wrestled with the philosophical arguments I've laid before you, and having watched the way these arguments play out in public life, I do not think that freedom of choice—even freedom of choice under fair conditions—is an adequate basis for a just society. What's more, the attempt to find neutral principles of justice seems to me misguided. It is not always possible to define our rights and duties without taking up substantive moral questions; and even when it's possible it may not be desirable. I'll now try to explain why.

The Claims of Community

The weakness of the liberal conception of freedom is bound up with its appeal. If we understand ourselves as free and independent selves, unbound by moral ties we haven't chosen, we can't make sense of a range of moral and political obligations that we commonly recognize, even prize. These include obligations of solidarity and loyalty, historic memory and religious faith—moral claims that arise from the communities and traditions that shape our identity. Unless we think of ourselves as encumbered selves, open to moral claims we have not willed, it is difficult to make sense of these aspects of our moral and political experience.

In the 1980s, a decade after Rawls's *A Theory of Justice* gave American liberalism its fullest philosophical expression, a number of critics (of which I was one) challenged the ideal of the freely choosing, unencumbered self along the lines I've just suggested. They rejected the claim for the priority of the right over the good, and argued that we can't reason about justice by abstracting from our aims and attachments.

They became known as the "communitarian" critics of contemporary liberalism.

Most of the critics were uneasy with the label, for it seemed to suggest the relativist view that justice is simply whatever a particular community defines it to be. But this worry raises an important point: Communal encumbrances can be oppressive. Liberal freedom developed as an antidote to political theories that consigned persons to destinies fixed by caste or class, station or rank, custom, tradition, or inherited status. So how is it possible to acknowledge the moral weight of community while still giving scope to human freedom? If the voluntarist conception of the person is too spare—if all our obligations are not the product of our will—then how can we see ourselves as situated and yet free?

Storytelling Beings

Alasdair MacIntyre offers a powerful answer to this question. In his book *After Virtue* (1981), he gives an account of the way we, as moral agents, arrive at our purposes and ends. As an alternative to the voluntarist conception of the person, MacIntyre advances a narrative conception. Human beings are storytelling beings. We live our lives as narrative quests. "I can only answer the question 'What am I to do?' if I can answer the prior question 'Of what story or stories do I find myself a part?'"[36]

All lived narratives, MacIntyre observes, have a certain teleological character. This does not mean they have a fixed purpose or end laid down by some external authority. Teleology and unpredictability coexist. "Like characters in a fictional narrative we do not know what will happen next, but none the less our lives have a certain form which projects itself toward our future."[37]

To live a life is to enact a narrative quest that aspires to a certain unity or coherence. When confronted with competing paths, I try to figure out which path will best make sense of my life as a whole, and of the things I care about. Moral deliberation is more about interpreting my life story than exerting my will. It involves choice, but the choice issues from the interpretation; it is not a sovereign act of will. At any given moment, others may see more clearly than I do which path, of the ones before me, fits best with the arc of my life; upon reflection, I may say that my friend knows me better than I know myself. The narrative account of moral agency has the virtue of allowing for this possibility.

It also shows how moral deliberation involves reflection within and about the larger life stories of which my life is a part. As MacIntyre writes, "I am never able to seek the good or exercise the virtues only *qua* individual."[38] I can make sense of the narrative of my life only by coming to terms with the stories in which I find myself. For MacIntyre (as for Aristotle), the narrative, or teleological, aspect of moral reflection is bound up with membership and belonging.

We all approach our own circumstances as bearers of a particular social identity. I am someone's son or daughter, someone's cousin or uncle; I am a citizen of this or that city, a member of this or that guild or profession; I belong to this clan, that tribe, this nation. Hence what is good for me has to be the good for one who inhabits these roles. As such, I inherit from the past of my family, my city, my tribe, my nation, a variety of debts, inheritances, rightful expectations and obligations. These constitute the given of my life, my moral starting point. This is in part what gives my own life its moral particularity.[39]

MacIntyre readily concedes that the narrative account is at odds with modern individualism. "From the standpoint of individualism I am what I myself choose to be." On the individualist view, moral reflection requires that I set aside or abstract from my identities and encumbrances: "I cannot be held responsible for what my country does or has done unless I choose implicitly or explicitly to assume such responsibility. Such individualism is expressed by those modern Americans who deny any responsibility for the effects of slavery upon black Americans, saying, 'I never owned any slaves.'"[40] (It should be noted that MacIntyre wrote these lines almost two decades before Congressman Henry Hyde made exactly this statement in opposing reparations.)

MacIntyre offers as a further example "the young German who believes that being born after 1945 means that what Nazis did to Jews has no moral relevance to his relationship to his Jewish contemporaries." MacIntyre sees in this stance a moral shallowness. It wrongly assumes that "the self is detachable from its social and historical roles and statuses."[41]

> The contrast with the narrative view of the self is clear. For the story of my life is always embedded in the story of those communities from which I derive my identity. I am born with a past; and to try to cut myself off from that past, in the individualist mode, is to deform my present relationships.[42]

MacIntyre's narrative conception of the person offers a clear contrast with the voluntarist conception of persons as freely choosing, unencumbered selves. How can we decide between the two? We might ask ourselves which better captures the experience of moral deliberation, but that is a hard question to answer in the abstract. Another way of assessing the two views is to ask which offers a more convincing account of moral and political obligation. Are we bound by some moral ties we haven't chosen and that can't be traced to a social contract?

Obligations Beyond Consent

Rawls's answer would be no. On the liberal conception, obligations can arise in only two ways—as natural duties we owe to human beings as such and as voluntary obligations we incur by consent.[43] Natural duties are universal. We owe them to persons as persons, as rational beings. They include the duty to treat persons with respect, to do justice, to avoid cruelty, and so on. Since they arise from an autonomous will (Kant) or from a hypothetical social contract (Rawls), they don't require an act of consent. No one would say that I have a duty not to kill you only if I promised you I wouldn't.

Unlike natural duties, voluntary obligations are particular, not universal, and arise from consent. If I've agreed to paint your house (in exchange for a wage, say, or to repay a favor), I have an obligation to do so. But I don't have an obligation to paint everyone's house. On the liberal conception, we must respect the dignity of all persons, but beyond this, we owe only what we agree to owe. Liberal justice requires that we respect people's rights (as defined by the neutral framework), not that we advance their good. Whether we must concern ourselves with the good of other people depends on whether, and with whom, we have agreed to do so.

One striking implication of this view is that "there is no political obligation, strictly speaking, for citizens generally." Although those who run for office voluntarily incur a political obligation (that is, to serve their country if elected), the ordinary citizen does not. As Rawls writes, "it is not clear what is the requisite binding action or who has performed it."[44] So if the liberal account of obligation is right, the average citizen has no special obligations to his or her fellow citizens, beyond the universal, natural duty not to commit injustice.

From the standpoint of the narrative conception of the person, the liberal account of obligation is too thin. It fails to account for the special responsibilities we have to one another as fellow citizens. More than this, it fails to capture those loyalties and responsibilities whose moral force consists partly in the fact that living by them is inseparable from understanding ourselves as the particular persons we are—as members of this family or nation or people; as bearers of that history; as citizens of this republic. On the narrative account, these identities are not contingencies we should set aside when deliberating about morality and justice; they are part of who we are, and so rightly bear on our moral responsibilities.

So one way of deciding between the voluntarist and narrative conceptions of the person is to ask if you think there is a third category of obligations—call them obligations of solidarity, or membership—that can't be explained in contractarian terms. Unlike natural duties, obligations of solidarity are particular, not universal; they involve moral responsibilities we owe, not to rational beings as such, but to those with whom we share a certain history. But unlike voluntary obligations, they do not depend on an act of consent. Their moral weight derives instead from the situated aspect of moral reflection, from a recognition that my life story is implicated in the stories of others.

THREE CATEGORIES OF MORAL RESPONSIBILITY

1. Natural duties: universal; don't require consent
2. Voluntary obligations: particular; require consent
3. Obligations of solidarity: particular; don't require consent

Solidarity and Belonging

Here are some possible examples of obligations of solidarity or membership. See if you think they carry moral weight, and if so, whether their moral force can be accounted for in contractarian terms.

Family obligations

The most elemental example is the special obligation of family members to one another. Suppose two children are drowning, and you have time to save only one. One child is your child, and the other is the child of a stranger. Would it be wrong to rescue your own child? Would it be better to flip a coin? Most people would say there's nothing wrong with rescuing your own child, and would find it odd to think that fairness requires flipping a coin. Lying behind this reaction is the thought that parents have special responsibilities for the welfare of their children. Some argue that this responsibility arises from consent; by choosing to have children, parents voluntarily agree to look after them with special care.

To set aside the matter of consent, consider the responsibility of children to their parents. Suppose two aging parents are in need of care; one is my mother, and the other is somebody else's mother. Most people would agree that, while it might be admirable if I could care for both, I have a special responsibility to look after my mother. In this case, it's not clear that consent can explain why this is so. I didn't choose my parents; I didn't even choose to have parents.

It might be argued that the moral responsibility to care for my mother derives from the fact that she looked after me when I was young. Because she raised me and cared for me, I have an obligation to repay the benefit. By accepting the benefits she conferred on me, I implicitly consented to pay her back when she was in need. Some may find this calculus of consent and reciprocal benefit too cold to account for familial obligations. But suppose you accept it. What would you say of a person whose parent was neglectful or indifferent? Would you say that the quality of the child-rearing determines the degree to which the son or daughter is responsible to help the parent in his or her time of need? Insofar as children are obligated to help even bad parents, the moral claim may exceed the liberal ethic of reciprocity and consent.

French resistance

Let's move from the family to communal obligations. During World War II, members of the French resistance piloted bombing runs over Nazi-occupied France. Although they aimed at factories and other military targets, they were not able to avoid civilian casualties. One day, a bomber pilot receives his orders and finds that his target is his home village. (The story may be apocryphal, but it raises an intriguing moral question.) He asks to be excused from the mission. He agrees that bombing this village is as necessary to the goal of liberating France as was the mission he carried out yesterday, and he knows that if he doesn't do it, someone else will. But he demurs on the grounds that he can't be the one to bomb and possibly kill some of his people, his fellow villagers. Even in a just cause, for him to carry out the bombing, he thinks, would be a special moral wrong.

What do you make of the pilot's stance? Do you admire it or consider it a form of weakness? Put aside the broader question of how many civilian casualties are justified in the cause of liberating France. The pilot was not questioning the necessity of the mission or the number of lives that would be lost. His point was that he could not be the one to take these particular lives. Is the pilot's reluctance mere squeamishness, or does it reflect something of moral importance? If we admire the pilot, it must be because we see in his stance a recognition of his encumbered identity as a member of his village, and we admire the character his reluctance reflects.

Rescuing Ethiopian Jews

In the early 1980s, a famine in Ethiopia drove some four hundred thousand refugees into neighboring Sudan, where they languished in refugee camps. In 1984, the Israeli government undertook a covert airlift called Operation Moses to rescue Ethiopian Jews, known as Falashas, and bring them to Israel.[45] Some seven thousand Ethiopian Jews were rescued before the plan was halted, after Arab governments pressured Sudan not to cooperate with Israel in the evacuation. Shimon Peres, the Israeli prime minister at the time, said, "We shall not rest until all our brothers and sisters from Ethiopia come safely back home."[46] In 1991, when civil war and famine threatened the remaining Ethiopian Jews, Israel carried out an even bigger airlift, which brought fourteen thousand Falashas to Israel.[47]

Did Israel do the right thing to rescue the Ethiopian Jews? It is hard to see the airlift as other than heroic. The Falashas were in desperate circumstances, and they wanted to come to Israel. And Israel, as a Jewish state founded in the wake of the Holocaust, was created to provide a homeland for Jews. But suppose someone posed the following challenge: Hundreds of thousands of Ethiopian refugees were suffering from famine. If, given its limited resources, Israel was able to rescue only a small portion of them, why shouldn't it have conducted a lottery to determine which seven thousand Ethiopians to save? Why wasn't the airlift of Ethiopian Jews, rather than Ethiopians generally, an act of unfair discrimination?

If you accept obligations of solidarity and belonging, the answer is obvious: Israel has a special responsibility to rescue Ethiopian Jews that goes beyond its duty (and that of all nations) to help refugees generally. Every nation has a duty to respect human rights, which requires that it provide help, according to its ability, to human beings anywhere who are suffering from famine, persecution, or displacement from their homes. This is a universal duty that can be justified on Kantian grounds, as a duty we owe persons as persons, as fellow human beings (category 1). The question we are trying to decide is whether nations have further, special responsibilities to care for their people. By referring to the Ethiopian Jews as "our brothers and sisters," the Israeli prime minister invoked a familiar metaphor of solidarity. Unless you accept some such notion, you would be hard pressed to explain why Israel should not have conducted its airlift by lottery. You would also have a hard time defending patriotism.

Is Patriotism a Virtue?

Patriotism is a much contested moral sentiment. Some view love of country as an unassailable virtue, while others see it as a source of mindless obedience, chauvinism, and war. Our question is more particular: Do citizens have obligations to one another that go beyond the duties they have to other people in the world? And if they do, can these obligations be accounted for on the basis of consent alone?

Jean-Jacques Rousseau, an ardent defender of patriotism, argues that communal attachments and identities are necessary supplements to our universal humanity. "It seems that the sentiment of humanity evaporates and weakens in being extended over the entire world, and that we cannot be affected by the calamities in Tartary or Japan the way we are by those of a European people. Interest and commiseration must somehow be limited and restrained to be active." Patriotism, he suggests, is a limiting principle that intensifies fellow feeling. "It is a good thing that the humanity concentrated among fellow citizens takes on new force through the habit of seeing each other and through the common interest that unites them."[48] But if fellow citizens are bound by ties of loyalty and commonality, this means they owe more to one another than to outsiders.

> Do we want people to be virtuous? Let us begin then by making them love their country. But how can they love it, if their country means nothing more to them than it does to foreigners, allotting to them only what it cannot refuse to anyone?[49]

Countries do provide more to their own people than they do to foreigners. U.S. citizens, for example, are eligible for many forms of public provision—public education, unemployment compensation, job training, Social Security, Medicare, welfare, food stamps, and so on—that foreigners are not. In fact, those who oppose a more generous immigration policy worry that the new entrants will take advantage of social programs American taxpayers have paid for. But this raises the question of why American taxpayers are more responsible for their own needy citizens than for those who live elsewhere.

Some people dislike all forms of public assistance, and would like to scale back the welfare state. Others believe we should be more generous than we are in providing foreign aid to assist people in developing countries. But almost everyone recognizes a distinction between welfare and foreign aid. And most agree that we have a special responsibility to meet the needs of our own citizens that does not extend to everyone in the world. Is this distinction morally defensible, or is it mere favoritism, a prejudice for our own kind? What, really, is the moral significance of national boundaries? In terms of sheer need, the billion people around the world who live on less than a dollar a day are worse off than our poor.

Laredo, Texas, and Juarez, Mexico, are two adjacent towns separated by the Rio Grande. A child born in Laredo is eligible for all of the social and economic benefits of the American welfare state, and has the right to seek employment anywhere in the United States when she comes of age. A child born on the other side of the river is entitled to none of these things. Nor does she have the right to cross the river. Through no doing of their own, the two children will have very different life prospects, simply by virtue of their place of birth.

The inequality of nations complicates the case for national community. If all countries had comparable wealth, and if every person were a citizen of some country or other, the obligation to take special care of one's own people would not pose a problem—at least not from the standpoint of justice. But in a world with vast disparities between rich and poor countries, the claims of community can be in tension with the claims of equality. The volatile issue of immigration reflects this tension.

Border patrols

Immigration reform is a political minefield. About the only aspect of immigration policy that commands broad political support is the resolve to secure the U.S. border with Mexico to limit the flow of illegal immigrants. Texas sheriffs recently developed a novel use of the Internet to help them keep watch on the border. They installed video cameras at places known for illegal crossings, and put live video feeds from the cameras on a Web site. Citizens who want to help monitor the border can go online and serve as "virtual Texas deputies." If they see anyone trying to cross the border, they send a report to the sheriff's office, which follows up, sometimes with the help of the U.S. Border Patrol.

When I heard about this Web site on National Public Radio, I wondered what motivates the people who sit at their computer screens and watch. It must be rather tedious work, with long stretches of inactivity and no remuneration. The reporter interviewed a South Texas truck driver who is among the tens of thousands who've logged on. After a long day of work, the trucker "comes home, sets his six-foot, six-inch, 250-pound frame in front of his computer, pops a Red Bull . . . and starts protecting his country." Why does he do it, the reporter asked? "This gives me a little edge feeling," the trucker replied, "like I'm doing something for law enforcement as well as for our own country."[50]

It's an odd expression of patriotism, perhaps, but it raises a question at the heart of the immigration debate: On what grounds are nations justified in preventing outsiders from joining their ranks?

The best argument for limiting immigration is a communal one. As Michael Walzer writes, the ability to regulate the conditions of membership, to set the terms of admission and exclusion, is "at the core of communal independence." Otherwise, "there could not be *communities of character*, historically stable, ongoing associations of men and women with some special commitment to one another and some special sense of their common life."[51]

For affluent nations, however, restrictive immigration policies also serve to protect privilege. Many Americans fear that allowing large numbers of Mexicans to immigrate to the United States would impose a significant burden on social services and reduce the economic well-being of existing citizens. It's not clear whether this fear is justified. But suppose, for the sake of argument, that open immigration would reduce the American standard of living. Would that be sufficient grounds for restricting it? Only if you believe that those born on the affluent side of the Rio Grande are entitled to their good fortune. Since the accident of birth is no basis for entitlement, however, it is hard to see how restrictions on immigration can be justified in the name of preserving affluence.

A stronger argument for limiting immigration is to protect the jobs and wage levels of low-skilled American workers, those most vulnerable to displacement by an influx of immigrants willing to work for less. But this argument takes us back to the question we are trying to resolve: Why should we protect our own most vulnerable workers if it means denying job opportunities to people from Mexico who are even less well-off?

From the standpoint of helping the least advantaged, a case could be made for open immigration. And yet, even people with egalitarian sympathies hesitate to endorse it.[52] Is there a moral basis for this reluctance? Yes, but only if you accept that we have a special obligation for the welfare of our fellow citizens by virtue of the common life and history we share. And this depends on accepting the narrative conception of personhood, according to which our identity as moral agents is bound up with the communities we inhabit. As Walzer writes, "It is only if patriotic sentiment has some moral basis, only if communal cohesion makes for obligations and shared meanings, only if there are members as well as strangers, that state officials would have any reason to worry especially about the welfare of their own people . . . and the success of their own culture and politics."[53]

Is it unfair to "Buy American"?

Immigration is not the only way that American jobs can be lost to outsiders. These days, capital and goods cross national boundaries more easily than people do. This, too, raises questions about the moral status of patriotism. Consider the familiar slogan "Buy American." Is it patriotic to buy a Ford rather than a Toyota? As cars and other manufactured goods are increasingly produced through global supply chains, it becomes harder to know exactly what counts as an American-made car. But let's assume we can identify goods that create jobs for Americans. Is that a good reason to buy them? Why should we be more interested in creating jobs for American workers than for workers in Japan or India or China?

In early 2009, the U.S. Congress passed and President Obama signed an economic stimulus package of $787 billion. The law contained a requirement that public works funded by the bill—roads, bridges, schools, and public buildings—use American-made steel and iron. "It just makes sense that, where possible, we try to stimulate our own economy, rather than the economy of other countries," explained Senator Byron Dorgan, (D-N.D.), a defender of the "Buy American" provision.[54] Opponents of the provision feared it would prompt retaliation against American goods by other countries, worsen the economic downturn, and wind up costing American jobs.[55] But no one questioned the assumption that the purpose of the stimulus package should be to create jobs in the United States rather than overseas. This assumption was made vivid in a term economists began using to describe the risk that U.S. federal spending would fund jobs abroad: *leakage*. A cover story in *BusinessWeek* focused on the leakage question: "How much of Obama's mammoth fiscal stimulus will 'leak' abroad, creating jobs in China, Germany, or Mexico rather than the U.S.?"[56]

At a time when workers everywhere are facing job losses, it is understandable that American policy-makers take as their first priority the protection of American jobs. But the language of leakage brings us back to the moral status of patriotism. From the standpoint of need alone, it is hard to argue for helping unemployed U.S. workers over unemployed workers in China. And yet few would quarrel with the notion that Americans have a special obligation to help their fellow citizens contend with hard times.

It is difficult to account for this obligation in terms of consent. I never agreed to help steelworkers in Indiana or farm workers in California. Some would argue that I've implicitly agreed; because I benefit from the complex scheme of interdependence represented by a national economy, I owe an obligation of reciprocity to the other participants in this economy—even though I've never met them, and even though I've never actually exchanged any goods or services with most of them. But this is a stretch. If we tried to trace the far-flung skein of economic exchange in the contemporary world, we would probably find that we rely as much on people who live half a world away as we do on people in Indiana.

So, if you believe that patriotism has a moral basis, if you believe that we have special responsibilities for the welfare of our fellow citizens, then you must accept the third category of obligation—obligations of solidarity or membership that can't be reduced to an act of consent.

Is Solidarity a Prejudice for Our Own Kind?

Of course, not everyone agrees that we have special obligations to our family, comrades, or fellow citizens. Some argue that so-called obligations of solidarity are actually just instances of collective selfishness, a prejudice for our own kind. These critics concede that we typically care more for our family, friends, and comrades than we do for other people. But, they ask, isn't this heightened concern for one's own people a parochial, inward-looking tendency that we should overcome rather than valorize in the name of patriotism or fraternity?

No, not necessarily. Obligations of solidarity and membership point outward as well as inward. Some of the special responsibilities that flow from the particular communities I inhabit I may owe to fellow members. But others I may owe to those with whom my community has a morally burdened history, as in the relation of Germans to Jews, or of American whites to African Americans. Collective apologies and reparations for historic injustices are good examples of the way solidarity can create moral responsibilities for communities other than my own. Making amends for my country's past wrongs is one way of affirming my allegiance to it.

Sometimes solidarity can give us special reason to criticize our own people or the actions of our government. Patriotism can compel dissent. Take for example two different grounds that led people to oppose the Vietnam War and protest against it. One was the belief that the war was unjust; the other was the belief that the war was unworthy of us and at odds with who we are as a people. The first reason can be taken up by opponents of the war whoever they are or wherever they live. But the second reason can be felt and voiced only by citizens of the country responsible for the war. A Swede could oppose the Vietnam War and consider it unjust, but only an American could feel ashamed of it.

Pride and shame are moral sentiments that presuppose a shared identity. Americans traveling abroad can be embarrassed when they encounter boorish behavior by American tourists, even though they don't know them personally. Non-Americans might find the same behavior disreputable but could not be embarrassed by it.

The capacity for pride and shame in the actions of family members and fellow citizens is related to the capacity for collective responsibility. Both require seeing ourselves as situated selves—claimed by moral ties we have not chosen and implicated in the narratives that shape our identity as moral agents.

Given the close connection between an ethic of pride and shame and an ethic of collective responsibility, it is puzzling to find political conservatives rejecting collective apologies on individualist grounds (as did Henry Hyde, John Howard, and others mentioned earlier). To insist that we are, as individuals, responsible only for the choices we make and the acts we perform makes it difficult to take pride in the history and traditions of one's country. Anyone anywhere can admire the Declaration of Independence, the Constitution, Lincoln's Gettysburg Address, the fallen heroes honored in Arlington National Cemetery, and so on. But patriotic pride requires a sense of belonging to a community extended across time.

With belonging comes responsibility. You can't really take pride in your country and its past if you're unwilling to acknowledge any responsibility for carrying its story into the present, and discharging the moral burdens that may come with it.

Can Loyalty Override Universal Moral Principles?

In most of the cases we've considered, the demands of solidarity seem to supplement rather than compete with natural duties or human rights. So it might be argued that these cases highlight a point that liberal philosophers are happy to concede: As long as we don't violate anyone's rights, we can fulfill the general duty to help others by helping those who are close at hand—such as family members or fellow citizens. There's nothing wrong with a parent rescuing his own child rather than another, provided he doesn't run over a stranger's child on the way to the rescue. Similarly, there's nothing wrong with a rich country setting up a generous welfare state for its own citizens, provided it respects the human rights of persons everywhere. Obligations of solidarity are objectionable only if they lead us to violate a natural duty.

If the narrative conception of the person is right, however, obligations of solidarity can be more demanding than the liberal account suggests—even to the point of competing with natural duties.

Robert E. Lee

Consider the case of Robert E. Lee, the commanding general of the Confederate army. Before the Civil War, Lee was an officer in the Union army. He opposed secession—in fact, he regarded it as treason. When war loomed, President Lincoln asked Lee to lead the Union forces. Lee refused. He concluded that his obligation to Virginia outweighed his obligation to the Union, and also his reported opposition to slavery. He explained his decision in a letter to his sons:

> With all my devotion to the Union, I have not been able to make up my mind to raise my hand against my relatives, my children, my home . . . If the Union is dissolved, and the Government disrupted, I shall return to my native State and share the miseries of my people. Save in her defense, I will draw my sword no more.[57]

Like the French resistance pilot, Lee could not countenance a role that would require him to inflict harm on his relatives, his children, his home. But his loyalty went further, even to the point of leading his people in a cause he opposed.

Since the cause of the Confederacy included not only secession but slavery, it is hard to defend Lee's choice. Still, it is hard not to admire the loyalty that gave rise to his dilemma. But why should we admire loyalty to an unjust cause? You might well wonder whether loyalty, under these circumstances, should carry any moral weight at all. Why, you might ask, is loyalty a virtue rather than just a sentiment, a feeling, an emotional tug that beclouds our moral judgment and makes it hard to do the right thing?

Here's why: Unless we take loyalty seriously, as a claim with moral import, we can't make sense of Lee's dilemma as a moral dilemma at all. If loyalty is a sentiment with no genuine moral weight, then Lee's predicament is simply a conflict between morality on the one hand and mere feeling or prejudice on the other. But by conceiving it that way, we misunderstand the moral stakes.[58]

The merely psychological reading of Lee's predicament misses the fact that we not only sympathize with people like him but also admire them, not necessarily for the choices they make, but for the quality of character their deliberation reflects. What we admire is the disposition to see and bear one's life circumstance as a reflectively situated being— claimed by the history that implicates me in a particular life, but self-conscious of its particularity, and so alive to competing claims and wider horizons. To have character is to live in recognition of one's (sometime conflicting) encumbrances.

Brothers' keepers I: The Bulger brothers

A more recent test of loyalty's moral weight involves two brotherly tales: The first is the story of William and James ("Whitey") Bulger. Bill and Whitey grew up together in a family of nine children in a

South Boston housing project. Bill was a conscientious student who studied the classics and got a law degree at Boston College. His older brother, Whitey, was a high-school dropout who spent his time on the streets committing larceny and other crimes.

Each rose to power in his respective world. William Bulger entered politics, became president of the Massachusetts State Senate (1978–1996), then served for seven years as president of the University of Massachusetts. Whitey served time in federal prison for bank robbery, then rose to become the leader of the ruthless Winter Hill Gang, an organized crime group that controlled extortion, drug deals, and other illegal activities in Boston. Charged with nineteen murders, Whitey fled to avoid arrest in 1995. He is still at large, and occupies a place on the FBI's "Ten Most Wanted" list.[59]

Although William Bulger spoke with his fugitive brother by phone, he claimed not to know his whereabouts, and refused to assist authorities in finding him. When William testified before a grand jury in 2001, a federal prosecutor pressed him without success for information on his brother: "So just to be clear, you felt more loyalty to your brother than you did to the people of the Commonwealth of Massachusetts?"

"I never thought about it that way," Bulger replied. "But I do have an honest loyalty to my brother, and I care about him . . . It's my hope that I'm never helpful to anyone against him . . . I don't have an obligation to help everyone catch him."[60]

In the taverns of South Boston, patrons expressed admiration for Bulger's loyalty. "I don't blame him for not telling on his brother," one resident told *The Boston Globe*. "Brothers are brothers. Are you going to squeal on your family?"[61] Editorial boards and newspaper reporters were more critical. "Instead of taking the righteous road," one columnist wrote, "he chose the code of the street."[62] Under public pressure for his refusal to assist in the search for his brother, Bulger resigned as president of the University of Massachusetts in 2003, though he was not charged with obstructing the investigation.[63]

Under most circumstances, the right thing to do is to help bring a murder suspect to justice. Can family loyalty override this duty? William Bulger apparently thought so. But a few years earlier, another figure with a wayward brother made a different call.

Brothers' keepers II: The Unabomber

For more than seventeen years, authorities had tried to find the domestic terrorist responsible for a series of package bombs that killed three people and injured twenty-three others. Because his targets included scientists and other academics, the elusive bomb maker was known as the Unabomber. To explain the cause behind his deeds, the Unabomber posted a thirty-five-thousand-word anti-technology manifesto on the Internet, and promised to stop bombing if *The New York Times* and *The Washington Post* both printed the manifesto, which they did.[64]

When David Kaczynski, a forty-six-year-old social worker in Schenectady, New York, read the manifesto, he found it eerily familiar. It contained phrases and opinions that sounded like those of his older brother, Ted, age fifty-four, a Harvard-trained mathematician turned recluse. Ted despised modern industrial society and was living in a mountain cabin in Montana. David had not seen him for a decade.[65]

After much anguish, in 1996 David informed the FBI of his suspicion that the Unabomber was his brother. Federal agents staked out Ted Kaczynski's cabin and arrested him. Although David had been given to understand that prosecutors would not seek the death penalty, they did. The prospect of bringing about the death of his brother was an agonizing thought. In the end, prosecutors allowed Ted Kaczynski to plead guilty in exchange for a sentence of life in prison without parole.[66]

Ted Kaczynski refused to acknowledge his brother in court and, in a book manuscript he wrote in prison, called him "another Judas Iscariot."[67] David Kaczynski tried to rebuild his life, which was indelibly marked by the episode. After working to spare his brother the death penalty, he became a spokesman for an anti–capital punishment group. "Brothers are supposed to protect each other," he told one audience, describing his dilemma, "and here, perhaps, I was sending my brother to his death."[68] He accepted the $1 million reward offered by the Justice Department for helping apprehend the Unabomber, but gave most of it to the families of those killed and injured by his brother. And he apologized, on behalf of his family, for his brother's crimes.[69]

What do you make of the way William Bulger and David Kaczynski contended with their brothers? For Bulger, family loyalty outweighed the duty to bring a criminal to justice; for Kaczynski, the reverse. Perhaps it makes a moral difference whether the brother at large poses a continuing threat. This seemed to weigh heavily for David Kaczynski: "I guess it's fair to say I felt compelled. The thought that another person would die and I was in the position to stop that—I couldn't live with that."[70]

However you judge the choices they made, it is hard to read their stories without coming to this conclusion: the dilemmas they faced make sense as moral dilemmas only if you acknowledge that the claims of loyalty and solidarity can weigh in the balance against other moral claims, including the duty to bring criminals to justice. If all our obligations are founded on consent, or on universal duties we owe persons as persons, it's hard to account for these fraternal predicaments.

Justice and the Good Life

We've now considered a range of examples meant to challenge the contractarian idea that we are the authors of the only moral obligations that constrain us: public apologies and reparations; collective responsibility for historic injustice; the special responsibilities of family members, and of fellow citizens, for one another; solidarity with comrades; allegiance to one's village, community, or country; patriotism; pride and shame in one's nation or people; fraternal and filial loyalties. The claims of solidarity seen in these examples are familiar features of our moral and political experience. It would be difficult to live, or to make sense of our lives, without them. But it is equally difficult to account for them in the language of moral individualism. They can't be captured by an ethic of consent. That is, in part, what gives these claims their moral force. They draw on our encumbrances. They reflect our nature as storytelling beings, as situated selves.

What, you may be wondering, does all this have to do with justice? To answer this question, let's recall the questions that led us down this path. We've been trying to figure out whether all our duties and obligations can be traced to an act of will or choice. I've argued that they cannot; obligations of solidarity or membership may claim us for reasons unrelated to a choice—reasons bound up with the narratives by which we interpret our lives and the communities we inhabit.

What exactly is at stake in this debate between the narrative account of moral agency and the one that emphasizes will and consent? One issue at stake is how you conceive human freedom. As you ponder the examples that purport to illustrate obligations of solidarity and membership, you might find yourself resisting them. If you are like many of my students, you might dislike or mistrust the idea that we're bound by moral ties we haven't chosen. This dislike might lead you to reject the claims of patriotism, solidarity, collective responsibility, and so on; or to recast these claims as arising from some form of consent. It's tempting to reject or to recast these claims because doing so renders them consistent with a familiar idea of freedom. This is the idea that says we are unbound by any moral ties we haven't chosen; to be free is to be the author of the only obligations that constrain us.

I am trying to suggest, through these and other examples we consider throughout this book, that this conception of freedom is flawed. But freedom is not the only issue at stake here. Also at stake is how to think about justice.

Recall the two ways of thinking about justice we've considered. For Kant and Rawls, the right is prior to the good. The principles of justice that define our duties and rights should be neutral with respect to competing conceptions of the good life. To arrive at the moral law, Kant argues, we must abstract from our contingent interests and ends. To deliberate about justice, Rawls maintains, we should set aside our particular aims, attachments, and conceptions of the good. That's the point of thinking about justice behind a veil of ignorance.

This way of thinking about justice is at odds with Aristotle's way. He doesn't believe that principles of justice can or should be neutral with respect to the good life. To the contrary, he maintains that one of the purposes of a just constitution is to form good citizens and to cultivate good character. He doesn't think it's possible to deliberate about justice without deliberating about the meaning of the goods—the offices, honors, rights, and opportunities—that societies allocate.

One of the reasons Kant and Rawls reject Aristotle's way of thinking about justice is that they don't think it leaves room for freedom. A constitution that tries to cultivate good character or to affirm a particular conception of the good life risks imposing on some the values of others. It fails to respect persons as free and independent selves, capable of choosing their ends for themselves.

If Kant and Rawls are right to conceive freedom in this way, then they are right about justice as well. If we are freely choosing, independent selves, unbound by moral ties antecedent to choice, then we need a framework of rights that is neutral among ends. If the self is prior to its ends, then the right must be prior to the good.

If, however, the narrative conception of moral agency is more persuasive, then it may be worth reconsidering Aristotle's way of thinking about justice. If deliberating about my good involves reflecting on the good of those communities with which my identity is bound, then the aspiration to neutrality may be mistaken. It may not be possible, or even desirable, to deliberate about justice without deliberating about the good life.

The prospect of bringing conceptions of the good life into public discourse about justice and rights may strike you as less than appealing—even frightening. After all, people in pluralist societies such as ours disagree about the best way to live. Liberal political theory was born as an attempt to spare politics and law from becoming embroiled in moral and religious controversies. The philosophies of Kant and Rawls represent the fullest and clearest expression of that ambition.

But this ambition cannot succeed. Many of the most hotly contested issues of justice and rights can't be debated without taking up controversial moral and religious questions. In deciding how to define the rights and duties of citizens, it's not always possible to set aside competing conceptions of the good life. And even when it's possible, it may not be desirable.

Asking democratic citizens to leave their moral and religious convictions behind when they enter the public realm may seem a way of ensuring toleration and mutual respect. In practice, however, the opposite can be true. Deciding important public questions while pretending to a neutrality that cannot be achieved is a recipe for backlash and resentment. A politics emptied of substantive moral engagement makes for an impoverished civic life. It is also an open invitation to narrow, intolerant moralisms. Fundamentalists rush in where liberals fear to tread.

If our debates about justice unavoidably embroil us in substantive moral questions, it remains to ask how these arguments can proceed. Is it possible to reason about the good in public without lapsing into wars of religion? What would a more morally engaged public discourse look like, and how would it differ from the kind of political argument to which we've become accustomed? These are not merely philosophical questions. They lie at the heart of any attempt to reinvigorate political discourse and renew our civic life.

10. JUSTICE AND THE COMMON GOOD

On September 12, 1960, John F. Kennedy, the Democratic candidate for president, gave a speech in Houston, Texas, on the role of religion in politics. The "religious issue" had dogged his campaign. Kennedy was a Catholic, and no Catholic had ever been elected president. Some voters harbored unspoken prejudice; others voiced the fear that Kennedy would be beholden to the Vatican in the conduct of his office or might impose Catholic doctrine on public policy.[1] Hoping to lay these fears to rest, Kennedy agreed to speak to a gathering of Protestant ministers about the role his religion would play in his presidency, should he be elected. His answer was simple: none. His religious faith was a private matter and would have no bearing on his public responsibilities.

"I believe in a president whose religious views are his own private affair," Kennedy stated. "Whatever issue may come before me as president—on birth control, divorce, censorship, gambling or any other subject—I will make my decision . . . in accordance with what my conscience tells me to be the national interest, and without regard to outside religious pressures or dictates."[2]

Kennedy did not say whether or how his conscience might have been shaped by his religious convictions. But he seemed to suggest that his beliefs about the national interest had little if anything to do with religion, which he associated with "outside pressures" and "dictates."

He wanted to reassure the Protestant ministers, and the American public, that he would not impose his religious beliefs—whatever they might be—on them.

The speech was widely regarded as a political success, and Kennedy went on to win the presidency. Theodore H. White, the great chronicler of presidential campaigns, praised the speech for defining "the personal doctrine of a modern Catholic in a democratic society."[3]

Forty-six years later, on June 28, 2006, Barack Obama, soon to become a candidate for his party's presidential nomination, gave a very different speech on the role of religion in politics. He began by recalling the way he had dealt with the religious issue in his U.S. Senate campaign two years earlier. Obama's opponent, a rather strident religious conservative, had attacked Obama's support for gay rights and abortion rights by claiming he was not a good Christian, and that Jesus Christ would not have voted for him.

"I answered with what has come to be the typically liberal response in such debates," Obama said, looking back. "I said that we live in a pluralistic society, that I can't impose my own religious views on another, that I was running to be the U.S. Senator of Illinois and not the Minister of Illinois."[4]

Although Obama easily won the Senate race, he now thought his response had been inadequate, and "did not adequately address the role my faith has in guiding my own values and my own beliefs."[5]

He proceeded to describe his own Christian faith and to argue for the relevance of religion to political argument. It was a mistake, he thought, for progressives to "abandon the field of religious discourse" in politics. "The discomfort of some progressives with any hint of religion has often prevented us from effectively addressing issues in moral terms." If liberals offered a political discourse emptied of religious content, they would "forfeit the imagery and terminology through which millions of Americans understand both their personal morality and social justice."[6]

Religion was not only a source of resonant political rhetoric. The solution to certain social problems required moral transformation.

"Our fear of getting 'preachy' may . . . lead us to discount the role that values and culture play in some of our most urgent social problems," Obama said. Addressing problems such as "poverty and racism, the uninsured and the unemployed," would require "changes in hearts and a change in minds."[7] So it was a mistake to insist that moral and religious convictions play no part in politics and law.

> Secularists are wrong when they ask believers to leave their religion at the door before entering into the public square. Frederick Douglass, Abraham Lincoln, William Jennings Bryan, Dorothy Day, Martin Luther King—indeed, the majority of great reformers in American history—were not only motivated by faith, but repeatedly used religious language to argue for their cause. So to say that men and women should not inject their "personal morality" into public policy debates is a practical absurdity. Our law is by definition a codification of morality, much of it grounded in the Judeo-Christian tradition.[8]

Many have noted the similarities between John F. Kennedy and Barack Obama. Both were young, eloquent, inspiring political figures whose election marked the turn to a new generation of leadership. And both sought to rally Americans to a new era of civic engagement. But their views on the role of religion in politics could hardly be more different.

The Aspiration to Neutrality

Kennedy's view of religion as a private, not public, affair reflected more than the need to disarm anti-Catholic prejudice. It reflected a public philosophy that would come to full expression during the 1960s and '70s—a philosophy that held that government should be neutral on moral and religious questions, so that each individual could be free to choose his or her own conception of the good life.

Both major political parties appealed to the idea of neutrality, but in different ways. Generally speaking, Republicans invoked the idea in economic policy, while Democrats applied it to social and cultural issues.[9] Republicans argued against government intervention in free markets on the grounds that individuals should be free to make their own economic choices and spend their money as they pleased; for government to spend taxpayers' money or regulate economic activity for public purposes was to impose a state-sanctioned vision of the common good that not everyone shared. Tax cuts were preferable to government spending, because they left individuals free to decide for themselves what ends to pursue and how to spend their own money.

Democrats rejected the notion that free markets are neutral among ends and defended a greater measure of government intervention in the economy. But when it came to social and cultural issues, they, too, invoked the language of neutrality. Government should not "legislate morality" in the areas of sexual behavior or reproductive decisions, they maintained, because to do so imposes on some the moral and religious convictions of others. Rather than restrict abortion or homosexual intimacies, government should be neutral on these morally charged questions and let individuals choose for themselves.

In 1971, John Rawls's *A Theory of Justice* offered a philosophical defense of the liberal conception of neutrality that Kennedy's speech had intimated.[10] In the 1980s, the communitarian critics of liberal neutrality questioned the vision of the freely choosing, unencumbered self that seemed to underlie Rawls's theory. They argued not only for stronger notions of community and solidarity but also for a more robust public engagement with moral and religious questions.[11]

In 1993, Rawls published a book, *Political Liberalism*, that recast his theory in some respects. He acknowledged that, in their personal lives, people often have "affections, devotions, and loyalties that they believe they would not, indeed could and should not, stand apart from. . . . They may regard it as simply unthinkable to view themselves apart from certain religious, philosophical, and moral convictions, or from certain enduring attachments and loyalties."[12] To this extent, Rawls accepted the possibility of thickly constituted, morally encumbered selves. But he insisted that such loyalties and attachments should have no bearing on our identity as citizens. In debating justice and rights, we should set aside our personal moral and religious convictions and argue from the standpoint of a "political conception of the person," independent of any particular loyalties, attachments, or conception of the good life.[13]

Why should we not bring our moral and religious convictions to bear in public discourse about justice and rights? Why should we separate our identity as citizens from our identity as moral persons more broadly conceived? Rawls argues that we should do so in order to respect "the fact of reasonable pluralism" about the good life that prevails in the modern world. People in modern democratic societies disagree about moral and religious questions; moreover, these disagreements are reasonable. "It is not to be expected that conscientious persons with full powers of reason, even after free discussion, will all arrive at the same conclusion."[14]

According to this argument, the case for liberal neutrality arises from the need for tolerance in the face of moral and religious disagreement. "Which moral judgments are true, all things considered, is not a matter for political liberalism," Rawls writes. To maintain impartiality between competing moral and religious doctrines, political liberalism does not "address the moral topics on which those doctrines divide."[15]

The demand that we separate our identity as citizens from our moral and religious convictions means that, when engaging in public discourse about justice and rights, we must abide by the limits of liberal public reason. Not only may government not endorse a particular conception of the good; citizens may not even introduce their moral and religious convictions into public debate about justice and rights.[16] For if they do, and if their arguments prevail, they will effectively impose on their fellow citizens a law that rests on a particular moral or religious doctrine.

How can we know whether our political arguments meet the requirements of public reason, suitably shorn of any reliance on moral or religious views? Rawls suggests a novel test: "To check whether we are following public reason we might ask: how would our argument strike us presented in the form of a supreme court opinion?"[17] As Rawls explains, this is a way to make sure that our arguments are neutral in the sense that liberal public reason requires: "The justices cannot, of course, invoke their own personal morality, nor the ideals and virtues of morality generally. Those they must view as irrelevant. Equally, they cannot invoke their or other people's religious or philosophical views."[18] When participating as citizens in public debate, we should observe a similar restraint. Like Supreme Court justices, we should set aside our moral and religious convictions, and restrict ourselves to arguments that all citizens can reasonably be expected to accept.

This is the ideal of liberal neutrality that John Kennedy invoked and Barack Obama rejected. From the 1960s through the 1980s, Democrats drifted toward the neutrality ideal, and largely banished moral and religious argument from their political discourse. There were some notable exceptions. Martin Luther King, Jr., invoked moral and religious arguments in advancing the cause of civil rights; the anti–Vietnam War movement was energized by moral and religious discourse; and Robert F. Kennedy, seeking the Democratic presidential nomination in 1968, tried to summon the nation to more demanding moral and civic ideals. But by the 1970s, liberals embraced the language of neutrality and choice, and ceded moral and religious discourse to the emerging Christian right.

With the election of Ronald Reagan in 1980, Christian conservatives became a prominent voice in Republican politics. Jerry Falwell's Moral Majority and Pat Robertson's Christian Coalition sought to clothe the "naked public square"[19] and to combat what they saw as the

moral permissiveness of American life. They favored school prayer, religious displays in public places, and legal restrictions on pornography,
abortion, and homosexuality. For their part, liberals opposed these policies, not by challenging the moral judgments case by case, but instead
by arguing that moral and religious judgments have no place in politics.

This pattern of argument served Christian conservatives well, and
gave liberalism a bad name. In the 1990s and early 2000s, liberals argued, somewhat defensively, that they, too, stood for "values," by which
they typically meant the values of tolerance, fairness, and freedom of
choice. (In an awkward reach for resonance, 2004 Democratic presidential nominee John Kerry used the words *value* or *values* thirty-two
times in his convention acceptance speech.) But these were the values
associated with liberal neutrality and the constraints of liberal public
reason. They did not connect with the moral and spiritual yearning
abroad in the land, or answer the aspiration for a public life of larger
meaning.[20]

Unlike other Democrats, Barack Obama understood this yearning
and gave it political voice. This set his politics apart from the liberalism
of his day. The key to his eloquence was not simply that he was adept
with words. It was also that his political language was infused with a
moral and spiritual dimension that pointed beyond liberal neutrality.

> Each day, it seems, thousands of Americans are going about their daily
> rounds—dropping off the kids at school, driving to the office, flying
> to a business meeting, shopping at the mall, trying to stay on their
> diets—and they're coming to realize that something is missing. They
> are deciding that their work, their possessions, their diversions, their
> sheer busyness, is not enough. They want a sense of purpose, a narra-
> tive arc to their lives. . . . If we truly hope to speak to people where
> they're at—to communicate our hopes and values in a way that's
> relevant to their own—then as progressives, we cannot abandon the
> field of religious discourse.[21]

Obama's claim that progressives should embrace a more capacious, faith-friendly form of public reason reflects a sound political instinct. It is also good political philosophy. The attempt to detach arguments about justice and rights from arguments about the good life is mistaken for two reasons: First, it is not always possible to decide questions of justice and rights without resolving substantive moral questions; and second, even where it's possible, it may not be desirable.

The Abortion and Stem Cell Debates

Consider two familiar political questions that can't be resolved without taking a stand on an underlying moral and religious controversy—abortion and embryonic stem cell research. Some people believe that abortion should be banned because it involves the taking of innocent human life. Others disagree, arguing that the law should not take sides in the moral and theological controversy over when human life begins; since the moral status of the developing fetus is a highly charged moral and religious question, they argue, government should be neutral on that question, and allow women to decide for themselves whether to have an abortion.

The second position reflects the familiar liberal argument for abortion rights. It claims to resolve the abortion question on the basis of neutrality and freedom of choice, without entering into the moral and religious controversy. But this argument does not succeed. For, if it's true that the developing fetus is morally equivalent to a child, then abortion is morally equivalent to infanticide. And few would maintain that government should let parents decide for themselves whether to kill their children. So the "pro-choice" position in the abortion debate is not really neutral on the underlying moral and theological question; it implicitly rests on the assumption that the Catholic Church's teaching on the moral status of the fetus—that it is a person from the moment of conception—is false.

To acknowledge this assumption is not to argue for banning abortion. It is simply to acknowledge that neutrality and freedom of choice are not sufficient grounds for affirming a right to abortion. Those who would defend the right of women to decide for themselves whether to terminate a pregnancy should engage with the argument that the developing fetus is equivalent to a person, and try to show why it is wrong. It is not enough to say that the law should be neutral on moral and religious questions. The case for permitting abortion is no more neutral than the case for banning it. Both positions presuppose some answer to the underlying moral and religious controversy.

The same is true of the debate over stem cell research. Those who would ban embryonic stem cell research argue that, whatever its medical promise, research that involves the destruction of human embryos is morally impermissible. Many who hold this view believe that personhood begins at conception, so that destroying even an early embryo is morally on a par with killing a child.

Proponents of embryonic stem cell research reply by pointing to the medical benefits the research may bring, including possible treatments and cures for diabetes, Parkinson's disease, and spinal cord injury. And they argue that science should not be hampered by religious or ideological interference; those with religious objections should not be allowed to impose their views through laws that would ban promising scientific research.

As with the abortion debate, however, the case for permitting embryonic stem cell research cannot be made without taking a stand on the moral and religious controversy about when personhood begins. If the early embryo is morally equivalent to a person, then the opponents of embryonic stem cell research have a point; even highly promising medical research would not justify dismembering a human person. Few people would say it should be legal to harvest organs from a five-year-old child in order to promote life-saving research. So the argument for permitting embryonic stem cell research is not neutral on the moral and religious controversy about when human personhood begins. It presupposes an answer to that controversy—namely that the pre-implantation embryo destroyed in the course of embryonic stem cell research is not yet a human being.[22]

With abortion and embryonic stem cell research, it's not possible to resolve the legal question without taking up the underlying moral and religious question. In both cases, neutrality is impossible because the issue is whether the practice in question involves taking the life of a human being. Of course, most moral and political controversies do not involve matters of life and death. So partisans of liberal neutrality might reply that the abortion and stem cell debates are special cases; except where the definition of the human person is at stake, we can resolve arguments about justice and rights without taking sides in moral and religious controversies.

Same-Sex Marriage

But this isn't true, either. Consider the debate over same-sex marriage. Can you decide whether the state should recognize same-sex marriage without entering into moral and religious controversies about the purpose of marriage and the moral status of homosexuality? Some say yes, and argue for same-sex marriage on liberal, nonjudgmental grounds: whether one personally approves or disapproves of gay and lesbian relationships, individuals should be free to choose their marital partners. To allow heterosexual but not homosexual couples to get married wrongly discriminates against gay men and lesbians, and denies them equality before the law.

If this argument is a sufficient basis for according state recognition to same-sex marriage, then the issue can be resolved within the bounds of liberal public reason, without recourse to controversial conceptions of the purpose of marriage and the goods it honors. But the case for same-sex marriage can't be made on nonjudgmental grounds. It depends on a certain conception of the telos of marriage—its purpose or point. And, as Aristotle reminds us, to argue about the purpose of a social institution is to argue about the virtues it honors and rewards. The debate over same-sex marriage is fundamentally a debate about whether gay and lesbian unions are worthy of the honor and recognition that, in our society, state-sanctioned marriage confers. So the underlying moral question is unavoidable.

To see why this is so, it's important to bear in mind that a state can take three possible policies toward marriage, not just two. It can adopt the traditional policy and recognize only marriages between a man and a woman; or it can do what several states have done, and recognize same-sex marriage in the same way it recognizes marriage between a man and a woman; or it can decline to recognize marriage of any kind, and leave this role to private associations.

These three policies can be summarized as follows:

1. Recognize only marriages between a man and a woman.
2. Recognize same-sex and opposite-sex marriages.
3. Don't recognize marriage of any kind, but leave this role to private associations.

In addition to marriage laws, states can adopt civil union or domestic partnership laws that grant legal protections, inheritance rights, hospital visitation rights, and child custody arrangements to unmarried couples who live together and enter into a legal arrangement. A number of states have made such arrangements available to gay and lesbian partners. In 2003, Massachusetts, by a ruling of its Supreme Court, became the first state to accord legal recognition to same-sex marriage (policy 2). In 2008, California's Supreme Court also ruled in favor of a right to same-sex marriage, but a few months after the ruling, a majority of the electorate overturned that decision in a state-wide ballot initiative. In 2009, Vermont became the first state to legalize gay marriage by legislation rather than by judicial ruling.[23]

Policy 3 is purely hypothetical, at least in the United States; no state has thus far renounced the recognition of marriage as a government function. But this policy is nonetheless worth examining, as it sheds light on the arguments for and against same-sex marriage.

Policy 3 is the ideal libertarian solution to the marriage debate. It does not abolish marriage, but it does abolish marriage as a state-sanctioned institution. It might best be described as the disestablishment of marriage.[24] Just as disestablishing religion means getting rid of an official state church (while allowing churches to exist independent of the state), disestablishing marriage would mean getting rid of marriage as an official state function.

The opinion writer Michael Kinsley defends this policy as a way out of what he sees as a hopelessly irresolvable conflict over marriage. Proponents of gay marriage complain that restricting marriage to heterosexuals is a kind of discrimination. Opponents claim that if the state sanctions gay marriage, it goes beyond tolerating homosexuality to endorsing it and giving it "a government stamp of approval." The solution, Kinsley writes, is "to end the institution of government-sanctioned marriage," to "privatize marriage."[25] Let people get married any way they please, without state sanction or interference.

> Let churches and other religious institutions continue to offer marriage ceremonies. Let department stores and casinos get into the act if they want. . . . Let couples celebrate their union in any way they choose and consider themselves married whenever they want. . . . And, yes, if three people want to get married, or one person wants to marry herself, and someone else wants to conduct a ceremony and declare them married, let 'em.[26]

"If marriage were an entirely private affair," Kinsley reasons, "all the disputes over gay marriage would become irrelevant. Gay marriage would not have the official sanction of government, but neither would straight marriage." Kinsley suggests that domestic partnership laws could deal with the financial, insurance, child support, and inheritance issues that arise when people co-habit and raise children together. He proposes, in effect, to replace all state-sanctioned marriages, gay and straight, with civil unions.[27]

From the standpoint of liberal neutrality, Kinsley's proposal has a clear advantage over the two standard alternatives (policies 1 and 2): It does not require judges or citizens to engage in the moral and religious controversy over the purpose of marriage and the morality of homosexuality. Since the state would no longer confer on any family units the honorific title of marriage, citizens would be able to avoid engaging in debate about the telos of marriage, and whether gays and lesbians can fulfill it.

Relatively few people on either side of the same-sex marriage debate have embraced the disestablishment proposal. But it sheds light on what's at stake in the existing debate, and helps us see why both proponents and opponents of same-sex marriage must contend with the substantive moral and religious controversy about the purpose of marriage and the goods that define it. Neither of the two standard positions can be defended within the bounds of liberal public reason.

Of course, those who reject same-sex marriage on the grounds that it sanctions sin and dishonors the true meaning of marriage aren't bashful about the fact that they're making a moral or religious claim. But those who defend a right to same-sex marriage often try to rest their claim on neutral grounds, and to avoid passing judgment on the moral meaning of marriage. The attempt to find a nonjudgmental case for same-sex marriage draws heavily on the ideas of nondiscrimination and freedom of choice. But these ideas cannot by themselves justify a right to same-sex marriage. To see why this is so, consider the thoughtful and nuanced opinion written by Margaret Marshall, chief justice of the Massachusetts Supreme Court, in the court's ruling in *Goodridge v. Dept. of Public Health* (2003), the same-sex marriage case.[28]

Marshall begins by recognizing the deep moral and religious disagreement the subject provokes, and implies that the court will not take sides in this dispute:

Many people hold deep-seated religious, moral, and ethical convictions that marriage should be limited to the union of one man and one woman, and that homosexual conduct is immoral. Many hold equally strong religious, moral and ethical convictions that same-sex couples are entitled to be married, and that homosexual persons should be treated no differently than their heterosexual neighbors. Neither view answers the question before us. "Our obligation is to define the liberty of all, not to mandate our own moral code."[29]

As if to avoid entering into the moral and religious controversy over homosexuality, Marshall describes the moral issue before the court in liberal terms—as a matter of autonomy and freedom of choice. The exclusion of same-sex couples from marriage is incompatible with "respect for individual autonomy and equality under law," she writes.[30] The liberty of "choosing whether and whom to marry would be hollow" if the state could "foreclose an individual from freely choosing the person with whom to share an exclusive commitment."[31] The issue, Marshall maintains, is not the moral worth of the choice, but the right of the individual to make it—that is, the right of the plaintiffs "to marry their chosen partner."[32]

But autonomy and freedom of choice are insufficient to justify a right to same-sex marriage. If government were truly neutral on the moral worth of all voluntary intimate relationships, then the state would have no grounds for limiting marriage to two persons; consensual polygamous partnerships would also qualify. In fact, if the state really wanted to be neutral, and respect whatever choices individuals wished to make, it would have to adopt Michael Kinsley's proposal and get out of the business of conferring recognition on any marriages.

The real issue in the gay marriage debate is not freedom of choice but whether same-sex unions are worthy of honor and recognition by the community—whether they fulfill the purpose of the social institution of marriage. In Aristotle's terms, the issue is the just distribution of offices and honors. It's a matter of social recognition.

Notwithstanding its emphasis on freedom of choice, the Massachusetts court made clear that it did not intend to open the way to polygamous marriage. It didn't question the notion that government may confer social recognition on some intimate associations rather than others. Nor did the court call for the abolition, or disestablishment, of marriage.

To the contrary, Justice Marshall's opinion offers a paean to marriage as "one of our community's most rewarding and cherished institutions."[33] It argues that eliminating state-sanctioned marriage "would dismantle a vital organizing principle of our society."[34]

Rather than abolish state-sanctioned marriage, Marshall argues for expanding its traditional definition to include partners of the same sex. In doing so, she steps outside the bounds of liberal neutrality to affirm the moral worth of same-sex unions, and to offer a view about the purpose of marriage, properly conceived. More than a private arrangement between two consenting adults, she observes, marriage is a form of public recognition and approval. "In a real sense, there are three partners to every civil marriage: two willing spouses and an approving State."[35] This feature of marriage brings out its honorific aspect: "Civil marriage is at once a deeply personal commitment to another human being and a highly public celebration of the ideals of mutuality, companionship, intimacy, fidelity, and family."[36]

If marriage is an honorific institution, what virtues does it honor? To ask that question is to ask about the purpose, or telos, of marriage as a social institution. Many opponents of same-sex marriage claim that the primary purpose of marriage is procreation. According to this argument, since same-sex couples are unable to procreate on their own, they don't have a right to marry. They lack, so to speak, the relevant virtue.

This teleological line of reasoning is at the heart of the case against same-sex marriage, and Marshall takes it on directly. She does not pre-

tend to be neutral on the purpose of marriage, but offers a rival interpretation of it. The essence of marriage, she maintains, is not procreation
but an exclusive, loving commitment between two partners—be they
straight or gay.

Now, how, you might ask, is it possible to adjudicate between rival
accounts of the purpose, or essence, of marriage? Is it possible to argue
rationally about the meaning and purpose of morally contested social
institutions such as marriage? Or is it simply a clash of bald assertions—some say it's about procreation, others say it's about loving
commitment—and there's no way of showing one to be more plausible
than the other?

Marshall's opinion offers a good illustration of how such arguments
can proceed. First, she disputes the claim that procreation is the primary purpose of marriage. She does so by showing that marriage, as
currently practiced and regulated by the state, does not require the
ability to procreate. Heterosexual couples who apply for marriage li-
censes are not asked about "their ability or intention to conceive children by coitus. Fertility is not a condition of marriage, nor is it grounds
for divorce. People who have never consummated their marriage, and
never plan to, may be and stay married. People who cannot stir from
their deathbed may marry." While "many, perhaps most married couples have children together (assisted or unassisted)," Marshall concludes, "it is the exclusive and permanent commitment of the marriage
partners to one another, not the begetting of children, that is the sine
qua non of civil marriage."[37]

So part of Marshall's argument consists of an interpretation of
the purpose or essence of marriage as it currently exists. Faced with
rival interpretations of a social practice—marriage-as-procreation
versus marriage-as-exclusive-and-permanent-commitment—how can
we determine which is more plausible? One way is to ask which account makes better sense of existing marriage laws, taken as a whole.
Another is to ask which interpretation of marriage celebrates virtues
worth honoring. What counts as the purpose of marriage partly de-

pends on what qualities we think marriage should celebrate and affirm. This makes the underlying moral and religious controversy unavoidable: What is the moral status of gay and lesbian relationships?

Marshall is not neutral on this question. She argues that same-sex relationships are as worthy of respect as heterosexual relationships. Restricting marriage to heterosexuals "confers an official stamp of approval on the destructive stereotype that same-sex relationships are inherently unstable and inferior to opposite-sex relationships and are not worthy of respect."[38]

So when we look closely at the case for same-sex marriage, we find that it cannot rest on the ideas of nondiscrimination and freedom of choice. In order to decide who should qualify for marriage, we have to think through the purpose of marriage and the virtues it honors. And this carries us onto contested moral terrain, where we can't remain neutral toward competing conceptions of the good life.

Justice and the Good Life

Over the course of this journey, we've explored three approaches to justice. One says justice means maximizing utility or welfare—the greatest happiness for the greatest number. The second says justice means respecting freedom of choice—either the actual choices people make in a free market (the libertarian view) or the hypothetical choices people *would* make in an original position of equality (the liberal egalitarian view). The third says justice involves cultivating virtue and reasoning about the common good. As you've probably guessed by now, I favor a version of the third approach. Let me try to explain why.

The utilitarian approach has two defects: First, it makes justice and rights a matter of calculation, not principle. Second, by trying to translate all human goods into a single, uniform measure of value, it flattens them, and takes no account of the qualitative differences among them.

The freedom-based theories solve the first problem but not the second. They take rights seriously and insist that justice is more than

mere calculation. Although they disagree among themselves about
which rights should outweigh utilitarian considerations, they agree that
certain rights are fundamental and must be respected. But beyond sin-
gling out certain rights as worthy of respect, they accept people's preferences as they are. They don't require us to question or challenge the
preferences and desires we bring to public life. According to these theories, the moral worth of the ends we pursue, the meaning and significance of the lives we lead, and the quality and character of the common
life we share all lie beyond the domain of justice.

This seems to me mistaken. A just society can't be achieved simply
by maximizing utility or by securing freedom of choice. To achieve a
just society we have to reason together about the meaning of the good
life, and to create a public culture hospitable to the disagreements that
will inevitably arise.

It is tempting to seek a principle or procedure that could justify,
once and for all, whatever distribution of income or power or opportunity resulted from it. Such a principle, if we could find it, would
enable us to avoid the tumult and contention that arguments about the
good life invariably arouse.

But these arguments are impossible to avoid. Justice is inescapably
judgmental. Whether we're arguing about financial bailouts or Purple
Hearts, surrogate motherhood or same-sex marriage, affirmative action or military service, CEO pay or the right to use a golf cart, questions of justice are bound up with competing notions of honor and
virtue, pride and recognition. Justice is not only about the right way to
distribute things. It is also about the right way to value things.

A Politics of the Common Good

If a just society involves reasoning together about the good life, it remains to ask what kind of political discourse would point us in this
direction. I don't have a fully worked out answer to this question, but
I can offer a few illustrative suggestions. First, an observation: Today,

most of our political arguments revolve around welfare and freedom—increasing economic output and respecting people's rights. For many people, talk of virtue in politics brings to mind religious conservatives telling people how to live. But this is not the only way that conceptions of virtue and the common good can inform politics. The challenge is to imagine a politics that takes moral and spiritual questions seriously, but brings them to bear on broad economic and civic concerns, not only on sex and abortion.

In my lifetime, the most promising voice in this direction was that of Robert F. Kennedy, as he sought the Democratic presidential nomination in 1968. For him, justice involved more than the size and distribution of the national product. It was also about higher moral purposes. In a speech at the University of Kansas on March 18, 1968, Kennedy spoke of the war in Vietnam, riots in America's cities, racial inequality, and the crushing poverty he had witnessed in Mississippi and Appalachia. He then turned from these explicit matters of justice to argue that Americans had come to value the wrong things. "Even if we act to erase material poverty," Kennedy said, "there is another greater task. It is to confront the poverty of satisfaction . . . that afflicts us all." Americans had given themselves over to "the mere accumulation of things."[39]

> Our Gross National Product now is over 800 billion dollars a year. But that Gross National Product counts air pollution and cigarette advertising, and ambulances to clear our highways of carnage. It counts special locks for our doors and the jails for the people who break them. It counts the destruction of the redwood and the loss of our natural wonder in chaotic sprawl. It counts napalm and counts nuclear warheads and armored cars for the police to fight the riots in our cities. It counts . . . the television programs which glorify violence in order to sell toys to our children. Yet the Gross National Product does not allow for the health of our children, the quality of their education or the joy of their play. It does not include the beauty of our poetry or the strength of our marriages, the intelligence of our

public debate or the integrity of our public officials. It measures neither our wit nor our courage, neither our wisdom nor our learning,
neither our compassion nor our devotion to our country. It measures
everything, in short, except that which makes life worthwhile. And
it can tell us everything about America except why we are proud to
be Americans.[40]

Listening to Kennedy, or reading this passage, you might say that
the moral criticism he leveled against the self-satisfaction and material
preoccupations of his time was independent of his point about the injustices of poverty, the Vietnam War, and racial discrimination. But he
saw them as connected. To reverse these injustices, Kennedy thought it
necessary to challenge the complacent way of life he saw around him.
He did not hesitate to be judgmental. And yet, by invoking Americans'
pride in their country, he also, at the same time, appealed to a sense of
community.

Kennedy was assassinated less than three months later. We can only
speculate whether the morally resonant politics he intimated would
have come to fruition had he lived.

Four decades later, during the 2008 presidential campaign, Barack
Obama also tapped Americans' hunger for a public life of larger purpose and articulated a politics of moral and spiritual aspiration. Whether
the need to contend with a financial crisis and deep recession will prevent him from turning the moral and civic thrust of his campaign into
a new politics of the common good remains to be seen.

What might a new politics of the common good look like? Here are
some possible themes:

1. Citizenship, sacrifice, and service

If a just society requires a strong sense of community, it must find a
way to cultivate in citizens a concern for the whole, a dedication to the
common good. It can't be indifferent to the attitudes and dispositions,

the "habits of the heart," that citizens bring to public life. It must find a way to lean against purely privatized notions of the good life, and cultivate civic virtue.

Traditionally, the public school has been a site of civic education. In some generations, the military has been another. I'm referring not mainly to the explicit teaching of civic virtue, but to the practical, often inadvertent civic education that takes place when young people from different economic classes, religious backgrounds, and ethnic communities come together in common institutions.

At a time when many public schools are in a parlous condition and when only a small fraction of American society serves in the military, it is a serious question how a democratic society as vast and disparate as ours can hope to cultivate the solidarity and sense of mutual responsibility that a just society requires. This question has recently reappeared in our political discourse, at least to some extent.

During the 2008 campaign, Barack Obama observed that the events of September 11, 2001, stirred in Americans a sense of patriotism and pride, and a new willingness to serve their country. And he criticized President George W. Bush for not summoning Americans to some form of shared sacrifice. "Instead of a call to service," Obama said, "we were asked to go shopping. Instead of a call for shared sacrifice, we gave tax cuts to the wealthiest Americans in a time of war for the very first time in our history."[41]

Obama proposed to encourage national service by offering students help with college tuition in exchange for one hundred hours of public service. "You invest in America, and America invests in you," he told young people as he campaigned across the country. The proposal proved to be one of his most popular, and in April 2009, he signed legislation to expand the AmeriCorps public service program and provide college money for students who volunteered in their communities. Despite the resonance of Obama's call to national service, however, more ambitious proposals for mandatory national service have not found their way onto the political agenda.

2. The moral limits of markets

One of the most striking tendencies of our time is the expansion of markets and market-oriented reasoning into spheres of life traditionally governed by non-market norms. In earlier chapters, we consider the moral questions that arise, for example, when countries hire out military service and the interrogation of prisoners to mercenaries or private contractors; or when parents outsource pregnancy and child-bearing to paid laborers in the developing world; or when people buy and sell kidneys on the open market. Other instances abound: Should students in underperforming schools be offered cash payments for scoring well on standardized tests? Should teachers be given bonuses for improving the test results of their students? Should states hire for-profit prison companies to house their inmates? Should the United States simplify its immigration policy by adopting the proposal of a University of Chicago economist to sell U.S. citizenship for a $100,000 fee?[42]

These questions are not only about utility and consent. They are also about the right ways of valuing key social practices—military service, child-bearing, teaching and learning, criminal punishment, the admission of new citizens, and so on. Since marketizing social practices may corrupt or degrade the norms that define them, we need to ask what non-market norms we want to protect from market intrusion. This is a question that requires public debate about competing conceptions of the right way of valuing goods. Markets are useful instruments for organizing productive activity. But unless we want to let the market rewrite the norms that govern social institutions, we need a public debate about the moral limits of markets.

3. Inequality, solidarity, and civic virtue

Within the United States, the gap between rich and poor has grown in recent decades, reaching levels not seen since the 1930s. Yet inequality has not loomed large as a political issue. Even Barack Obama's modest proposal to return income tax rates to where they stood in the 1990s prompted his 2008 Republican opponents to call him a socialist who wanted to spread the wealth.

The dearth of attention to inequality in contemporary politics does not reflect any lack of attention to the topic among political philosophers. The just distribution of income and wealth has been a mainstay of debate within political philosophy from the 1970s to the present. But the tendency of philosophers to frame the question in terms of utility or consent leads them to overlook the argument against inequality most likely to receive a political hearing and most central to the project of moral and civic renewal.

Some philosophers who would tax the rich to help the poor argue in the name of utility; taking a hundred dollars from a rich person and giving it to a poor person will diminish the rich person's happiness only slightly, they speculate, but greatly increase the happiness of the poor person. John Rawls also defends redistribution, but on the grounds of hypothetical consent. He argues that if we imagined a hypothetical social contract in an original position of equality, everyone would agree to a principle that would support some form of redistribution.

But there is a third, more important reason to worry about the growing inequality of American life: Too great a gap between rich and poor undermines the solidarity that democratic citizenship requires. Here's how: As inequality deepens, rich and poor live increasingly separate lives. The affluent send their children to private schools (or to public schools in wealthy suburbs), leaving urban public schools to the children of families who have no alternative. A similar trend leads to the secession by the privileged from other public institutions and facilities.[43] Private health clubs replace municipal recreation centers and swimming pools. Upscale residential communities hire private security guards and rely less on public police protection. A second or third car removes the need to rely on public transportation. And so on. The affluent secede from public places and services, leaving them to those who can't afford anything else.

This has two bad effects, one fiscal, the other civic. First, public services deteriorate, as those who no longer use those services become less willing to support them with their taxes. Second, public institutions such as schools, parks, playgrounds, and community centers cease to be places where citizens from different walks of life encounter one another. Institutions that once gathered people together and served as informal schools of civic virtue become few and far between. The hollowing out of the public realm makes it difficult to cultivate the solidarity and sense of community on which democratic citizenship depends.

So, quite apart from its effects on utility or consent, inequality can be corrosive to civic virtue. Conservatives enamored of markets and liberals concerned with redistribution overlook this loss.

If the erosion of the public realm is the problem, what is the solution? A politics of the common good would take as one of its primary goals the reconstruction of the infrastructure of civic life. Rather than focus on redistribution for the sake of broadening access to private consumption, it would tax the affluent to rebuild public institutions and services so that rich and poor alike would want to take advantage of them.

An earlier generation made a massive investment in the federal highway program, which gave Americans unprecedented individual mobility and freedom, but also contributed to the reliance on the private automobile, suburban sprawl, environmental degradation, and living patterns corrosive to community. This generation could commit itself to an equally consequential investment in an infrastructure for civic renewal: public schools to which rich and poor alike would want to send their children; public transportation systems reliable enough to attract upscale commuters; and public health clinics, playgrounds, parks, recreation centers, libraries, and museums that would, ideally at least, draw people out of their gated communities and into the common spaces of a shared democratic citizenship.

Focusing on the civic consequences of inequality, and ways of reversing them, might find political traction that arguments about income distribution as such do not. It would also help highlight the connection between distributive justice and the common good.

4. A politics of moral engagement

Some consider public engagement with questions of the good life to be a civic transgression, a journey beyond the bounds of liberal public reason. Politics and law should not become entangled in moral and religious disputes, we often think, for such entanglement opens the way to coercion and intolerance. This is a legitimate worry. Citizens of pluralist societies do disagree about morality and religion. Even if, as I've argued, it's not possible for government to be neutral on these disagreements, is it nonetheless possible to conduct our politics on the basis of mutual respect?

The answer, I think, is yes. But we need a more robust and engaged civic life than the one to which we've become accustomed. In recent decades, we've come to assume that respecting our fellow citizens' moral and religious convictions means ignoring them (for political purposes, at least), leaving them undisturbed, and conducting our public life—insofar as possible—without reference to them. But this stance of avoidance can make for a spurious respect. Often, it means suppressing moral disagreement rather than actually avoiding it. This can provoke backlash and resentment. It can also make for an impoverished public discourse, lurching from one news cycle to the next, preoccupied with the scandalous, the sensational, and the trivial.

A more robust public engagement with our moral disagreements could provide a stronger, not a weaker, basis for mutual respect. Rather than avoid the moral and religious convictions that our fellow citizens bring to public life, we should attend to them more directly—sometimes by challenging and contesting them, sometimes by listening to and learning from them. There is no guarantee that public deliberation about hard moral questions will lead in any given situation to agreement—or even to appreciation for the moral and religious views of others. It's always possible that learning more about a moral or religious doctrine will lead us to like it less. But we cannot know until we try.

A politics of moral engagement is not only a more inspiring ideal than a politics of avoidance. It is also a more promising basis for a just society.

NOTES

Chapter 1: Doing the Right Thing

1. Michael McCarthy, "After Storm Come the Vultures," *USA Today*, August 20, 2004, p. 6B.
2. Joseph B. Treaster, "With Storm Gone, Floridians Are Hit with Price Gouging," *New York Times*, August 18, 2004, p. A1; McCarthy, "After Storm Come the Vultures."
3. McCarthy, "After Storm Come the Vultures"; Treaster, "With Storm Gone, Floridians Are Hit with Price Gouging"; Crist quoted in Jeff Jacoby, "Bring on the 'Price Gougers,'" *Boston Globe*, August 22, 2004, p. F11.
4. McCarthy, "After Storm Come the Vultures"; Allison North Jones, "West Palm Days Inn Settles Storm Gouging Suit," *Tampa Tribune*, October 6, 2004, p. 3.
5. Thomas Sowell, "How 'Price Gouging' Helps Floridians," *Tampa Tribune*, September 15, 2004; also published as "'Price Gouging' in Florida," *Capitalism Magazine*, September 14, 2004, at www.capmag.com/article.asp?ID=3918.
6. Ibid.
7. Jacoby, "Bring on the 'Price Gougers.'"
8. Charlie Crist, "Storm Victims Need Protection," *Tampa Tribune*, September 17, 2004, p. 17.
9. Ibid.
10. Jacoby, "Bring on the 'Price Gougers.'"
11. Lizette Alvarez and Erik Eckholm, "Purple Heart Is Ruled Out for Traumatic Stress," *New York Times*, January 8, 2009.

12. Ibid.

13. Tyler E. Boudreau, "Troubled Minds and Purple Hearts," *New York Times*, January 26, 2009, p. A21.

14. Alvarez and Eckholm, "Purple Heart Is Ruled Out."

15. Boudreau, "Troubled Minds and Purple Hearts."

16. S. Mitra Kalita, "Americans See 18% of Wealth Vanish," *Wall Street Journal*, March 13, 2009, p. A1.

17. Jackie Calmes and Louise Story, "418 Got A.I.G. Bonuses; Outcry Grows in Capital," *New York Times*, March 18, 2009, p. A1; Bill Saporito, "How AIG Became Too Big to Fail," *Time*, March 30, 2009, p. 16.

18. AIG CEO Edward M. Liddy quoted in Edmund L. Andrews and Peter Baker, "Bonus Money at Troubled A.I.G. Draws Heavy Criticism," *New York Times*, March 16, 2009; see also Liam Pleven, Serena Ng, and Sudeep Reddy, "AIG Faces Growing Wrath Over Payments," *Wall Street Journal*, March 16, 2009.

19. *New York Post*, March 18, 2009, p. 1.

20. Shailagh Murray and Paul Kane, "Senate Will Delay Action on Punitive Tax on Bonuses," *Washington Post*, March 24, 2009, p. A7.

21. Mary Williams Walsh and Carl Hulse, "A.I.G. Bonuses of $50 Million to Be Repaid," *New York Times*, March 24, 2009, p. A1.

22. Greg Hitt, "Drive to Tax AIG Bonuses Slows," *Wall Street Journal*, March 25, 2009.

23. Not all recipients of the disputed A.I.G. bonuses were responsible for having made the risky investments that created the havoc. Some had joined the financial products division after the crash, to help clean up the mess. One such executive published an op-ed piece complaining that the public outrage had failed to distinguish between those responsible for the reckless investments and those who had had no part in them. See Jake DeSantis, "Dear AIG, I Quit!," *New York Times*, March 24, 2009. Unlike DeSantis, Joseph Cassano, president of A.I.G.'s financial products for thirteen years, made $280 million before leaving the company in March 2008, shortly before the credit default swaps he championed ruined the company.

24. Senator Sherrod Brown quoted in Jonathan Weisman, Naftali Bendavid, and Deborah Solomon, "Congress Looks to a Tax to Recoup Bonus Money," *Wall Street Journal*, March 18, 2009, p. A2.

25. President Barack Obama, remarks by the president, the White House, March 16, 2009, at www.whitehouse.gov/the_press_office/Remarks-by-the-President-to-small-business-owners.

26. Michael Shnayerson, "Wall Street's $16 Billion Bonus," *Vanity Fair*, March 2009.

27. President Barack Obama, remarks by the president on executive compensation, the White House, February 4, 2009, at www.whitehouse.gov/blog_post/new_rules.

28. Senator Grassley made his comments on WMT radio in Iowa. They are reprinted in *The Caucus*, a blog on the *New York Times* website. See Kate Phillips, "Grassley: AIG Must Take Its Medicine (Not Hemlock)," March 17, 2009, at www.thecaucus.blogs.nytimes.com/2009/03/17/grassley-aig-should-take-its-medicine-not-hemlock.

29. Ibid. See also Kate Phillips, "Senator Wants Some Remorse from C.E.O.'s," *New York Times*, March 18, 2009, p. A15.

30. Alan Schwartz, former chief executive of Bear Stearns, quoted in William D. Cohen, "A Tsunami of Excuses," *New York Times*, March 12, 2009.

31. Ibid.

32. Shnayerson, "Wall Street's $16 Billion Bonus."

33. David R. Francis, "Should CEO Pay Restrictions Spread to All Corporations?," *Christian Science Monitor*, March 9, 2009.

34. Ibid.

35. CEO pay figures from analysis of 2004–2006 data by Towers Perrin, cited in Kenji Hall, "No Outcry About CEO Pay in Japan," *BusinessWeek*, February 10, 2009.

36. The classic formulations of the trolley case are Philippa Foot, "The Problem of Abortion and the Doctrine of Double Effect," in *Virtues and Vices and Other Essays in Moral Philosophy* (Oxford, UK: Basil Blackwell, 1978), p. 19, and Judith Jarvis Thomson, "The Trolley Problem," *Yale Law Journal* 94 (May 1985): 1395–415.

37. The following account is drawn from Marcus Luttrell, with Patrick Robinson, *Lone Survivor: The Eyewitness Account of Operation Redwing and the Lost Heroes of SEAL Team 10* (New York: Little, Brown and Company, 2007).

38. Ibid., p. 205.

39. Ibid.

40. Ibid., pp. 206–207.

Chapter 2: The Greatest Happiness Principle / Utilitarianism

1. *Queen v. Dudley and Stephens*, 14 Queens Bench Division 273, 9 December 1884. Quotes from newspaper account in "The Story of the Mignonette," *The Illus-*

trated London News, September 20, 1884. See also A. W. Brian Simpson, *Cannibalism and the Common Law* (Chicago: University of Chicago Press, 1984).

2. Jeremy Bentham, *Introduction to the Principles of Morals and Legislation* (1789), J. H. Burns and H.L.A. Hart, eds. (Oxford University Press, 1996), chap. 1.

3. Ibid.

4. Jeremy Bentham, "Tracts on Poor Laws and Pauper Management," 1797, in John Bowring, ed., *The Works of Jeremy Bentham*, vol. 8 (New York: Russell & Russell, 1962), pp. 369–439.

5. Ibid., p. 401.

6. Ibid., pp. 401-402.

7. Ibid., p. 373.

8. Ursula K. Le Guin, "The Ones Who Walked Away from Omelas," in Richard Bausch, ed., *Norton Anthology of Short Fiction* (New York: W. W. Norton, 2000).

9. Gordon Fairclough, "Philip Morris Notes Cigarettes' Benefits for Nation's Finances," *Wall Street Journal*, July 16, 2001, p. A2. The text of the report, "Public Finance Balance of Smoking in the Czech Republic," November 28, 2000, as prepared for Philip Morris by Arthur D. Little International, Inc., is available online at www.mindfully.org/Industry/Philip-Morris-Czech-Study.htm and at www.tobaccofreekids.org/reports/philipmorris/pmczechstudy.pdf.

10. Ellen Goodman, "Thanks, but No Thanks," *Boston Globe*, July 22, 2001, p. D7.

11. Gordon Fairclough, "Philip Morris Says It's Sorry for Death Report," *Wall Street Journal*, July 26, 2001, p. B1.

12. The court case was *Grimshaw v. Ford Motor Co.*, 174 *Cal. Reporter* 348 (Cal. Ct. App. 1981). The cost-benefit analysis was reported in Mark Dowie, "Pinto Madness," *Mother Jones*, September/October 1977. For a similar General Motors case, see Elsa Walsh and Benjamin Weiser, "Court Secrecy Masks Safety Issues," *Washington Post*, October 23, 1988, pp. A1, A22.

13. W. Kip Kiscusi, "Corporate Risk Analysis: A Reckless Act?," *Stanford Law Review* 52 (February 2000): 569.

14. Katharine Q. Seelye and John Tierney, "E.P.A. Drops Age-Based Cost Studies," *New York Times*, May 8, 2003, p. A26; Cindy Skrzycki, "Under Fire, E.P.A. Drops the 'Senior Death Discount,'" *Washington Post*, May 13, 2003, p. E1; Robert Hahn and Scott Wallsten, "Whose Life Is Worth More? (And Why Is It Horrible to Ask?)," *Washington Post*, June 1, 2003.

15. Orley Ashenfelter and Michael Greenstone, "Using Mandated Speed Limits to Measure the Value of a Statistical Life," *Journal of Political Economy* 112, Supplement (February 2004): S227–67.

16. Edward L. Thorndike, *Human Nature and the Social Order* (New York: Macmillan, 1940). Abridged version edited by Geraldine Joncich Clifford, (Boston: MIT Press, 1969), pp. 78–83.

17. Ibid., p. 43.

18. Ibid.

19. John Stuart Mill, *On Liberty* (1859), Stefan Collini, ed. (Cambridge University Press, 1989), chap. 1.

20. Ibid.

21. Ibid., chap. 3.

22. Ibid.

23. Ibid.

24. The quote comes from an obscure writing by Bentham, *The Rationale of Reward*, published in the 1820s. Bentham's statement was brought to prominence by John Stuart Mill. See Ross Harrison, *Bentham* (London: Routledge, 1983), p. 5.

25. John Stuart Mill, *Utilitarianism* (1861), George Sher, ed. (Hackett Publishing, 1979), chap. 2.

26. Ibid.

27. Ibid., chap. 4.

28. Ibid., chap. 2.

29. Ibid.

30. I draw here and in the following paragraphs on the excellent account by Joseph Lelyveld, "English Thinker (1748–1832) Preserves His Poise," *New York Times*, June 18, 1986.

31. "Extract from Jeremy Bentham's Last Will and Testament," May 30, 1832, on the Web site of the Bentham Project, University College London, at www.ucl .ac.uk/Bentham-Project/info/will.htm.

32. These and other anecdotes are related on the Web site of the Bentham Project, University College London, at www.ucl.ac.uk/Bentham-Project/info/jb.htm.

33. Ibid.

Chapter 3: Do We Own Ourselves? / Libertarianism

1. Matthew Miller and Duncan Greenberg, "The Forbes 400," *Forbes*, September 17, 2008, at www.forbes.com/2008/09/16/forbes-400-billionaires-lists -400list08_cx_mn_0917richamericans_land.html.

2. Lawrence Michel, Jared Bernstein, and Sylvia Allegretto, *The State of Working America 2006/2007: An Economic Policy Institute Book*, Ithaca, N.Y.: ILR Press, an

imprint of Cornell University Press, 2007, using data from Edward N. Wolff (2006), at www.stateofworkingamerica.org/tabfig/05/SWA06_05_Wealth .pdf. See also Arthur B. Kennickell, "Currents and Undercurrents: Changes in the Distribution of Wealth, 1989–2004," Federal Reserve Board, Washington, D.C., January 30, 2006, at www.federalreserve.gov/pubs/oss/oss2/papers/ concentration.2004.5.pdf.

3. Friedrich A. Hayek, *The Constitution of Liberty* (Chicago: University of Chicago Press, 1960).

4. Milton Friedman, *Capitalism and Freedom* (Chicago: University of Chicago Press, 1962), p. 188.

5. Ibid., p. 111.

6. Ibid., pp. 137–60.

7. Robert Nozick, *Anarchy, State, and Utopia* (New York: Basic Books, 1974), p. ix.

8. Ibid., pp. 149–60.

9. Ibid., pp. 160–64.

10. Ibid., p. 169.

11. Ibid., p. 172.

12. Ibid., p. 171.

13. Monica Davey, "Kevorkian Speaks After His Release From Prison," *New York Times*, June 4, 2007.

14. Mark Landler, "Eating People Is Wrong! But Is It Homicide? Court to Rule," *New York Times*, December 26, 2003, p. A4.

15. Mark Landler, "German Court Convicts Internet Cannibal of Manslaughter," *New York Times*, January 31, 2004, p. A3; Tony Paterson, "Cannibal of Rotenburg Gets 8 Years for Eating a Willing Victim," *The Independent* (London), January 31, 2004, p. 30.

16. Luke Harding, "German Court Finds Cannibal Guilty of Murder," *The Guardian* (London), May 10, 2006, p. 16.

17. Karen Bale, "Killer Cannibal Becomes Veggie," *Scottish Daily Record*, November 21, 2007, p. 20.

Chapter 4: Hired Help / Markets and Morals

1. James W. Geary, *We Need Men: The Union Draft in the Civil War* (DeKalb: Northern Illinois University Press, 1991), pp. 3–48; James M. McPherson, *Battle Cry*

of Freedom: The Civil War Era (New York: Oxford University Press, 1988), pp. 490–94.

2. McPherson, *Battle Cry*, pp. 600–11.

3. Ibid.; Geary, *We Need Men*, pp. 103–50.

4. McPherson, *Battle Cry*, p. 601; Geary, *We Need Men*, p. 83.

5. Geary, *We Need Men*, p. 150, and *The Civil War: A Film by Ken Burns*, episode 5, "The Universe of Battle," chapter 8.

6. Jeffrey M. Jones, "Vast Majority of Americans Opposed to Reinstating Military Draft," Gallup News Service, September 7, 2007, at www.gallup.com/poll/28642/Vast-Majority-Americans-Opposed-Reinstituting-Military-Draft.aspx.

7. Hon. Ron Paul (R-Texas), "3000 American Deaths in Iraq," U.S. House of Representatives, January 5, 2007; at www.ronpaullibrary.org/document.php?id=532.

8. "Army Recruitment in FY 2008: A Look at Age, Race, Income, and Education of New Soldiers," National Priorities Project; data from chart 6: Active-duty Army: Recruits by Neighborhood Income, 2005, 2007, 2008; at www.nationalpriorities.org/militaryrecruiting2008/active_duty_army/recruits_by_neighborhood_income.

9. Ibid. A study by the Heritage Foundation challenges this finding, in part by showing that officers come disproportionately from more affluent zip codes. See Shanea J. Watkins and James Sherk, "Who Serves in the U.S. Military? Demographic Characteristics of Enlisted Troops and Officers," Heritage Center for Data Analysis, August 21, 2008, at www.heritage.org/Research/National Security/cda08-05.cfm.

10. "Military Recruitment 2008: Significant Gap in Army's Quality and Quantity Goals," National Priorities Project; data from Table 1: Educational Attainment, FY 2008, at www.nationalpriorities.org/militaryrecruiting2008/army2008 edattainment.

11. David M. Kennedy, "The Wages of a Mercenary Army: Issues of Civil-Military Relations," *Bulletin of the American Academy* (Spring 2006): 12–16. Kennedy cites Andrew Bacevich, *The New American Militarism: How Americans Are Seduced by War* (New York: Oxford University Press, 2005), p. 28.

12. Kathy Roth-Douquet and Frank Schaeffer, *AWOL: The Unexcused Absence of America's Upper Classes from Military Service* (New York: HarperCollins, 2006).

13. Arielle Gorin, "Princeton, in the Nation's Service?," *The Daily Princetonian*, January 22, 2007. The Princeton figures are from Charles Moskos, a sociologist

who studies the military. Moskos is quoted in Julian E. Barnes and Peter Spie-gel, "Expanding the Military, Without a Draft," *Los Angeles Times*, December 24, 2006.

14. *USA Today* reports that, according to the U.S. Senate Library, at least 9 of the 535 members of Congress have sons or daughters who have served in Iraq. Kathy Kiely, "Lawmakers Have Loved Ones in Combat Zone," *USA Today*, January 23, 2007.

15. Charles Rangel, "Why I Want the Draft," *New York Daily News*, November 22, 2006, p. 15.

16. Ibid.

17. Kennedy, "The Wages of a Mercenary Army"; see also David M. Kennedy, "The Best Army We Can Buy," *New York Times*, July 25, 2005, p. A19.

18. Ibid., p. 13.

19. Ibid., p. 16.

20. Jean-Jacques Rousseau, *The Social Contract* (1762), Book III, chap. 15, translated by G.D.H. Cole (London: J. M. Dent and Sons, 1973).

21. Doreen Carvajal, "Foreign Legion Turns to Internet in Drive for Recruits," *Boston Sunday Globe*, November 12, 2006; Molly Moore, "Legendary Force Updates Its Image: Online Recruiting, Anti-Terrorist Activities Routine in Today's French Foreign Legion," *Washington Post*, May 13, 2007, p. A14.

22. Julia Preston, "U.S. Military Will Offer Path to Citizenship," *New York Times*, February 15, 2009, p. 1; Bryan Bender, "Military Considers Recruiting Foreigners," *Boston Globe*, December 26, 2006, p. 1.

23. T. Christian Miller, "Contractors Outnumber Troops in Iraq," *Los Angeles Times*, July 4, 2007.

24. Peter W. Singer, "Can't Win with 'Em, Can't Go to War Without 'Em: Private Military Contractors and Counterinsurgency," Brookings Institution, *Foreign Policy Paper Series*, September 2007, p. 3.

25. According to U.S. Department of Labor insurance claims, 1,292 contractors had been killed as of April 2008. Figures quoted in Peter W. Singer, "Outsourcing the Fight," *Forbes*, June 5, 2008. On contractor deaths not being counted by the U.S. military, see Steve Fainaru, "Soldier of Misfortune: Fighting a Parallel War in Iraq, Private Contractors Are Officially Invisible—Even in Death," *Washington Post*, December 1, 2008, p. C1.

26. Evan Thomas and March Hosenball, "The Man Behind Blackwater," *Newsweek*, October 22, 2007, p. 36.

NOTES TO PAGES 89–99 279

27. Prince quoted in Mark Hemingway, "Warriors for Hire: Blackwater USA and the Rise of Private Military Contractors," *The Weekly Standard*, December 18, 2006.

28. The billion-dollar figure for Blackwater in Iraq is from Steve Fainaru, *Big Boy Rules: America's Mercenaries Fighting in Iraq* (New York: Da Capo, 2008), quoted in Ralph Peters, "Hired Guns," *Washington Post*, December 21, 2008.

29. Ginger Thompson and James Risen, "Five Guards Face U.S. Charges in Iraq Deaths," *New York Times*, December 6, 2008.

30. Singer, "Can't Win with 'Em," p. 7.

31. The facts of the case presented in this and the following paragraphs are drawn from the court opinions: In re *Baby M*, 217 New Jersey Superior Court, 313 (1987), and *Matter of Baby M*, Supreme Court of New Jersey, 537 *Atlantic Reporter*, 2d Series, 1227 (1988).

32. In re *Baby M*, 217 New Jersey Superior Court, 313 (1987).

33. Ibid., p. 374–75.

34. Ibid., p. 376.

35. Ibid., p. 372.

36. Ibid., p. 388.

37. *Matter of Baby M*, Supreme Court of New Jersey, 537 *Atlantic Reporter*, 2d Series, 1227 (1988).

38. Ibid., p. 1248.

39. Ibid.

40. Ibid., p. 1249.

41. Ibid.

42. Ibid., pp. 1248–49.

43. Elizabeth S. Anderson, "Is Women's Labor a Commodity?" *Philosophy and Public Affairs* 19 (Winter 1990): 71–92.

44. Ibid., p. 77.

45. Ibid., pp. 80–81.

46. Ibid., p. 82.

47. Susannah Cahalan, "Tug O' Love Baby M All Grown Up," *New York Post*, April 13, 2008.

48. Lorraine Ali and Raina Kelley, "The Curious Lives of Surrogates," *Newsweek*, April 7, 2008; Debora L. Spar, *The Baby Business* (Cambridge, Mass.: Harvard Business School Press, 2006), pp. 83–84.

49. In Spar, *The Baby Business*. Spar has since become president of Barnard College.

50. Ibid., p. 79.

51. Ibid.

52. Ibid., p. 80.

53. Ibid., p. 81.

54. Ibid.

55. Sam Dolnick, "World Outsources Pregnancies to India," Associated Press Online, December 30, 2007.

56. Ibid. See also Amelia Gentleman, "India Nurtures Business of Surrogate Motherhood," *NewYork Times*, March 10, 2008, p. 9.

57. Dolnick, "World Outsources Pregnancies to India."

58. Ibid.

59. Gentleman, "India Nurtures Business of Surrogate Motherhood."

60. The woman and her economic situation are reported in Dolnick, "World Outsources Pregnancies to India."

61. Ibid.

Chapter 5: What Matters Is the Motive / Immanuel Kant

1. See Christine M. Korsgaard, "Introduction," Immanuel Kant, *Groundwork of the Metaphysics of Morals* (Cambridge: Cambridge University Press, 1997), pp. vii–viii.

2. Immanuel Kant, *Groundwork for the Metaphysics of Morals* (1785), translated by H. J. Paton (NewYork: Harper Torchbooks, 1964), 442. Since readers will use various editions of Kant's *Groundwork*, I cite the standard page numbers, drawn from the edition of the *Groundwork* published by the Royal Prussian Academy in Berlin. Most contemporary editions of the *Groundwork* use these page references.

3. Ibid.

4. Ibid., 394.

5. Ibid., 390.

6. I am indebted to Lucas Stanczyk for this formulation of Kant's view.

7. Ibid., 397.

8. Hubert B. Herring, "Discounts for Honesty," *NewYork Times*, March 9, 1997.

9. Kant, *Groundwork*, p. 398.

10. Ibid.

11. Ibid.

12. "Misspeller Is a Spelling Bee Hero" (UPI), *NewYork Times*, June 9, 1983.

13. Kant, *Groundwork*, p. 412.

14. Ibid., 395.

15. Kant uses this phrase in an essay he wrote several years after the *Groundwork*. See Immanuel Kant, "On the Common Saying: 'This May Be True in Theory, But It Does Not Apply in Practice'" (1793), in Hans Reiss, ed., *Kant's Political Writings*, translated by H. B. Nisbet (Cambridge, UK: Cambridge University Press, 1970), p. 73.

16. Kant, *Groundwork*, p. 414.

17. Ibid., 416.

18. Ibid., 425. See also 419–20.

19. Ibid., 421.

20. Ibid., 422.

21. Ibid., 428.

22. Ibid.

23. Ibid., 429.

24. Ibid.

25. Ibid., 433.

26. Ibid., 440.

27. Ibid., 447.

28. Ibid., 452.

29. Ibid.

30. Ibid., 453.

31. Ibid., 454.

32. Ibid., 454.

33. Ibid., 456.

34. Immanuel Kant, "Duties Toward the Body in Respect of Sexual Impulse" (1784–85), translated by Louis Infield and published in Immanuel Kant, *Lectures on Ethics* (Cambridge, Mass.: Hackettt Publishing, 1981), p. 164. This text is based on lecture notes taken by students who attended Kant's lectures.

35. Ibid.

36. Ibid., p. 165.

37. Ibid.

38. Ibid., pp. 165–66.

39. Ibid., p. 167.

40. Immanuel Kant, "On a Supposed Right to Lie Because of Philanthropic Concerns" (1799), translated by James W. Ellington and published as a supplement to Immanuel Kant, *Grounding for the Metaphysics of Morals* (Cambridge, Mass.: Hackett Publishing, 1993), p. 64.

41. Ibid., p. 65.

42. Kant quoted in Alasdair MacIntyre, "Truthfulness and Lies: What Can We Learn from Kant?" in Alasdair MacIntyre, *Ethics and Politics: Selected Essays*, vol. 2 (Cambridge, UK: Cambridge University Press, 2006), p. 123.

43. Ibid.

44. House Judiciary Committee, December 8, 1998. Exchange transcribed from CNN coverage. A partial transcript of the exchange can be found at www.cnn .com/ALLPOLITICS/stories/1998/12/08/as.it.happened.

45. Immanuel Kant, "On the Common Saying: 'This May Be True in Theory, but It Does Not Apply in Practice,'" (1793), translated by H. B. Nisbet and published in Hans Reiss ed., *Kant's Political Writings* (Cambridge: Cambridge University Press, 1970), pp. 73–74.

46. Ibid., p. 79.

47. Ibid.

Chapter 6: The Case for Equality / John Rawls

1. John Locke, *Second Treatise of Government* (1690), in Peter Laslett, ed., *Locke's Two Treatises of Government*, 2d ed. (Cambridge, UK: Cambridge University Press, 1967), sec. 119.

2. John Rawls, *A Theory of Justice* (Cambridge, Mass.: The Belknap Press of Harvard University Press, 1971).

3. See the excellent history of contract law, P. S. Atiyah, *The Rise and Fall of Freedom of Contract* (New York: Oxford University Press, 1979; also Charles Fried, *Contract as Promise* (Cambridge, Mass.: Harvard University Press, 1981).

4. Associated Press, "Bill for Clogged Toilet: $50,000," *Boston Globe*, September 13, 1984, p. 20.

5. David Hume, *Treatise of Human Nature* (1739–40), Book III, part II, sec. 2 (New York: Oxford University Press, 2nd ed., 1978).

6. Ibid., Book III, part III, sec. 5.

7. The story is related in Atiyah, *The Rise and Fall of Freedom of Contract*, pp. 487–88; Atiyah cites E. C. Mossner, *Life of David Hume* (Edinburgh: Kelson, 1954), p. 564.

8. Hume quoted in Atiyah, *Rise and Fall*, p. 487.

9. Steve Lee Myers, "'Squeegees' Rank High on Next Police Commissioner's Priority List," *New York Times*, December 4, 1993, pp. 23–24.

10. Rawls, *A Theory of Justice*, sec. 24.

11. Ibid., sec. 12.

12. Ibid.

13. Ibid.

14. Ibid.

15. Kurt Vonnegut, Jr., "Harrison Bergeron" (1961), in Vonnegut, *Welcome to the Monkey House* (New York: Dell Publishing, 1998), p. 7.

16. Ibid., pp. 10–11.

17. Rawls, *A Theory of Justice*, sec. 17.

18. Ibid., sec. 12.

19. Ibid., sec. 48.

20. Ibid.

21. Rawls, *A Theory of Justice* (2d ed., 1999), sec. 17.

22. Ibid., sec. 48.

23. Woody Allen, *Stardust Memories*, United Artists, 1980.

24. Milton and Rose Friedman, *Free to Choose* (New York: Houghton Mifflin Harcourt, 1980), pp. 136–37.

25. Rawls, *A Theory of Justice*, sec. 17.

26. Ibid. In the revised edition of *A Theory of Justice* (1999), Rawls dropped the phrase about sharing one another's fate.

Chapter 7: Arguing Affirmative Action

1. The facts of Hopwood's case are presented in *Cheryl J. Hopwood v. State of Texas*, United States Court of Appeals for the Fifth Circuit, 78 F.3d 932 (1996), and in Richard Bernstein, "Racial Discrimination or Righting Past Wrongs?," *New York Times*, July 13, 1994, p. B8. The district court opinion pointed out, in a footnote, that Hopwood's LSAT score, in the eighty-third percentile, placed her "well below the median LSAT for nonminorities in the 1992 entering class." See *Cheryl J. Hopwood v. State of Texas*, United States District Court for the Western District of Texas, 861 F. Supp. 551 (1994), at 43.

2. Michael Sharlot, quoted in Sam Walker, "Texas Hunts for Ways to Foster Diversity," *Christian Science Monitor*, June 12, 1997, p. 4.

3. Bernstein, "Racial Discrimination or Righting Past Wrongs?"

4. *Regents of University of California v. Bakke*, 438 U.S. 265 (1978).

5. *Grutter v. Bollinger*, 539 U.S. 306 (2003).

6. Ethan Bronner, "Colleges Look for Answers to Racial Gaps in Testing," *New York Times*, November 8, 1997, pp. A1, A12.

7. Michael Sharlot, then the acting dean of the University of Texas Law School, quoted in Bernstein, "Racial Discrimination or Righting Past Wrongs?"

8. *Regents of University of California v. Bakke*, 438 U.S. 265 (1978), appendix to opinion of Justice Powell, pp. 321–24.

9. Ibid., 323.

10. Ronald Dworkin, "Why Bakke Has No Case," *New York Review of Books*, vol. 24, November 10, 1977.

11. Ibid.

12. Lowell quote from "Lowell Tells Jews Limit at Colleges Might Help Them," *New York Times*, June 17, 1922, pp. 3.

13. Dartmouth quotes from William A. Honan, "Dartmouth Reveals Anti-Semitic Past," *New York Times*, November 11, 1997, p. A16.

14. Dworkin, "Why Bakke Has No Case."

15. An excellent account of the Starrett City quotas is Jefferson Morley, "Double Reverse Discrimination," *The New Republic*, July 9, 1984, pp. 14–18; see also Frank J. Prial, "Starrett City: 20,000 Tenants, Few Complaints," *New York Times*, December 10, 1984.

16. These hypothetical letters are adapted from Michael J. Sandel, *Liberalism and the Limits of Justice* (Cambridge, UK: Cambridge University Press, 2d ed., 1998).

Chapter 8: Who Deserves What? / Aristotle

1. Callie Smartt's story was reported in Sue Anne Pressley, "A 'Safety' Blitz," *Washington Post*, November 12, 1996, pp. A1, A8. The analysis I present here draws on Michael J. Sandel, "Honor and Resentment," *The New Republic*, December 23, 1996, p. 27; reprinted in Michael J. Sandel, *Public Philosophy: Essays on Morality in Politics* (Cambridge, Mass.: Harvard University Press, 2005), pp. 97–100.

2. Aristotle, *The Politics*, edited and translated by Ernest Barker (New York: Oxford University Press, 1946), Book III, chap. xii [1282b].

3. Ibid.

4. A. A. Milne, *Winnie-the-Pooh* (1926; New York: Dutton Children's Books, 1988), pp. 5–6.

5. Aristotle, *The Politics*, Book III, chap. ix [1280b].

6. Ibid. [1280a].

7. Ibid. [1280b].

8. Ibid.

9. Ibid., [1281a]; Book III, chap. xii [1282b].

10. Ibid., Book I, chap. ii [1253a].

11. Ibid.

12. Ibid.

13. Aristotle, *Nicomachean Ethics*, translated by David Ross (New York: Oxford University Press, 1925), Book II, chap. 3 [1104b].

14. Ibid., Book II, chap. 1 [1103a].

15. Ibid. [1103a–1103b].

16. Ibid. [1003b].

17. Judith Martin, "The Pursuit of Politeness," *The New Republic*, August 6, 1984, p. 29.

18. Aristotle, *Nicomachean Ethics*, Book II, chap. 2 [1104a].

19. Ibid., Book II, chap. 9 [1109a].

20. Ibid., Book VI, chap. 6 [1140b].

21. Ibid., Book VI, chap. 7 [1141b].

22. Ibid., Book VI, chap. 5 [1140b].

23. Ibid., Book VI, chap. 7 [1141b].

24. I am indebted here to the illuminating discussion in Bernard Williams, *Shame and Necessity* (Berkeley: University of California Press, 1993), pp. 103–29.

25. Aristotle, *The Politics*, Book I, chap. v [1254a].

26. Ibid. [1254b].

27. Ibid. [1254b].

28. Ibid. [1255a].

29. Ibid., Book I, chap. vi [1254b].

30. Ibid. [1255b].

31. Ibid., Book I, chap. iii [1253b].

32. For an illuminating discussion of this point, see Russell Muirhead, *Just Work* (Cambridge, Mass.: Harvard University Press, 2004).

33. *PGA Tour v. Martin*, 532 U.S. 661 (2001).

34. Ibid., Justice Scalia dissent, at 700.

35. Ibid., Justice Stevens opinion, at 682.

36. Ibid., at 687.

37. Ibid.

38. Ibid., Justice Scalia dissent, at 701.

39. Tom Kite, "Keep the PGA on Foot," *New York Times*, February 2, 1998.

Chapter 9: What Do We Owe One Another? / Dilemmas of Loyalty

1. Elazar Barkan, *The Guilt of Nations* (New York: W. W. Norton, 2000), offers a good overview of post–World War II restitutions and apologies. On German reparations to Israel and Jews, see pp. 3–29. See also Howard M. Sachar, *A History of Israel* (London: Basil Blackwell, 1976), pp. 464–70.

2. Konrad Adenauer speech to Bundestag quoted in "History of the Claims Conference," at the official website of the Conference on Jewish Material Claims Against Germany, at www.claimscon.org/?url=history.

3. Johannes Rau quoted in Karin Laub, "Germany Asks Israel's Forgiveness over Holocaust," Associated Press, in *The Independent*, February 16, 2000.

4. Barkan, *The Guilt of Nations*, pp. 46–64. Hiroko Tabuchi, "Historians Find New Proof on Sex Slaves," Associated Press, April 17, 2007.

5. Barkan, *The Guilt of Nations*.

6. Norimitsu Onishi, "Call by U.S. House for Sex Slavery Apology Angers Japan's Leader," *New York Times*, August 1, 2007.

7. Barkan, *The Guilt of Nations*, pp. 245–48; "Australia Apologizes 'Without Qualification,'" Interview with Professor Patty O'Brien, Center for Australian and New Zealand Studies, Georgetown University, on National Public Radio, February 14, 2008.

8. Barkan, *The Guilt of Nations*.

9. Tim Johnston, "Australia Says 'Sorry' to Aborigines for Mistreatment," *New York Times*, February 13, 2008; Misha Schubert and Sarah Smiles, "Australia Says Sorry," *The Age* (Melbourne, Australia), February 13, 2008.

10. Barkan, *The Guilt of Nations*, pp. 30–45.

11. Ibid., pp. 216–31.

12. Ibid., pp. 283–93; Tamar Lewin, "Calls for Slavery Restitution Getting Louder," *New York Times*, June 4, 2001.

13. On Rep. John Conyers's bill to study reparations, see www.conyers.house .gov/index.cfm?FuseAction=Issues.Home&Issue_id=06007167-19b9-b4b1- 125c-df3de5ec97f8.

14. Walter Olson, "So Long, Slavery Reparations," *Los Angeles Times*, October 31, 2008, A19.

15. Survey research by Michael Dawson, reported in Harbour Fraser Hodder, "The Price of Slavery," *Harvard Magazine*, May–June 2003, pp. 12–13; see also Alfred L. Brophy, "The Cultural War over Reparations for Slavery," *DePaul Law Review* 53 (Spring 2004): 1201–11.

16. Wendy Koch, "Virginia First State to Express 'Regret' over Slavery," *USA Today*, February 26, 2007, p. 5A. On slaveholding population of Virginia and other states, see Christine Vestal, "States Lead Slavery Apology Movement," Stateline .org, April 4, 2008, at www.stateline.org/live/details/story?contentId =298236.

17. Vestal, "States Lead Slavery Apology Movement." See also "Apologies for Slavery," *State Legislatures*, June 2008, p. 6.

18. Darryl Fears, "House Issues an Apology for Slavery," *Washington Post*, July 30, 2008, p. A3; House Resolution 194: "Apologizing for the Enslavement and Racial Segregation of African-Americans," *Congressional Record House* 154, no. 127 (July 29, 2008): 7224–27,

19. For an insightful analysis of this issue, see David Miller, *National Responsibility and Global Justice* (New York: Oxford University Press, 2008), pp. 135–62.

20. Gay Alcorn, "The Business of Saying Sorry," *Sydney Morning Herald*, June 20, 2001, p. 17.

21. Henry Hyde quoted in Kevin Merida, "Did Freedom Alone Pay a Nation's Debt?," *Washington Post*, November 23, 1999.

22. Williams quoted in Lewin, "Calls for Slavery Restitution Getting Louder."

23. Tom Hester, Jr., "New Jersey Weighs Apology for Slavery," *Boston Globe*, January 2, 2008.

24. Darryl Fears, "Slavery Apology: A Sincere Step or Mere Politics?," *Washington Post*, August 2, 2008.

25. John Locke, *Second Treatise of Government* (1690), sec. 95, in John Locke, *Two Treatises of Goverment*, ed. Peter Laslett (Cambridge: Cambridge University Press, 3rd ed., 1988).

26. Aristotle, *The Politics*, Book VII, 1323a, translated by Ernest Barker (New York: Oxford University Press, 1946).

27. Immanuel Kant, *Critique of Practical Reason* (1788), translated by Lewis White Beck (Indianapolis: Library of Liberal Arts, 1956), pp. 66–67.

28. John Rawls, *A Theory of Justice* (Cambridge, Mass.: Harvard University Press, 1971), sec. 33, p. 211.

29. Ibid., sec. 84, p. 560.

30. Ibid., sec. 85, p. 561.

31. Ibid., sec. 84, p. 560.

32. For elaboration of this point, see Michael J. Sandel, *Democracy's Discontent* (Cambridge, Mass.: Harvard University Press, 1996), pp. 280–84; also James Holt, "The New Deal and the American Anti-Statist Tradition," in John Brae-

man, Robert H. Bremner, and David Brody, eds., *The New Deal: The National Level* (Columbus: Ohio State University Press, 1975), pp. 27–49.

33. Franklin D. Roosevelt, "Message to Congress on the State of the Union," January 11, 1944, in *Public Papers and Addresses*, vol. 13, pp. 40–42.

34. Robert Nozick, *Anarchy, State, and Utopia* (New York: Basic Books, 1974), p. 33.

35. Barry Goldwater, *The Conscience of a Conservative* (1960; Washington, D.C.: Regnery, Gateway edition, 1990), pp. 52–53, 66–68.

36. Alasdair MacIntyre, *After Virtue* (Notre Dame, Ind.: University of Notre Dame Press, 1981), p. 201.

37. Ibid.

38. Ibid., p. 204.

39. Ibid., pp. 204–205.

40. Ibid., p. 205.

41. Ibid.

42. Ibid.

43. John Rawls, *A Theory of Justice*, pp. 108–17.

44. Ibid., p. 114.

45. "Airlift to Israel Is Reported Taking Thousands of Jews from Ethiopia," *New York Times*, December 11, 1984; Hunter R. Clark, "Israel an Airlift to the Promised Land," *Time*, January 14, 1985.

46. Peres quoted in Anastasia Toufexis, "Israel Stormy Skies for a Refugee Airlift," *Time*, January 21, 1985.

47. Stephen Spector, *Operation Solomon: The Daring Rescue of the Ethiopian Jews* (New York: Oxford University Press, 2005). See also the website of the Israel Association for Ethiopian Jews: www.iaej.org.il/pages/history.htm.

48. Jean-Jacques Rousseau, "Discourse on Political Economy" (1755), translated by Donald A. Cress (Cambridge, Mass.: Hackett Publishing), p. 173.

49. Ibid., p. 174.

50. John Burnett, "A New Way to Patrol the Texas Border: Virtually," *All Things Considered*, National Public Radio, February 23, 2009. See www.npr.org/templates/story/story.php?storyId=101050132.

51. Michael Walzer, *Spheres of Justice* (New York: Basic Books, 1983), p. 62.

52. For a thoughtful argument in favor of open borders, see Joseph H. Carens, "Aliens and Citizens: The Case for Open Borders," *The Review of Politics* 49 (Spring 1987).

53. Ibid., pp. 37–38.

54. Byron Dorgan, "Spend Money on U.S. Goods," *USA Today*, February 2, 2009, p. 14A.

55. Douglas A. Irwin, "If We Buy American, No One Else Will," *New York Times*, February 1, 2009; Anthony Faiola, "'Buy American' Rider Sparks Trade Debate," *Washington Post*, January 29, 2009.

56. Michael Mandel, "Can Obama Keep New Jobs at Home?," *BusinessWeek*, November 25, 2008.

57. Lee quoted in Douglas Southall Freeman, *R. E. Lee* (New York: Charles Scribner's Sons, 1934), pp. 443, 421. See also Morton Grodzins, *The Loyal and the Disloyal* (Chicago: University of Chicago Press, 1965), pp. 142–43.

58. In this and the following paragraph I draw on Sandel, *Democracy's Discontent*, pp. 15–16.

59. Dick Lehr, "Bulger Brothers Find Their Worlds Colliding," *Boston Globe*, December 4, 2002, p. B1; Eileen McNamara, "Disloyalty to the Dead," *Boston Globe*, December 4, 2002; www.fbi.gov/wanted/topten/fugitives/bulger.htm.

60. Scot Lehigh, "Bulger Chose the Code of the Streeet," *Boston Globe*, December 4, 2002, p. A19.

61. Nicolas Zamiska, "In South Boston, Belief and Sympathy," *Boston Globe*, June 20, 2003, p. A22.

62. Lehigh, "Bulger Chose the Code of the Street."

63. Shelley Murphy, "No U.S. Charges Against Bulger," *Boston Globe*, April 4, 2007, p. A1.

64. David Johnston and Janny Scott, "Prisoner of Rage: The Tortured Genius of Theodore Kaczynski," *New York Times*, May 26, 1996.

65. Ibid.

66. David Johnston, "Judge Sentences Confessed Bomber to Four Life Terms," *New York Times*, May 5, 1998.

67. William Glaberson, "In Book, Unabomber Pleads His Case," *New York Times*, March 1, 1999.

68. William Glaberson, "The Death Penalty as a Personal Thing," *New York Times*, October 18, 2004.

69. Matthew Purdy, "Crime, Punishment and the Brothers K.," *New York Times*, August 5, 2001.

70. Johnston and Scott, "Prisoner of Rage."

Chapter 10: Justice and the Common Good

1. Theodore H. White, *The Making of the President 1960* (New York: Atheneum Publishers, 1961), pp. 295–98.
2. Address of Senator John F. Kennedy to the Greater Houston Ministerial Association, Houston, Texas, September 12, 1960, at www.jfklibrary.org/ Historical+Resources/Archives/Reference+Desk/Speeches/JFK/JFK+Pre -Pres/1960/Address+of+Senator+John+F.+Kennedy+to+the+Greater+ Houston+Ministerial+Association.htm.
3. White, *The Making of the President 1960*, p. 298.
4. Barack Obama, "Call to Renewal Keynote Address," Washington, D.C., June 28, 2006, at www.barackobama.com/2006/06/28/call_to_renewal_key note_address.php.
5. Ibid.
6. Ibid.
7. Ibid.
8. Ibid.
9. For elaboration of this theme, see Michael J. Sandel, *Democracy's Discontent: America in Search of a Public Philosophy* (Cambridge, Mass.: Harvard University Press, 1996), pp. 278–85.
10. John Rawls, *A Theory of Justice* (Cambridge, Mass.: Harvard University Press, 1971).
11. Alasdair MacIntyre, *After Virtue* (Notre Dame, Ind.: University of Notre Dame Press, 1981); Michael J. Sandel, *Liberalism and the Limits of Justice* (Cambridge, UK: Cambridge University Press, 1982); Michael Walzer, *Spheres of Justice* (New York: Basic Books, 1983); Charles Taylor, "The Nature and Scope of Distributive Justice," in Charles Taylor, *Philosophy and the Human Sciences, Philosophical Papers*, vol. 2 (Cambridge, UK: Cambridge University Press), p. 289.
12. John Rawls, *Political Liberalism* (New York: Columbia University Press, 1993), p. 31.
13. Ibid., pp. 29–31.
14. Ibid., p. 58.
15. Ibid., pp. xx, xxviii.
16. Ibid., p. 215.
17. Ibid., p. 254.
18. Ibid., p. 236.

19. The phrase is from Richard John Neuhaus, *The Naked Public Square* (Grand Rapids, Mich.: William B. Eerdmans, 1984).

20. See Michael J. Sandel, *Public Philosophy: Essays on Morality in Politics* (Cambridge, Mass.: Harvard University Press, 2005), pp. 2–3.

21. Obama, "Call to Renewal Keynote Address."

22. I take up the question of the moral status of the embryo in Michael J. Sandel, *The Case Against Perfection* (Cambridge, Mass.: Harvard University Press, 2007), pp.102–28.

23. Connecticut (2008) and Iowa (2009) legalized same-sex marriage through rulings of their state supreme courts.

24. See Tamara Metz, "Why We Should Disestablish Marriage," in Mary Lyndon Shanley, *Just Marriage* (New York: Oxford University Press, 2004), pp. 99–108.

25. Michael Kinsley, "Abolish Marriage," *Washington Post*, July 3, 2003, p. A23.

26. Ibid.

27. Ibid.

28. *Hillary Goodridge vs. Department of Public Health*, Supreme Judicial Court of Massachusetts, 440 Mass. 309 (2003).

29. Ibid., p. 312. The sentence quoted in the court's opinion ("Our obligation is to define the liberty of all, not to mandate our own moral code") is from *Lawrence v. Texas*, 539 U.S. 558 (2003), the U.S. Supreme Court decision that overturned a Texas law banning homosexual practices. The *Lawrence* opinion, in turn, had quoted this sentence from *Planned Parenthood v. Casey*, 505 U.S. 833 (1992), a U.S. Supreme Court decision that dealt with abortion rights.

30. Ibid.

31. Ibid., p. 329.

32. Ibid., p. 320.

33. Ibid., p. 313.

34. Ibid., p. 342.

35. Ibid., p. 321.

36. Ibid., p. 322.

37. Ibid., p. 331.

38. Ibid., p. 333.

39. Robert F. Kennedy, "Remarks at the University of Kansas," March 18, 1968, at www.jfklibrary.org/Historical+Resources/Archives/Reference+Desk/Speeches/RFK/RFKSpeech68Mar18UKansas.htm.

40. Ibid.

41. Barack Obama, "A New Era of Service," University of Colorado, Colorado Springs, July 2, 2008, in *Rocky Mountain News*, July 2, 2008.

42. Gary Becker, "Sell the Right to Immigrate," The Becker-Posner Blog, February 21, 2005, at www.becker-posner-blog.com/archives/2005/02/sell_the _right.html.

43. See Robert B. Reich, *The Work of Nations* (New York: Alfred A. Knopf, 1991), pp. 249–315.

ACKNOWLEDGMENTS

This book began life as a course. For almost three decades, I've had the privilege of teaching political philosophy to Harvard undergraduates. And in many of those years, I've taught a course called "Justice." The course exposes students to some of the great philosophical writings about justice, and also takes up contemporary legal and political controversies that raise philosophical questions.

Political philosophy is an argumentative subject, and part of the fun of the Justice course is that the students get to argue back—with the philosophers, with one another, and with me. So I would like, first of all, to record my appreciation to the thousands of undergraduates who have joined me in this journey over the years. Their lively engagement with questions of justice is reflected, I hope, in the spirit of this book. I am also grateful to the several hundred graduate students and law students who have helped me teach the course. Their probing questions in our weekly staff meetings not only kept me on my toes but also deepened my understanding of the philosophical themes we together were imparting to our students.

Writing a book is very different from teaching a course, however similar the subject matter. So in many ways, writing this book involved starting from scratch. For support while writing, I am grateful to the Harvard Law School's faculty summer research workshop. I am also indebted to the Carnegie Scholars Program of the Carnegie Corporation of New York, which has supported my work on the moral limits of markets. I am especially grateful to Vartan Gregorian, Patricia Rosenfield, and Heather McKay for their kindness, patience, and support. The portions of this book that touch on markets and morals represent the beginning of a project I still owe them.

I was the beneficiary of a splendid team at Farrar, Straus and Giroux. Jonathan Galassi, Paul Elie, Jeff Seroy, and Laurel Cook were a pleasure to work with from start to finish, as was my literary agent, Esther Newberg. Their love of books, and of bookmaking, informs everything they do, and makes life easy for an author. I am deeply grateful for their help.

My sons, Adam and Aaron, have been subjected to arguments about justice around the dinner table from the time they could hold a spoon. Their moral seriousness, brilliance, and passion have been challenging, enriching, and a pleasure to behold. When in doubt, we all turn to Kiku, our moral and spiritual touchstone, my soul mate. I dedicate this book to her with love.

INDEX